America in Conflict

The Deepening Values Divide

Rogene A. Buchholz

Hamilton Books
A member of
The Rowman & Littlefield Publishing Group
Lanham • Boulder • New York • Toronto • Plymouth, UK

Copyright © 2007 by
Hamilton Books
4501 Forbes Boulevard
Suite 200
Lanham, Maryland 20706
Hamilton Books Acquisitions Department (301) 459-3366

Estover Road
Plymouth PL6 7PY
United Kingdom

All rights reserved
Printed in the United States of America
British Library Cataloging in Publication Information Available

Library of Congress Control Number: 2007921285
ISBN-13: 978-0-7618-3719-0 (paperback : alk. paper)
ISBN-10: 0-7618-3719-1 (paperback : alk. paper)

∞™ The paper used in this publication meets the minimum
requirements of American National Standard for Information
Sciences—Permanence of Paper for Printed Library Materials,
ANSI Z39.48—1992

To Lauren, Aliisa, Mark, Michelle, and Stanford
whose values reflect the highest ideals of this country

Contents

Acknowledgments vii

Introduction ix

Part I Values and Policy

1 War 3
2 Freedom 44
3 Taxes 70
4 Environment 83

Part II Values and Religion

5 Fundamentalist Christianity 107
6 Fundamentalism in Government 129
7 Church and State 143

Part III Values and Democracy

8 Religion and a Democratic Society 163
9 Revitalizing Democracy 180

10 The Future of America	198
Sources	225
Bibliography	227
Index	231
About the Author	243

Acknowledgments

This book was started soon after the invasion of Iraq took place as a way to deal with the frustrations I was experiencing. Before the invasion I paced the floor night after night in utter disbelief that we were actually going to involve ourselves in what I thought from the very beginning would be a fiasco. All the propaganda coming from the administration as to how the Iraqi's would embrace democracy and all would be well once Saddam was removed from power seemed to me to be sheer fantasy. After I started writing, the book branched out into other areas and I realized that I might have something that could be of interest to other people. So perhaps I should first acknowledge the role that Bush's foreign policy played in providing the initial motivation for this book.

The amount of space I ended up devoting to religion and the role it plays in public life started with a course I audited at the University of Colorado at Denver (UCD). As a retired Professor of Business Ethics, it has been my practice to audit at least one course a semester at this university. This particular course was entitled Church and State: Religion and Contemporary Political Issues taught by Dr. Sharon L. Coggan of the Religious Studies Department. This course provided me with the motivation to read further on this issue and include religion and the role it plays in public life as a major part of my book. Another course that was very useful as far as the religious element is concerned was a course in The Philosophy of Religion taught by Dr. Robert Metcalf of the Philosophy Department at UCD, and he and his wife, Lucy Dwight, read an early draft of the chapters that dealt with religion and made many suggestions for improvement. Additionally, I have audited several courses taught by Dr. Myra Bookman also a professor at UCD that contributed to the breadth and depth of my thinking about social issues and the role of religion in society.

Another person to whom I am indebted is Arshad Kahn who was supportive of my writing the book and very helpful with suggestions relative to getting the book published. He put me in touch with a professional editor who edited the book in its entirety. Her name is Judy King from Houston, Texas, and I am also indebted to her for her help in making this a more readable book. The people at Hamilton Books, inlcuding David Chao the Acquisitions Editor and Michael Marino the Manager of Editorial Administration, were a pleasure to work with and I am indebted to them for bringing this book to fruition.

However, the person who most deserves an acknowledgement for her help with this book is my wife Sandy, who read the entire manuscript and made many suggestions for improvement that I took into account. She provided a balance to my tendency to be dogmatic on things I believe in strongly and constantly reminded that there are always two sides to an issue and those who differ from me may have something to say that is important to take into account. At times I also let my disgust with some of the policies and prouncements of the Bush administration get out of control which, in turn, clouded my judgments and made me unreasonable. On those occasions she kept me from going overboard and reminded me that shouting obscenities was not going to accomplish anything. In addition she suggested the title for the book. To her I owe a great deal of gratitude for making the book a much better product than it would otherwise have been.

Introduction

Before the next presidential election the country needs to engage in a conversation about a host of issues that are not getting enough attention. It needs to talk about the Iraqi War and what we owe the Iraqi people for having invaded their country and created the conditions for violence to escalate. It needs to talk about the doctrine of preemption that got us into Iraq and under what conditions, if any, this doctrine makes sense. It needs to talk about terrorism and how we can adequately protect ourselves against this kind of threat without sacrificing our civil liberties and our moral standards regarding treatment of prisoners. The country needs to discuss rising inequalities and tax policies that are fair to all Americans. The country needs to take global warming and a host of environmental issues seriously and consider solutions that work for the country as a whole. And most importantly, the role of religion in public life needs to be discussed and debated extensively. All this needs to be done before we elect another leader.

But a conversation about these and other issues is made difficult by the values divide that exists in this country. Something is going on in this society that has divided America into two camps who can't talk to each other, do not seek to understand each other's concerns, and have no respect for each other's positions. This divide is most often called the culture wars, but this term does adequately capture the difference in values and worldviews the two camps represent. Most Americans find themselves on one side or another of this divide and are caught up in this conflict. While there are many reasons for this divide, I want to highlight one element in this equation, the role that religious fundamentalism plays in this society and the contribution it makes to dividing the country. The culture wars are in some sense a war over religion and the role it should play in public life.

The election of George W. Bush in 2004 for another four years caused many of us to consider the values that are guiding this country. There have been many explanations for the way the election turned out, but there are at least two such theories I do not accept. The first is that Kerry ran a poor campaign and did not have a clear message he could communicate to the American people. The second is that the majority of the populace is stupid or ignorant in some sense and did not vote in its own self-interest but was manipulated by the Bush campaign to support policies not in their best interests.

As to the first explanation, Kerry had his flaws, to be sure, but he was a credible candidate who eventually got his act together and presented the public with clear alternatives to Bush on everything from taxes to the war on terror. Many pundits think he did better than Bush not only in the first debate, but in all three debates, and looked more presidential and in control of himself. Despite the fact that he lost, Kerry managed to garner more votes than did Gore in the 2000 election. And with the switch of a mere 60,000 votes in Ohio, he would have been our next president.

As for the second theory, while the American people may be ignorant about many things in our government, like who is chief justice of the Supreme Court and even the name of their senators and representatives, I do not believe they are stupid when it comes to voting in their own interests. Thus it may be that the majority of the voters in this country chose what they actually want—more wars to impose democracy on other people, more security and less freedom, more economic policies that favor the rich and impose more of the tax burden on the middle class, and more exploitation of the environment to support our life style.

And this is what frightens me and makes me wonder about the future of this country and its democratic system of government. Some have said that the 2004 election was mainly about values as if every election isn't about values of some kind or other. But the values reflected in the Bush administration, and apparently in 51 percent of the American populace, are not the values that have guided this country during the 74 years I have lived, and perhaps throughout its entire history. Values seem to have changed quite dramatically for Bush supporters as the values exemplified in the Bush administration are not those I came to cherish and believe are consistent with a democratic society.

This is not a book that looks at the values divide from an objective standpoint and analyzes what could be going on from an unbiased position. It should already be quite clear that I have a certain set of values I hold dear and am evaluating what is going on in the country and in the Bush administration from this perspective. Lest I appear too partisan however, the Democrats will come in for their share of criticism as they have been anything but moral paragons and defenders of values I think are important. But the Bush administration has taken the country down a new path that reflects different values from the traditional ones I believe have informed this country. The Bush administration and its policies will thus capture the majority of my attention.

The book consists of three parts. The first part focuses on major policy areas of the Bush administration and what I call its relentless assult on American values that undergird our society. The war in Iraq will be discussed forwards and backwards, the Patriot Act and the search for security in a new kind of world, Bush's tax cuts and their implications for the society, and the real war this administration is carrying on with respect to the environment. Important values are at stake in these policy areas, values with respect to how and when we use our military power, values related to the balance between freedom and security, fairness and equity in our tax system, and values regarding the environment. In these pages I want to clarify what the different value positions are in these policy areas.

The second part of the book will deal with religious fundamentalism in this country and the values it is trying to promote in society. The primary focus will be on such a religious approach in the United States, but I will also mention Islamic fundamentalism where it is appropriate. In this section I make the case that the worst thing that happened to the Republican Party over the past several decades was to be captured by the religious right and become its political arm, so to speak. This is also the worst thing that has happened to the country as it contributes to the lack of civility and inability to compromise in Congress as well as influencing the policies of the Bush administration that have further alienated a significant portion of the population as well as foreign countries. There are few moderates in Congress anymore as many have quit because the job is no longer tenable under the conditions that exist there. The division in Congress reflects the division in the country at large, a division that has been created by the approach to public policy issues taken by the religious right and the values it is trying to promote.

The involvement of the religious right in public policy has been democracy's greatest problem for the past several decades and threatens the separation of church and state that was of great concern to the founders of the country. While the religious right started all this political involvement, the Catholic Church also got into the act during the 2004 election by threatening to withhold communion from politicians who did not adhere to the party line on abortion and other issues. With the exception of immigration and, of course, terrorism, the public policy agenda in this country is largely set by the concerns of the religious right. The issues that receive the most discussion are abortion, gay marriage, and stem cell research, all issues of major concern to these religious groups. Poverty, inequality of wealth and income, a host of environmental issues, and the safety and well-being of consumers and workers are not even on the agenda anymore.

The last part of book discusses the future of America and what Bush's second term holds for the country. One chapter focuses on problems with democracy by looking at how the religious right's involvement in politics threatens the very democracy we so cherish and would like to impose on others. Another chapter discusses what needs to be done to restore a viable democracy, such as fixing the Electoral College, changing the way states are redistricted, and other such problems in our democracy. This chapter will also discuss what the Democrats need to do to remain a viable political alternative in this country. The final chapter discusses what the Bush administration is doing in its second term and what this means for the country's future.

Two things got under my skin more than anything else that motivated me to write this book. First of all I got sick and tired of the macho attitude this administration exemplified. First there was the "bin Laden dead or alive" rhetoric. Then the ultimatum to Saddam to get out of his country in 48 hours or he was, in effect, dead meat. After the war was supposedly over, we have Bush strutting around a carrier deck in a flight suit, in effect saying to the world how we showed those Iraqis what America is made of. Soon after that was the "bring it on" remark and the insurgents have indeed brought it on much longer than expected. And then there was the remark that we were not going to ask the UN for permission to defend our national interest. This remark was the last straw.

Of course we aren't going to ask the UN for permission. And neither is any other country in the world. Any country, from the smallest to the largest, is not going to ask anyone for permission to deal with a threat to its security. It might ask the UN for help, but not for permission. So what's the big deal? Many people stood up an applauded and said, "right on!" to this remark. Why do we have to state the obvious in such belligerent terms as if to prove to ourselves and the rest of the world how tough we are? Is this the mark of a mature nation that knows how to use its power responsibly?

After these remarks I concluded that Bush as still going through adolescence and taking the whole country with him through that experience. But then came Kerry during the Democratic convention trotting out his Vietnam buddies to show how tough he was, leading me to conclude that perhaps the whole country is going through adolescence and Bush only reflects this characteristic of the country at large. The country seems to have a need these days to prove how tough it is and how independent it is and how able it is to go it alone without any help or assistance. These are characteristics of an adolescent trying to grow up and find him or herself, and it seems as if the country is trying to grow up and find itself and determine its role in the world as the only superpower left standing.

The second thing I got tired of relates to all the talk about religion that pervades our discourse on so many issues. Religion used to be largely a private matter, but in the past decade or so it has entered the public arena in a way that seems unprecedented. Almost every politician has to parade his or her religion before the public and tout his or her faith as if to prove to the American public that he or she believes in something beyond politics. Issues such as stem cell research, abortion, gay marriage, and the teaching of intelligent design in public schools are all tied up with religion. This again seems to reflect a great deal of immaturity and anxiety about morals and how life should be lived. People who are confident in their faith do not need to make a public show of how religious they are and prove anything to anybody.

The United States I grew up in and served for four years of my life in the military is no longer the county I knew and whose values I could support wholeheartedly. It has become more of a threat to the world than I could ever have imagined. Its economic and military power is now unchecked as it alone is the world's superpower. There is no other nation that can provide a check and balance on the use of this power as the Soviet Union did for many decades. China is years away from being enough of a power to serve this function. The morals of the Bush administration that have guided the use of this power are tainted with lies and deceptions that are at least as great as those which got us into the Vietnam fiasco.

As the old saying goes, absolute power corrupts absolutely, and what this administration has done with its unilateral approach to preemptive or preventive war proves that thesis unequivocally. Add to that the decline of an internal moral compass that can guide the nation in a responsible use of that power and we have a recipe for disaster. The country is beginning to question the direction this administration has taken as the results of the 2006 election show conclusively. Many believe something has gone wrong and the country needs a change of direction. But what direction the Democrats will take us in is anybody's guess at this point.

Hopefully this book will contribute to a conversation about issues by clarifying the values at at stake in policy decisions. This country has been a great place to grow up in and work in, as the freedoms and opportunities we have are essential for human life to flourish. We should not give them up out of fear or anger at being attacked by terrorists. Thus I am really writing this book out of concern for the country and what it will be like when my grandchildren come of age and play their roles in society. Hopefully it will still be a country with values reflecting the highest ideals of a democratic society and providing its citizens with opportunities like those I had available when I was deciding what to do with my life. To these grandchildren this book is dedicated.

Part I

VALUES AND POLICY

Chapter One

War

The war in Iraq has been one of the most controversial, if not the most controversial, war in which this country has ever become engaged. Dozens of books and thousands of articles have been written about the subject, some supporting the war wholeheartedly and others questioning the entire enterprise. Several support the initial invasion but are critical about the lack of postwar planning and the way the Bush administration has handled the situation after declaring the mission accomplished. It should come as no surprise that there is extensive discussion about this war as it is a radical departure from previous wars this country has fought and represents something of a watershed in the use of military power to accomplish political objectives.

THE COMMITMENT

The picture that emerges with respect to Iraq is that this administration was committed to go to war with Iraq and force a regime change from the very first day it took office. The Bush administration had people in high places, including the vice-president, who had Iraq in their sights and were only looking for a justification to put their commitment into action. Only 10 days after the inauguration, according to Paul O'Neill, the first Treasury secretary of the Bush administration, the focus of foreign policy was already on Iraq and on how to dispose of Saddam Hussein. There was never a discussion as to why this action was advisable; it was more a matter of building a case against Saddam and figuring out how he could be disposed of and Iraq changed into a new country.[1]

This commitment came in large part from the Project for a New American Century (PNAC), a neoconservative think tank "dedicated to a few fundamental propositions that American leadership is both good for America and for the world, and that such leadership requires military strength, diplomatic energy and commitment to moral principle."[2] In its statement of principles, PNAC asked "Does the United States have the resolve to shape a new century favorable to American principles and interests?" This document goes on to say "America has a vital role in maintaining peace and security in Europe, Asia, and the Middle East. If we shirk our responsibilities, we invite challenges to our fundamental interests. The history of the 20th century should have taught us that it is important to shape circumstances before crises emerge, and to meet threats before they become dire."[3] The document lists four consequences of this doctrine for foreign policy:

- We need to increase defense spending significantly if we are to carry out our global responsibilities today and modernize our armed forces for the future.
- We need to strengthen our ties to democratic allies and to challenge regimes hostile to our interests and values.
- We need to promote the cause of political and economic freedom abroad.
- We need to accept responsibility for America's unique role in preserving and extending an international order friendly to our security, our prosperity, and our principles.[4]

This document lays the groundwork for American intervention anywhere in the world and advocates a preemptive strategy to meet threats before they materialize. The goal of this organization seems to be to extend American hegemony across the world by force of arms, if necessary, as a show of resolve to promote American values throughout the world. It is an arrogant document that believes America has a right to impose its will on the rest of the world and shape it according to its own interests. There is nothing in this document regarding respect for diversity and rights of other nations to pursue their own interests and develop their own future free from domination by a foreign power.

Vice-President Dick Cheney, former Defense Secretary Donald Rumsfeld, and former Deputy Defense Secretary Paul Wolfowitz were members of this organization. Thus people at the very top levels of the Bush administration shared these views of American foreign policy and were more than happy to be put in positions where they could implement this vision for America. Iraq was unfinished business for these people, and their interests meshed with Bush's own personal vendetta against Saddam and, as it later became apparent, his conviction that he was chosen by both God and history to liberate Iraq and bring democracy to the Middle East.

The goal was and is to establish a democracy in Iraq more in tune with Western values that would hopefully spread to other countries in the region. Democracy would, it is believed, promote our interests in a stable Middle East by reducing the threat of terrorism and to keeping the oil flowing so our way of life can continue. This war wasn't only about oil, as some would have us believe, but take oil out of the equation and one has to wonder if we would really care what happened in these Middle Eastern countries as long as there was no threat of terrorism from them that would directly affect our country.

An important part of the motivation for war was the matter of showing our resolve. As O'Neill stated in his book: "A weak but increasingly obstreperous Saddam might be useful as a demonstration model of America's new, unilateral resolve. If it could effectively be shown that he possessed, or was trying to build, weapons of mass destruction—creating an `asymmetric threat,' in the neoconservative parlance, to U.S. power in the region—his overthrow would help `dissuade' other countries from doing the same."[5] We would show the world not to mess with America, an extension of the "Don't Mess with Texas" signs that appear alongside highways in that state in reference to litter. Bush himself stated over and over again "We had to show the world that the United States means what it says." It was important for the United States not just to be respected, but also feared because of its military might that was now unopposed in the world.

JUSTIFICATION

The 9/11 attacks opened the door to manufacture a justification for disposing of Saddam and forcing regime change. Even though it seemed certain that al Qaeda was responsible for these attacks, Bush immediately wanted to start building a case against Saddam and find a way to prove his involvement in the attacks.[6] But Afghanistan had to be dealt with first as after all that is where al Qaeda had established its base of operations and where its training facilities were located. Thus Bush bided his time to get his ducks in order and then attacked the country. This action was absolutely justifiable and we had international support to mount this attack. While there has been criticism about the way this campaign was conducted, it was quickly successful in driving the Taliban from power and establishing a new regime.[7]

Once we had the Taliban on the run however and it became clear we were not going to get Osama bin Laden anytime soon, attention shifted to the real goal of this administration. Planning for an invasion of Iraq was begun even before the Taliban were routed. The Bush administration mounted a masterful propaganda campaign to convince the American public that Saddam had weapons of mass destruction and links to al Qaeda and thus constituted an immediate threat to the country and the world. They also created the impression that Iraq was involved in the 9/11 attacks, so that the polls showed a great number of Americans believed this was the case. Later on Bush explicitly denied this connection, but the impression remained.[8]

The administration kept sounding a constant drumbeat for war with all the "no doubt" statements about Saddam having weapons of mass destruction. The president stated that "intelligence gathered by this and other governments leaves no doubt that the Iraq regime continues to possess and conceal some of the most lethal weapons ever devised." Vice-president Cheney said "There is no doubt that Saddam Hussein now has weapons of mass destruction." When asked about the location of the WMDs, Donald Rumsfeld, the secretary of defense, answered, "We know where they are."[9] On another occasion Cheney declared that the high-strength aluminum tubes Saddam had imported constituted "irrefutable evidence" that Saddam was reconstituting his nuclear weapons program.[10] And for George Tenet, the head of the CIA, justification for the war was a "slam dunk," two words he came to regret he had ever uttered.[11]

Thus a preemptive strike was justified because Bush had the sacred constitutional duty to protect the country from threats of this nature.[12] Where propaganda didn't work, the administration tried to bully the United Nations and European countries into submission, and we had the audacity to criticize France for not going along with this charade. Before anybody realized it, we were amassing troops in great numbers in Kuwait, getting ready to strike into Iraq. The Democrats proved to be just as warmongering as anyone else as a bipartisan Congress gave the president carte blanche to go to war with little opposition. Everyone seemed ready to rush into war with Iraq, the press included, and there was something of a gleeful attitude in the country as if going to war were like a going on a new and exciting adventure.

Meanwhile the UN weapons inspectors were doing their job, and the buildup of troops had a beneficial effect in getting Saddam to open up more places for inspection. However these inspectors could find nothing in the way of weapons of mass destruction. After it has recently became abundantly clear there are no such weapons, most commentators focused on intelligence failures on the part of the CIA, and at least two commissions were formed to look into this problem and eventually blamed the intelligence community and let the administration off the hook.[13] But there was no intelligence failure. The Bush administration had the best intelligence anyone could hope for available to them from these UN inspectors who were on the ground in Iraq having access to places and people they never had before. Yet the administration chose to discredit this whole process, focusing instead on surveillance photos from the CIA they could interpret any way they wanted.[14]

Thus every factory was producing chemical weapons, every truck was a mobile biological weapons lab, and every aluminum tube had something to do with nuclear bombs. O'Neill describes a meeting of the National Security Council when a grainy photograph of a factory was laid out on the table that George Tenet, director of the Central Intelligence Agency (CIA), believed might be a plant producing either chemical or biological materials for weapons manufacture. O'Neill mentioned that he had seen a lot of factories around the world that looked like the one in the photograph and asked what made us suspect that this one produced chemical or biological agents for weapons. Tenet mentioned a few items of circumstantial evidence but had to admit that there was "no confirming intelligence" as to the materials being produced.[15]

Perhaps the most flagrant fabrication of evidence was reference to Iraq's purchase of uranium from Africa in Bush's State of the Union address, a claim that was already highly dubious at the time it was uttered. Officials writing the speech originally wanted to refer specifically to Niger, but after being told there were problems with this information, substituted the more vague Africa reference. They then referred to the information as coming from British sources in order to make the point without having to vouch for its authenticity. The whole claim was later proven to be a total fabrication.[16] After a former Ambassador by the name of Joseph Wilson was hired by the CIA to investigate this claim and found it to have no basis, his wife, a CIA operative was outed supposedly to undermine her husband's criticism of the use of this information.

This sparked another investigation into the source of the leak leading to the indictment of I. Lewis "Scooter" Libby, a top aid to Vice President Dick Cheney. Libby was charged with lying and obstructing justice, and later revealed that the president himself had ordered declassification of parts of a pre-war intelligence report and indirectly authorized Libby to leak this information to reporters to rebut critics who said the administration was exaggerating the nuclear threat posed by Iraq. This information suggested that Saddam Hussein was trying to buy uranium ore from Niger for nuclear weapons.[17]

A former national intelligence officer responsible for the Middle East from 2000 to 2005 states that intelligence was misused publicly to justify decisions that had already been made and that the intelligence community's work was politicized. The administration "cherry picked" raw intelligence that had not been analyzed or interpreted to make it case to the public.[18] A reporter who covers national security for the New York Times describes what I call the "culture of deceit" that existed at the CIA where, because of pressure from the administration, only information supportive of its position surfaced and information that did not support its case, even information from inside Iraq itself that denied the existence of WMDs, was buried.[19]

And so it went with most of the so-called evidence supporting a justification for the war against Saddam. This was not a preemptive war based on incontrovertible evidence that an attack of any kind was imminent. The truth is that there was nothing Saddam or anyone else could have done to stop the invasion.[20] We were going to war with Iraq period. Talk about resolve. The result was that the United States invaded a country that had not done us any harm, that was boxed in by no-fly zones and economic sanctions, and that posed no threat to this country. These are not the values of the country I grew up in and served for four years of my life. We do not attack people for no good reason, just to change the world to our likeness. We are not called to rid the world of all the bad guys and play Texas Ranger all over the globe.[21]

There is no moral justification for this war on any grounds. The war was illegal from an international perspective and had absolutely no legitimacy. The war violated Resolution 1441 adopted by the United Nations Security Council in November 2002, and thus we went to war outside the framework of international law and became a law unto ourselves. Under this resolution the United Nations reserved for itself the right to make a decision whether Iraq was or was not in compliance with its obligations. This was not a decision for the U.S. or any other country to make. Thus we tried hard to obtain a second resolution declaring Iraq was in violation and authorizing the use of force. When it became apparent this was not going to happen, we acted as if a second resolution was not necessary and was of no importance.[22]

The war also violated the United Nations charter which obligated member states to refrain "from the threat or use of force against the territorial integrity or political independence of any state." There was only one exception: that force could be employed in self or collective defense against an armed attack.[23] Thus it seems clear that Bush's real justification for invading Iraq was not a commitment to uphold international law and, in going to the UN, he was not acting in good faith. Bush took his case to the UN hoping the decision would go his way and thus giving him some cover from criticism, but he had already decided to invade Iraq no matter what the UN did.

As for legitimacy, Robert W. Tucker and David C. Hendrickson writing in Foreign Affairs argue that Bush's doctrine of preventive war, which was misnamed the "strategy of preemption," replaced the doctrines of containment and deterrence that governed our relations with the Soviet Union and called into question all four of the pillars that supported U.S. legitimacy after the Second World War. These four pillars were (1) commitment to international law, (2) acceptance of consensual decision making, (3) reputation for moderation, and (4) identification with the preservation of peace. According to the authors, the Bush doctrine was severely wanting in all four of these elements.[24]

Even if weapons of mass destruction had been found in Iraq, a preemptive strategy would have been unconvincing because the possession of such weapons is not proof of an impending attack. As for deposing a tyrant and freeing the Iraqi people, what this means is that the United States on its own can decide to invade any nation that fails some kind of democratic litmus test and force regime change. The fact of the matter is that the Bush administration does not care about international law or is it concerned about legitimacy at an international level. It is so certain about its moral cause that none of this makes any difference. As a result the United States is a rouge and lawless nation feared by the rest of the world. It can attack when and where it pleases for any reason it deems legitimate. The United States has become a self-appointed judge, jury, and executioner on the world stage.

The values I grew up with are that we do not attack someone unless we ourselves are attacked. Afghanistan was thus justified after the Taliban refused to turn over the al Qaeda terrorists and the Bush administration deserves credit for taking the fight to the enemy. But the job in this country was left incomplete because of our shift to Iraq, and the warlords and the Taliban are both resurgent, particularly in the countryside. According to an editorial in Kabul's Anis, several hundred warlords and drug lords still command the loyalty of thousands of rifle-packing militants. Democracy won't work under the gun, and the editorial goes on to state that if the parlimentary elections scheduled for fall 2005 were held today, "those who control the guns would control the votes."[25]

Why wasn't Afghanistan enough? Why couldn't it have served as a model of democracy for the rest of the Arab world? Why wasn't it enough of a demonstration of America's new resolve? Why Iraq? If we needed to pick a fight with someone else to show our resolve, why not pick on someone more nearly our own size? Like North Korea maybe. There was ample reason at the time to believe that country actually was developing weapons of mass destruction along with the missile capability to deliver those weapons to other countries like the United States where it perceives a threat to its existence. We opened the door to preemptive strikes, and if North Korea should ever launch a missile in our direction, we have no moral grounds to oppose such an action. Perception of a threat that justifies a preemptive strike is obviously in the eye of the beholder.

Our actions make a rethinking of this traditional approach to war and respect for the sovereignty of nations imperative. The new world of terrorism may require a preemptive strike in certain circumstances to protect American citizens from experiencing another 9/11 attack. Bush has a point. Perhaps the old doctrines of containment and deterrence do not work against terrorism, and we need to take the fight to the enemy under certain conditions to confront the worst threats before they emerge. A statement appearing in a document called "The National Security Strategy of the United States of America" issued by the White House in September 2002 makes the case for a preemptive strike.

> ... the United States can no longer solely rely on a reactive posture as we have in the past. The inability to deter a potential attacker, the immediacy of today's threats, and the magnitude of potential harm that could be caused by our adversaries' choice of weapons do not permit that option. We cannot let our enemies strike first.[26]

This idea needs extensive discussion in the world community as to the conditions under which such a strike is morally justified as it is a radical departure from the traditional approach to war and respect for the sovereignty of nations. Bush had an opportunity to lead the world in this discussion but instead chose to act unilaterally in this matter and assume we had all the right answers. But what constitutes a threat that justifies such action? What standards of intelligence should apply? It would certainly seem that the "beyond a reasonable doubt" standard of our court system is a good candidate. And most important of all who makes the decisions? Discussion of these issues has never taken place, and it did not take place in either the Bush or Kerry campaigns.[27]

Certainly Saddam was a brutal dictator who at times made war on his own people. And the world is undoubtedly a better place because he is no longer in power. But again who decides what dictators among the many in the world deserve to be taken out? At best this war can only be seen as a preventive war, and this is much more problemmatical than a preemptive war where a threat actually exists. Many countries have the capability of developing weapons of mass destruction, some with much more capability than Saddam had at the point of invasion. How do we decide which ones are justified to invade to destroy this capability? Do we rely solely on Bush's instincts and his belief that he was "called" for the task? Is this a sound basis for foreign policy?

NO WEAPONS AND NO COOPERATION

The Bush doctrine of preemption requires near perfect intelligence about the enemy's intentions and capabilities. After Saddam did not use any biological or chemical weapons to defend himself and after we did not find any such weapons initially, we should have begun to doubt our intelligence. But not this administration. They continued to insist that WMDs were there and would be found. All we had to do was look harder, a claim that began to have less and less credibility. If they were that hard to find with complete access to the country, how could we have had any confidence before we occupied the country that they were actually there? While we could not give the UN weapons inspectors another 10 days to search for them before the war started, we now said we needed months to find them.

Then came the official denials of any weapons of mass destruction in Iraq and of any links to al Qaeda. David Kay led the 2003 search for WMDs in Iraq, and in his report to Congress admitted stocks of such weapons had not yet been found. But he also added that "we are not yet at the point where we can say definitively either that such weapons do not exist or that they existed before the war and our only task is to find where they have gone."[28] When he left his post in early 2004, however, he was more certain that Iraq did not have weapons of mass destruction before the war and was critical of the National Security Council for not protecting the president from faulty pre-war intelligence.[29]

The most definitive statement on WMDs came in a 1,000–page report from his replacement, the administration's new chief weapons inspector in Iraq, Charles Duelfer. The report concluded that at the time of the invasion Iraq had no stockpiles of biological or chemical weapons and there were no active programs to produce them. Its capacity to produce such weapons had significantly eroded by the time of the invasion. Iraq had "essentially destroyed" its illicit weapons ability by the end of 1991, the report said, and eliminated in 1996 its last secret factory which was a biological-weapons facility. Duelfer concluded that between 1991 and 2003 Saddam had in effect sacrificed his illicit weapons program to the long-term goal of winning an end to UN sanctions.[30]

However, even though he had destroyed his WMDs to escape the sanctions, he still wanted to perpetuate the belief that he had them, mainly, the report suggests, to keep Iran in check. Saddam apparently considered WMDs as essential in this effort, and while the U.S. was focused on the threat Iraq posed, he was focused on maintaining the fiction of WMDs as a strategic deterrent to keep Iran from invading or otherwise interfering in his country. This presented Saddam with a difficult balancing act in getting rid of his WMDs to win relief from the sanctions while at the same time pretending he still had them for regional security. This balancing act did not work to his advantage.[31]

This report was the result of some 15 months of work by the Iraq Survey Group, a military and intelligence team of more than 1,200 people who inspected scores of sites, interviewed hundreds of former Iraqi scientists and officials, and reviewed thousands of documents in an effort to reach a definitive judgment.[32] This report clearly destroyed the rationale used by the Bush administration to justify the war: that Iraq actually possessed chemical and biological weapons and was reconstituting its nuclear weapons program. The report also however opened the door for the administration to justify the invasion on different grounds.

Duelfer argued that Saddam was using this period to exploit avenues opened by the sanctions, like the oil-for-food program, to lay the groundwork for a long-term program to restart weapons production once the sanctions were lifted. Supporters of the war used this statement as proof that Saddam needed to be taken out, that he was a threat to world peace, and had never given up his dream of reshaping world history. They argued that the report provided the best argument yet that the war was necessary. The issue was when—not if—Saddam would put his banned weapons programs back on track.[33] These arguments make clear, however, that this war was not a preemptive war, but at best a preventive war that is much more problemmatical.

There was still the argument that Saddam had shipped his WMDs to Syria before the war began. People who refused to believe that Saddam had no weapons of mass destruction latched onto this possibility as a last-ditch effort to salvage some credibility about Saddam's possession of such weapons. This argument was put to rest by the CIA, which concluded there was no indication Iraq had shipped any weapons of mass destruction to Syria before or during the invasion.[34] This finding dashed any hope that such weapons ever existed when we invaded Iraq and forced the administration to turn to other rationales for the war.

The second pillar of the Bush administration's justification for war was, of course, alleged links between Saddam and al Qaeda, linkage that was crucial to the case for war in that Saddam then had the capability to provide terrorists with biological and chemical weapons. The 9/11 commission quashed this argument with its findings that there was no "collaborative relationship" between Saddam and the terrorist organization. Based on its examination of relevant classified information, the commission found that while there had been contacts between Iraq and al Qaeda, they could find no evidence of actual cooperation.[35]

The commission said that Osama bin Laden had "explored possible cooperation with Iraq" while in Sudan through 1996, but "Iraq apparently never responded." There were also contacts between Iraq and al Qaeda after bin Laden went to Afghanistan in 1996, "but they do not appear to have resulted in a collaborative relationship."[36] It also stated that while Osama bin Laden had made a request to establish training camps in Iraq and had asked for help in obtaining weapons, Iraq ignored these requests. And a meeting alleged to have taken place in Prague between Mohamed Atta, leader of the 9/11 hijackers, and a senior Iraqi intelligence official a few months before the attacks never took place.[37]

This meeting had been used by the administration as clear evidence of cooperation between Saddam and al Qaeda and to show that Saddam was somehow involved in the 9/11 attacks, an impression the administration went out of its way to create.[38] Cheney and other top government officials often asserted there were extensive ties between Iraq and al Qaeda, saying the evidence of a link was "overwhelming." The public came to believe this as polls showed that almost half of the public thought there was "clear evidence that Iraq was supporting al Qaeda has been found."[39] Even after this report President Bush continued to insist that the existence of "numerous contacts" between Saddam and al Qaeda showed that Saddam was a threat to the United States.[40]

In a speech to the UN in September 2004 Bush defended the invasion of Iraq and rebutted the assertion by Secretary-General Kofi Annan that the war violated international law because it lacked UN authority. Bush argued that the U.S. and its allies were enforcing a Security Council resolution threatening "serious consequences" if Saddam did not disarm, disclose Iraq's banned weapons, and permit inspectors to roam the country. "The Security Council promised serious consequences for his defiance," Bush said, "and the commitments we make must have meaning." Of course Saddam did allow the weapons inspectors more access to the country and they could find no weapons of mass destruction, and we now know that Saddam had nothing to disclose or disarm. Apparently the president does not see the contradictions in his own statements.[41]

Thus every major claim justifying the invasion including the existence of weapons of mass destruction to cooperation with terrorist networks was shown to be wrong. None of these revelations, however, have seemed to faze this administration as Bush has continued to this day to maintain he did the right thing in invading Iraq and that freeing Iraq from Saddam's brutal tyranny was a noble cause no matter what the casualties. Whether or not Saddam was an imminent threat to us makes no difference, as we were justified to invade the country under any circumstances. The Bush administration has used so many rationales for the war that it is impossible to keep track of them. As one rationale became discredited, they came up with another one and seemed to have an endless series of rationalizations.

DEMOCRACY IN IRAQ

Removing Saddam from power, as bad as he was, created a power vacuum that may take years to resolve. We didn't fill that vacuum because we were not willing to commit at least 500,000 troops we didn't have so there was virtually a soldier on every street corner in every major city in Iraq to keep order.[42] The Iraqi Governing Council didn't fill that vacuum as they did not have legitimacy. Neither did the government under Prime Minister Allawi, which was only temporary until elections could be held to establish a legitimate government. Much has been made of these elections and the new government being established, but whether they can bring things under control remains to be seen. They have had trouble getting themselves organized and whether they can draw up a constitution acceptable to all parties is not certain. One of the big questions concerns the role religion is to play in governing the country, whether it is to be a secular government or one founded on Islamic principles.[43]

After the elections there was much praise for the Bush administration and its role in promoting democracy in Iraq, forgetting that it was the threat of an armed rebellion from Grand Ayatollah Ali al-Sistani and the Shiite community that brought about the elections. Al-Sistani, the country's most powerful Shiite leader, rejected the U.S. plan to transfer power through a provisional legislature selected by 18 regional caucuses and insisted on direct elections. How much credit can Bush take for the elections and how much real control do we have over what happens there? And as one commentator reminds us, in 1967 U.S. officials were heartened by the size of the turnout in South Vietnam's presidential election despite a Vietcong terrorist campaign to disrupt the voting.[44] Yet these elections did not prevent a takeover of the country and our ultimate expulsion.

Meanwhile the insurgency continues. In July 2003 President Bush said, "Bring them on" and indeed they have come on far stronger than we imagined. We do not have the force necessary to deal with the security situation in Iraq. At first the administration said the violence in Iraq was the work of a few deadenders. Then they later claimed it was fueled by a handful of foreign terrorists. They refused to accept that there was a political dimension to the insurgency that fed off the anger of the Sunnis, who saw themselves as being displaced from the power they had held for many decades. Whether they can be brought into the power structure and pacified in some way is a vital question.

While there was some hope that the insurgents were on the wane in early 2005, a new wave of bombings emerged that made people think twice about an early end to the struggle. What goals do the insurgents have beyond killing people and wreaking as much havoc as possible? According to some experts, the bombings are signs of a deeper struggle that the attempt to create a democracy in Iraq has brought about and involves several factions within Iraq itself that are at war with each other. Democracy is anathema to everything jihadist forces stand for and above all is against the rule of God as it is based on the right to choose your religion.⁴⁵ The insurgents aim to create an Islamic state in Iraq and turn the country into a terrorist haven.⁴⁶

My greatest fear, however, is that the major ethnic groups in Iraq are going to end up fighting each other for power and control of the country. In January 2003, an independent panel that advises the director of the CIA called the National Intelligence Council warned Bush that an American-led invasion of Iraq would result in a deeply divided society prone to violent internal conflict.⁴⁷ In September 2004 Britain's's highly regarded Royal Institute of International Affairs concluded that Iraq would be lucky to avoid a breakup and civil war and could become the spark for regional upheaval. The report also suggests that the best the U.S. and its allies can hope for is a "muddle through" scenario, holding the country together but failing to create a full-fledged democracy friendly to the West.⁴⁸

The bombing of the Askareiyah shrine in Samarra in February 2006 which was one of the most revered Shiite shrines sparked sectarian violence that claimed the lives of hundreds of people. The official word on this violence was that Iraq was not yet engaged in a civil war, but might be teetering at the brink.⁴⁹ Few people wanted to admit that Iraq might be engaged in a civil war, but at least one commentator disagreed with this assessment and stated that Iraq's civil war had begun months before this incident.⁵⁰ Thus it looked as if my worst fears were coming to fruition, and that we may have destablized Iraq to the point where a full-scale civil war is inevitable.

Throw foreign terrorists into this mix who seem to have plunging the country into a civil war as their goal, and you have a conflict that may go on for years and will result in many more dead Iraqis, including many innocent women and children.⁵¹ Has this war really accomplished anything other than destabilizing the region and opening it up to continued conflict? Will Iraq ever be able to establish anything like a functioning democracy? And even if they do, is this an acceptable justification for making war on these people; in other words does democracy justify the means of establishing it with a military invasion?

These ethnic groupings have never liked each other which is an understatement, as some things I have read from experts on the Middle East suggested the Shiites and Sunnis hate each other more than they hate the Americans.⁵² The country was cobbled together by the British after the First World War, putting the Kurds, Sunnis, and Shiites together and hoping the arrangement would work out satisfactorily. It may have taken somebody like Saddam to hold that country together, given the hatred between these ethnic groupings. He may have played a role much like Tito did in Yugoslavia. This is not to suggest that the tactics Saddam used to keep the country together are morally acceptable, only to say that he may have served an important function that in our zeal to dispose of him we failed to recognize and thus failed to develop a plan to fill the vacuum of power we created.

People like bin Laden could not have been more pleased by our invasion. Iraq is the second holiest land in Islam, according to Anonymous, but Islam had been suppressed by Saddam while the Sunni minority long dominated and brutalized the Shiite majority. Order was kept by the Baathists, who prevented a long overdue civil war. If Saddam were to fall, it could be expected that regional powers like Iran and Saudi Arabia would intervene to stop the creation of a Sunni or Shiite successor state. In short Iraq without Saddam would become a "failed state" bedeviled by its neighbors and a place where terrorist organizations would thrive.[53]

The idea that we could "build" a democracy in Iraq like one can build a house is ludicrous.[54] Democracy in Western societies was the product of centuries of evolution regarding social and political thought. It took the courage of revolutionaries who challenged the divine right of kings to rule their subjects. Democracy came from within people who wanted to govern themselves and enjoy the fruits of their own labors. It was not imposed from without. Iraqis have known nothing but arbitrary rule for years. They have long endured violence, poverty, and fear. They have had no experience with democracy and the rule of law and all the rest that goes along with democracy. How can a democracy be "built" in this environment? People like Wolfowitz who believed democracy would just emerge in Iraq were ignorant of history. He would do well to have read the words of Henry Kissinger, former secretary of state under the Nixon administration:

> Democracy in the West evolved over centuries. It required first a church independent of the state; then the Reformation, which imposed pluralism of religion; the Enlightenment, which asserted the autonomy of reason from both church and state; the Age of Discovery, which broadened horizons; and finally capitalism, with its emphasis on competition and the market. None of these conditions exists in the Islamic world. Instead, there is a merging of religion and politics inimical to pluralism. . . . The emergence of democratic institutions and of the arrangements which hold them together cannot be engineered as an act of will, it requires patience and modesty."[55]

When we think democracy can be exported much like some kind of product and believe this can be done speedily and on the cheap, we betray, according to Anonymous, ignorance of foreign lands, cultures, and histories as well as the creeds and ambitions of other peoples. And we equally ignore the bloody struggles and heroic accomplishments of our own history. Attempting the impossible is to ignore the road that America itself traveled on the road to democracy and forcing upon other people a system of government and society they may not want.⁵⁶ There is a staggering incompatibility between American democracy and contemporary Muslim society, "between a world where both Caesar and God each receive their due, and one where God and Caesar are the same."⁵⁷

> In both Afghanistan and Iraq we have won the war, but we stand in danger of losing what we won because our foreign policy suffers from the King George Syndrome. Freedom is neither a spontaneous nor a universal aspiration. Other goods captivate the minds of other people from other lands, order, honor, and tribal loyalties being the most obvious. And because these other goods orient these peoples no less powerfully than freedom orients us, we are apt to be sorely surprised when people who are liberated turn to new tyrants who can assume order; to terrorists who die for the honor of their country or Islam; and to tribal warlords whose winner-take-all mentality is corrosive to pluralism and toleration that are the very hallmarks of modern democracy.⁵⁸

How many wars is it going to take, how many people have to be killed, how much money has to be spent before we learn we cannot remake the world to be more to our liking and serve our interests? We could not build a democratic society in Vietnam; it will not happen in Iraq either. Does a Republican administration think it has the wisdom and power to do this when a Democratic administration failed with 500,000 troops and all the resolve in the world? The people who are causing all the ruckus in Iraq are called insurgents, but I wish we would have used another term. An insurgent is someone who rises up against established authority. George Washington was an insurgent in this sense.

Did we think other countries in the Middle East would idly stand by while we created a democracy next door? A functioning democracy in Iraq would provoke democratic activism on an even greater scale than has already appeared in Lebanon and Egypt among oppressed people in those countries. Other governments in the region do not want rebellion in their countries that would threaten their autocratic rule and unfettered access to oil wealth. Perhaps they are actively supporting the terrorists or merely giving them aid and comfort. In any event they have a vested interest in keeping the violence going and seeing American troops stay in the country, according to one theory. As long as the troops are there, Iraq is not really independent or democratic. The goal of the terrorists may be to make sure Iraq remains unable to provide for its own security.⁵⁹

The insurgency is not only a struggle against the United States; it is also a struggle to gain political dominance. Granted they use violence and killing to accomplish what they want, but we must never forget that we had our own civil war to resolve the issue of slavery. Whenever there is some decrease in insurgent activity, we must not be lulled into thinking we are getting the upper hand and that the insurgency is defeated. If I were the leader of this insurgency, I would adopt a strategy of lying low for a while to convince everyone that it is safe for the Americans to leave. They are not going to drive us out of the country as did the North Vietnamese and Viet Cong, thus their best strategy is to keep a low profile for a while.

Keep enough attacks going so that suspicions are not aroused, but keep the majority of your powder dry for another day. After having failed to prevent the elections, the best bet is to wait until the Americans leave and then come on with a full force of attacks on the existing Iraqi government and security forces. Once the Americans are gone, they are not likely to come back and the insurgents will have free run of the entire country to wreak havoc and spread terror among the Iraqi people. Will the Iraqis themselves be strong enough at that point to resist these attacks? Or will the country sink deeper and deeper into chaos? Whether the troops stay or leave, the U.S. is in a no-win situation.

We announced "mission accomplished" much too quickly, but of course it gave Bush a chance for a great photo op as he strutted across the deck on the aircraft carrier off the San Diego harbor. We did not have a plan for Iraq after the invasion had accomplished its objectives. The idea that the Iraqis would welcome us with open arms and immediately get down to the business of building a democracy was totally unrealistic. We are now bogged down in fighting Saddam's kind of war, a war we can't win and that could go on forever. Saddam was a tyrant, to be sure, but he wasn't dumb, and there is now ample evidence that Saddam planned for a war of insurgency.

What Bush calls success may have been nothing more than being sucked into a strategy of insurgency that may have been planned by Saddam Hussein months before the invasion. Secret intelligence reports indicate that Saddam dispatched more than 1,000 security and intelligence officers to military facilities near Baghdad, where they underwent guerrilla training. Knowing he could not win a war by confronting the U.S. military head on, he began laying the foundation for the insurgency that has gone on since Bush declared "mission accomplished" and claimed many more lives of U.S service men and women than were lost in the initial invasion itself to say nothing of the Iraqi people who are now the primary targets.[60]

Regarding the restoration of order, we created policy as we went along. First it was the creation of local caucuses. Then the Iraqi Governing Council. Then we backed Brahimi's plan to abolish this council and instead appoint a president, two vice-presidents, a prime minister, and a group of technocrats to run ministries and prepare the country for elections which finally took place. Now we have the new government trying to get itself up and running. Talk about flip-flopping. Does anyone know what they are doing? Hopefully the

Iraqi people can make something constructive out of this mess and create a new society and a new identity as a nation without annihilating each other in the process. But I am not particularly hopeful. How can they engage in peaceful negotiations after inflicting so much pain on each other?

When is all this going to end? Do we really know how the war against the insurgency is going? The various forces engaged in Iraq do not agree on a unified system for measuring successes and failures in the campaign against the insurgents. How can we tell if we are winning or losing? Nothing has gone as it was supposed to from the beginning, and perhaps there is a lesson to be learned here. Once the initial mistake was made—and that means the invasion itself—nothing thereafter can go right. Eventually it seems as if we will have to pull at least the majority of our troops out of the country. People in this country will eventually grow weary of the continued bloodshed. But when? The insurgents seem to have an inexhaustible supply of lethal explosives and willing martyrs and look as if they can keep on going forever.[61]

We have done nothing but create a total mess and destabilize the entire region. We have not just made a mistake; we have committed a colossal blunder of historic proportions. But is the American public willing to pay for this blunder? While many Americans still support the war and think it was the right thing to do, how long will they stay the course?[62] Are they willing to see an increase in taxes of some kind to pay for this war rather than pass the cost on to their children and grandchildren? Other than for the people who have lost family members and friends, have the rest of us had to sacrifice anything?

It seems to me that if we are really serious about stabilizing Iraq and giving the new government a chance to take hold, we would put enough troops into the country to quell the violence. Even if it takes a million soldiers, we owe this to Iraq having overthrown the old order and created the conditions for the current chaos. This would mean the draft would have to be reinstituted, of course, and taxes would have to be raised. But if this war is worth fighting the country should be called upon to make sacrifices. Realistically, however, when the sons and daughters of members of Congress began to be drafted and when the sons and daughters of big donors to the Republican party were drafted to serve in Iraq we would be out of there in a hurry. Commitment to this war is only skin deep, in my opinion.

Joe Klein writing in Time warns against the dangers of what he calls "yellow ribbon patriotism," that the country does not really understand what the soldiers are going through in Iraq. America by and large is at peace and only a few of its citizens are at war putting their lives at risk and paying the price. If the war in Iraq is worth fighting why isn't it worth paying for rather than passing the cost on to future generations? There are no war-bond drives as there were in World War II. The president has not issues a national call to service. People are not being asked to collect clothing for the children of Iraq. If the public at large does not really acknowledge this war and feel some of the agony, how can the nation engage in a long overdue conversation about the war and whether it is still worth fighting?[63]

It is a mystery to me why there is not more moral outrage in the country. Why aren't the people losing loved ones in Iraq not outraged as the body bags, which are kept well hidden from public view, keep returning? We make the dead into heroes, and deservedly so, but this fails to recognize the human cost of this war on the part of people who have lost a loved one or of the soldiers who come back wounded and maimed. Why aren't we all sickened at the sight of bus loads of children being blown into oblivion? During the Vietnam War we protested everything in sight and the students at Kent State put their lives on the line for their convictions. All the protesting made a difference: Johnson finally got the message and decided not to run for a second term. Where do we see this kind of courage and outrage today? Do people just not care? There have been some protests, to be sure, but they have not involved enough people or been consistent enough to make a difference.

One has to wonder why impeachment proceedings were not started against this administration many years ago when it became apparent that we went to war under false pretenses. The Republicans were so quick to impeach Clinton for some foolish, half-baked sexual affair that he indeed lied about under oath. But Clinton's behavior was not an impeachable offense as it did not constitute high crimes and misdemeanors against the state. Bush on the other hand has misled the American people about things of far greater consequence, about weapons of mass destruction, about links to al Qaeda, about the real reasons for this war, and on and on.

The result of these deceptions has been the death of more than 3,000 American soldiers, numerous deaths of soldiers and citizens from other countries and countless Iraqis, the loss of respect in the international community, an increase in the risk from terrorism as more and more people hate America with a vengeance, the expenditure of at least $300 billion and counting, and the sacrifice of our future as the national debt climbs to staggering proportions.[64] Bush not only wants guns and butter; he wants guns, butter, and tax cuts and to hell with the consequences. If Clinton committed impeachable offenses, are not Bush's actions far closer to "high crimes and misdemeanors" against the United States of America?[65]

This war is the most reckless, arrogant, and irresponsible use of American power since Vietnam and perhaps in our entire history. At least in Vietnam a war was already going on. We did not start it, and there was some plausible threat to American interests if communism spread to other countries, the so-called domino theory. The perpetuators of this war need to be held accountable. If Iraq sinks into a full-scale civil war, Bush, Cheney, Rumsfeld, Wolfowitz, Rice, and Powell ought to be indicted by the International Court of Justice for war crimes against the Iraqi people. At the very least Bush needed to be sent back permanently to his Crawford ranch, where he spends much of his time anyhow, so he could play Texas Ranger without hurting anyone.[66]

It is interesting to note that most of the people responsible for this war have not had any active military experience. This includes President Bush, Vice-President Cheney, and Deputy Defense Secretary Paul Wolfowitz. Cheney, described as a powerful, steamrolling force in favor of the war, accepted a series of student and family-related draft deferments during the Vietnam War and in 1989 reportedly announced that he "had other priorities in the `60s than military service."[67] Bush sat out the war in the Texas National Guard, what we used to call "weekend warriors" but in the Iraqi War have been called up to active duty. There is still some question as to whether Bush fulfilled his obligations to the Guard, but all this was tabled as a result of the unfortunate CBS scandal involving Dan Rather and his unsupported story about Bush's record.[68] Meanwhile Kerry volunteered for Vietnam service and received several medals for his valor and was questioned by the Swift Boat Veterans, who spread doubts during the 2004 campaign about his service record. It seems obvious that patriotism was not in and that what counted during the campaign was the ability to talk tough. It was the chickenhawks, as they have been called, who prevailed.

WHAT THE WAR IN IRAQ IS ABOUT

There is most likely no single reason for this war as the administration would have us believe. Already in May of 2004 a researcher turned up 23 different rationales offered by the Bush administration in the year following the 9/11 attacks. This research was based on a computer analysis of public statements from Bush administration officials and key members of Congress. The rationales ranged from possession of weapons of mass destruction to spreading Western-style democracy. Some gained currency, according to the researcher, as earlier rationales failed. For example the war over WMDs that never existed gave way to transformation of the Middle East and liberating the Iraqi people. One surprising finding is that the media often introduced ideas about the dangers Iraq posed for the United States even before the Bush administration.[69] Regarding the legitimacy of the war, the researcher had this to say:

> . . . it's tempting to say that if they have 23 reasons for going to war, we probably should have gone. On the other hand, I find myself thinking that if they had

to keep coming up with new reasons for going to war, we probably shouldn't have done it. It's almost like the decision came first, then the rationales."[70]

It has been claimed that Iraq was a hotbed of terrorism and that this alone justified the invasion, citing early links to a radical Islamist group in northern Iraq that went by the name of Ansar al-Islam, a group that had probably taken refuge in Iraq after being driven out of Afghanistan. If there were any such links, it is most likely that Saddam supported this group in the hopes of destabilizing the Kurdish attempt to create a ministate. Saddam had been unable to control the northern part of his country since 1991 when the no-fly zone was created by the U.S. and England and enforced by the U.S. military.[71]

But even if this link existed and this reason was an adequate justification to invade another country, it is clear that Saudi Arabia was the most logical target for such an invasion. Eleven of the fifteen hijackers came from that country, Osama bin Laden was a Saudi, and we know the country was funding al Qaeda. Even later most of the suicide bombers in Iraq were believed to come from Saudi Arabia.[72] Talk about a hotbed of terrorism. Of course if we had invaded Saudi Arabia, Bush would not have been able to hold hands with his good friend from that country, Crown Prince Abdullah.[73] One thing is certain, Iraq is definitely a hotbed of terrorist activity now, so maybe we should start all over and invade it again.

Bush is something of a Wilsonian who believes that the United States has both a moral and a practical duty to spread its values throughout the world. While he did not campaign as one, he became a Wilsonian after 9/11, and his insistence that freedom is a universal yearning is similar to the rhetoric of Woodrow Wilson himself.[74] Wilson only wanted to make the world safe for democracy. Today's goal is to make the whole world democratic, but this attempt to spread American values around the world leads to imperialism, a theme that is found in many articles and books.[75] Anonymous, for example, accuses American elites of being so full of themselves that they cannot imagine that the rest of the world does not want to be like us and that an American empire in the 21st century is not only our destiny, it is our duty to mankind, "especially to the unwashed, unlettered, undemocratic, unwhite, unshaved, and antifeminist Muslim masses."[76]

Perhaps the best book to deal with the theme of imperialism is entitled The Empire Has No Clothes by Ivan Eland of the Independent Institute. Eland argues that the fight against communism and now against terrorism is a cloak for expanding America's empire. With the demise of the former Soviet Union, the rationale has changed from the need to contain the spread of communism to one of spreading democracy, free markets, and human rights around the globe.[77] Of course every American president denies that America seeks to establish an empire and does not seek an expansion of territory,[78] yet more than a decade after the end of the Cold War, the United States has about 250,000 troops stationed overseas in 38 countries and at sea and legally binding commitments to provide security to at least 36 countries.[79] Defense spending is now 10 percent higher than the Cold War average.[80] The informal empire of the United States stretches around the world, even larger than the more formal British empire at the height of its powers.[81]

The founders of the republic would be appalled, says Eland, to find out that America is now a militaristic global empire on a mission to convert the world to democracy and free markets while at the same time destroying its own republic. The country some time ago abandoned a foreign policy that had served the republic well for some 175 years, a policy that took advantage of America's uniquely secure geography to exercise a policy of military restraint overseas and stay out of disputes among other nations where possible.[82] Since the end of the Cold War, the Clinton and two Bush administrations have regarded the entire world as their playgound.

Wars that seek to expand this empire can be expensive. The Vietnam War, which started modestly, ended up costing $500 billion in current dollars. The war in Iraq will end up costing more than $300 billion when all is said and done. Such wars can be ruinous to a country's economy. The Soviet Union collapsed, Eland argues, because its nonviable economic system could not support its overextended foreign and military policies. Reagan's buildup of our defense capabilities put added pressure on the Soviet Union, but it probably would have collapsed even without this pressure. There is a lesson here for the United States: While it has military dominance in the world, it no longer has the economic dominance to match—witness our increased budget deficit. Everything depends on a strong economy.[83] In the 20th century alone, nine empires collapsed because of imperial overstretch.[84]

Eland also links imperialism to terrorism and argues that an interventionist foreign policy designed to maintain an informal American empire is the main reason the United States has a problem with terrorism.[85] If the United States refrained from getting involved in civil wars in the Middle East, for example, the terrorist groups involved in those conflicts would have no incentive to attack our country. This war is being conducted by militant Islamic fundamentalists who believe that many secular governments in Islamic countries backed by the United States are corrupt. Osama bin Laden and others like him want to cleanse the faith of this corrupt power structure and get the United States out of their territory.[86] If we had not involved ourselves in this Islamic civil war by supporting the Saudi government and stationing our forces on Saudi soil, al Qaeda would have had no reason to attack this country, but this fact is often overlooked in the rhetoric that claims these terrorists are out to destroy our way of life and our freedoms. This fear can be manipulated by those in power to garner support for further empire building.[87]

Eland believes we must rediscover the founders' preference for a foreign policy of military restraint overseas and resurrect the constraints built into the Constitution on the president's war-making powers.[88] The U.S. should intervene overseas only in the rare cases where its vital interests are actually at stake or when the balance of power breaks down in any one of a small number of regions.[89] The United States needs to monitor the balance of power in only two key regions, Europe and East Asia, and take some kind of action only if regional powers or organizations fail to maintain that balance of power. Using military power to defend a narrower set of interests will save the taxpayers a great deal of money and actually increase the security of Americans by giving terrorists less of a reason to attack this country.[90] Getting rid of our informal empire and interventionist foreign policy will also save the American republic from further erosion of its essential liberties.[91]

What about oil as a reason for our intervention in the Middle East? Are we hooked on cheap oil to keep our economy humming and preserve our way of life? Is this what the war is about? Certainly the first Gulf War was largely about oil as we could not let Saddam come to dominate a large part of the world's oil supply. Was the same true here, that we wanted to have control of an alternative source of oil in Iraq, as it has the largest oil reserves of any country in the Middle East outside of Saudi Arabia? Those oil fields were undeveloped under Saddam and were not fulfilling their potential. Was our goal to install a new regime under our control who would develop these fields?

Andrew J. Bacevich, writing in the Wilson Quarterly, argues that America's political and military efforts in the Middle East go by many names, but all of these undertakings grow from a decision that the American way of life requires unlimited access to foreign oil. This decision was made by, of all people, Jimmy Carter, who, in response to the Iranian Revolution and the Soviet invasion of Afghanistan, enunciated what came to be known as the Carter doctrine. In one of his State of the Union addresses, he stated, "An attempt by any outside force to gain control of the Persian Gulf region will be regarded as an assult on the vital interests of the United States of America, and such an assault will be repelled by any means necessary, including military force."[92]

Carter initiated a contest for control of the region. The overarching motive for this action was preservation of the American way of life as Carter realized that what Americans demanded from their government was more freedom, defined as more choice; more opportunity; and above more abundance measured in material terms. That abundance depended on assured access to lots of cheap oil. The Carter doctrine came to be held as sacrosanct, according to Bacevich, and each of his successors has expanded U.S. military involvement and operations in the region.[93] This involvement has gradually converted the Persian Gulf into World War IV's principal theater of operations to guarantee the ever-increasing affluence that underwrites the modern American conception of liberty.[94]

Bush's response to 9/11 openly acknowledged the existence of a conflict in which the U.S. had been engaged for the previous 20 years. World War IV became the centerpiece of his presidency.[95] A pacified Middle East brought into compliance with American ideological norms and policed by the American military could be counted on to provide plentiful supplies of oil and accept the presence of a Jewish state in its midst.[96] But as Bacevich wrote his article, the outcome of World War IV hangs very much in the balance and, even if the U.S. prevails, the future is no less discouraging. The collision between American interests and a noncompliant world will provide the impetus for more conflicts, dooming the United States to fight perpetual wars in a vain effort to satisfy our craving for limitless freedom.[97]

Spending hundreds of billions of dollars to defend our oil interests in the Middle East is not worth it, say some experts. According to one analysis, the Pentagon spent an estimated $30 to $60 billion per year to defend oil imports from the Gulf region during the 1990s that were worth, on average, only about $10 billion annually.[98] We get about 23.5 percent of our oil imports from the Gulf region, a lower percentage of our total petroleum consumption than Japanese or European countries, yet these nations provide few military forces to defend their supplies. Persian Gulf countries are more dependent on oil than we are as it makes up a greater share of their exports than it does our imports.[99] Thus the Carter doctrine is outdated and we need to think more seriously about our need for Middle Eastern oil and its importance to our way of life. We need an energy policy that is not based on drilling our way to energy independence, a goal that is impossible to achieve, but one based on energy conservation and increased reliance on renewable sources of energy.[100]

CONSEQUENCES

The Bush administration had a grand vision regarding the outcome of the war in Iraq, one in which the consequences were a win-win situation for virtually everyone involved. The threat that Saddam posed to the United States and the world would be removed and Bush would receive world accolades for having taken this bold step against a brutal dictator. The Iraqi people would be freed from his rule and able to establish a democracy in which freedom for all the people of Iraq would prevail. The oil fields in Iraq would be modernized so that more oil could be produced to reduce our dependence on Saudi Arabia for the cheap oil we need to keep our economy going. And Bush's friends in corporate America, like Haliburton, would be rewarded with lucrative contracts to rebuild the country and so would be additionally motivated to contribute even more money to his campaign to keep the Bush administration in power. It was a rosy scenario to be sure, as noted by one author quoted below:

> The policy makers in the Bush administration also grandly assumed and asserted that U.S. soldiers would be greeted by the Iraqi masses with flowers as conquering heroes; that after short, low-intensity occupation of three months or so, democracy would flourish; that the deep-seated historical antagonisms among Shiites, Baathists, and Kurds would not create postwar conflict; that Iraqi oil production could be dramatically boosted from 3 million barrels a day to 6 million; that the invasion would create a reverse domino effect in which one autocratic regime after another in Iraq, Libya, and Iran would fall, paving the way for a new democratic Middle East.[101]

The Bush administration did little or no planning for what would happen after the country was conquered, assuming that the Iraqis would take over their country and run it effectively after Saddam was removed from power. Bush did not listen to the advice of his secretary of state who warned that after the invasion we would own the country and be responsible for putting it back together. Our priorities were to win the war as quickly as possible and get out to let the rebuilding of the country begin. More than three years later, the country is anything but put together and a struggle is still going on to fill the power vacuum we created. So one consequence of this war was to throw the country into something of a civil war over who should govern the country and what kind of a society should Iraq become. This struggle could go on for years.

Far from reducing the threat of terrorism, the invasion of Iraq has only increased the threat and Iraq has indeed become a hotbed of terrorism. According to a report released in January 2005 by the National Intelligence Council, Iraq has replaced Afghanistan as the training ground for the next generation of "professionalized" terrorists. This report took a year to produce and is based on the analysis of 1,000 U.S. and foreign experts. The report states that before the invasion Saddam had only circumstantial ties with several members of al Qaeda. Osama bin Laden rejected the notion of forming some kind of alliance with Saddam because Saddam rejected radical Islamic ideals and ran a secular government.[102]

But after Saddam was overthrown and instability increased, hundreds of foreign terrorists flooded into the country across its unguarded borders. They were able to utilize tons of weapons in unprotected caches that they are now using against the U.S. military and Iraqis themselves. These foreign terrorists have been forming tactical, ever-changing alliances with former Baathists who were removed from power and other insurgents. The conflict in Iraq that we started has only deepened solidarity among Muslims and has helped spread radical Islamic ideology throughout the country and the region. Instead of spreading democracy throughout the region, the war appears to be spreading terrorism.[103]

The threat of terrorism around the world has increased in recent years, so much so that the State Department, which usually puts hard data in its annual report on terrorism, decided in May 2005 it would no longer release the numbers but just talk about terrorism in a general way without quantifying whether attacks are up or down. The U.S. Congress however was briefed on the numbers and some went public. The number of terrorist attacks worldwide more than tripled in a year, going from 172 to 655, and this does not include attacks by insurgents in Iraq even though they are called terrorists. The old report was generally considered to be the last word on trends in global terrorism.[104]

The administration appears to be beginning to think about a shift in its terror policies to cope with the transformation of al Qaeda into a far more amorphous, diffuse, and difficult-to-target organization from the one that was behind the 9/11 attacks. This shift involves moving away from efforts to capture and kill al Qaeda leaders to a broader "strategy against violent extremism." There are few specifics as to what this new policy means, but much of the discussion has apparently focused on how to deal with the rise of a new generation of terrorists who will survive the conflict in Iraq and disperse all over the world to merge with local extremist movements.[105]

Another part of this new strategy is an increase of public diplomacy efforts to win over Arab public sentiment. The United States has embarked on a campaign of what has been called political warfare in Arab countries. It is spending tens of millions of dollars on everything from psychological operations teams and CIA covert operatives to openly funded media and think tanks. This campaign is an attempt to win the hearts and minds of the Arab people by influencing not only Muslim societies but Islam itself. Many Arab leaders believe that America is at war with Islam, according to a report by the Center for Strategic and International Studies, which also concludes that U.S.- Arab relations are at their lowest point in generations. For millions of Muslims the toppling of Saddam confirmed the picture of the United States as an imperialistic country bent on controlling the Middle Eastern countries.[106]

What about an exit strategy? At what point do our troops leave Iraq and come home? Or will they be there for the forseeable future? If we leave now further chaos in Iraq will surely be the result.[107] But if our rationale for staying the course is based on the same faulty assumption that we can build a democracy where none existed before, we are most likely to be sorely disappointed. Can anything good come out of an endeavor based on lies and deceptions? In March 2006 Bush stated that our troops would remain in Iraq until at least 2009, and that the decision to remove all U.S. forces would belong "to future presidents and future governments of Iraq."[108] In other words, he is going to leave it to someone else to clean up the mess he created, but when he leaves office he can claim to have stayed the course. This is leadership?

In the 1991 Gulf War there were those who wanted our troops to push on to Baghdad and force a regime change at that point when we had Saddam on the run. But George H. W. Bush's then secretary of defense said, "Once you've got Baghdad, it's not clear what you do with it. It's not clear what kind of government you would put in. . . . How much credibility is the government going to have if it's set up by the United States military? . . . To have American military forces engaged in a civil war inside Iraq would fit the definition of Quagmire, and we have absolutely no desire to get bogged down in that fashion." These were the words of a younger, but seemingly wiser, Dick Cheney.[109] George H. W. Bush himself said in defense of his decision not to advance to Baghdad:

> Trying to eliminate Saddam . . . would have incurred incalculable human and political costs. . . . We would have been forced to occupy Baghdad and in effect, rule Iraq. . . . There was no viable "exit strategy" we could see, violating another of our principles. Furthermore, we had been self-consciously trying to set a pattern for handling aggression in the post-Cold War world. Going in and occupying Iraq, thus unilaterally exceeding the United Nations' mandate, would have destroyed the precedent of international response to aggression that we hoped to establish.[110]

Would that George W. Bush had listened to his earthly father rather than some supernatural being that he used to justify his grand vision for the Middle East. Meanwhile our soldiers continue to be killed day by day and make the ultimate sacrifice for this folly, but it not only our troops and their friends and loved ones who are paying a price. Small communities across America are beginning to feel the effects of this war. Time magazine reports the story of a small town in Arkansas where the mayor, police chief, and eight other citizens went off to Iraq as part of the National Guard callup. They all returned unharmed, but while they were gone, nothing progressed in the town and now there is no money to do things in the town that need doing. This gives the Republican mayor mixed emotions after he had witnessed the waste of resources in trying to rebuild Iraq, money that could be used to rebuild our infrastructure in this country.[111]

Meanwhile recruitment of new people for the Army has fallen off dramatically. In April 2005 the Army was about one-third short of its recruiting goal as concerns about serving in Iraq began to affect parents and young people across the country. This was the third month in a row that recruitment had fallen short of targets, and each month had gotten worse. In February the gap was 27 percent, and in March it was 31 percent. In May the unofficial shortage was about 25 percent, but the target had been lowered by 1,350 recruits to "adjust for changing market conditions." These shortfalls have led to speculation that the draft might be reinstituted, but there is little support for this in Congress or in the country at large.[112]

With regard to more global and long-term consequences, one major possibility is a realignment of power in the Middle East with the emergence of a "Shia crescent" in the region. The Sunni-Shia civil war in Iraq could erupt into a wider war across the Arab world, with the Shia, dominated by Iran, gaining control of the Iraqi, Saudi, and Caspian oil and gas fields which would be placed under the protection of Iran's nuclear arsenal. This would give Iran unprecedented power and give it great power status, something that has not been accomplished in the Middle East since the collapse of the Ottoman Empire. How the Western world would live with this empire dependent as they are on its oil and gas must be something keeping statesmen up at night.[113]

Another long-term consequence of the Bush doctrine is to overthrow the international system in effect until 9/11, a system established by the Treaty of Westphalia in 1648 to govern relations between nations. This treaty was established after the Thirty Years War in Europe, when nearly 30 percent of Central Europe's population was killed in what was nominally a conflict over religious beliefs. The principle established in this treaty was one of sovereignty within a country's borders and noninterference across those borders. Threats to this order were defined as movements of military units across established frontiers.[114] This treaty, with some exceptions, has by and large governed relations between countries for thousands of years.

The 9/11 attacks brought an end to this order as threats were no longer identical with state action. The terror we face today is mostly unconnected to a particular state and, according to Fareed Zakaria, states have been getting out of the terror business since the late 1980s. Terrorist groups can be harbored in any country, even the United States, and draw on support from private individuals and groups, not from the states themselves. In Afghanistan it was less a case of a state sponsoring a terror group and more a case of a terror group sponsoring a state. What we are faced with are dozens of such groups around the world connected by a global ideology.[115]

The Bush doctrine went beyond traditional understandings of what constitutes a preemptive or preventive war, and beyond most accepted notions of the limits imposed by international law and the sovereignty of independent states. It asserted that "the best defense is a good offense" and went on to say that "we will not hesitate to act alone, if necessary, to exercise our right of self-defense by acting preemptively." This new doctrine seemed to be demolishing the whole structure of international law as it had developed since the 17th century. In view of what this doctrine has led to, this shift in thinking has not received anything like the attention it deserves. What has not been brought into public focus for discussion is under what conditions a preemptive war is justified and who has the legitimacy to make such a decision.

The doctrine of preemption that Bush proclaimed cannot replace the old international order as no nation can organize a new international system by itself. Nor does this country want to encourage every state to define preemption based on its national interest. This makes an international organization like the United Nations more important than ever despite this administration's disdain for such organizations. The United States cannot go it alone, but we can take the lead in establishing a new global order by being willing to discuss international principles of preemption and the means for carrying out a preemptive strategy, even while reserving, as Kissinger says, "the right to defend national security alone as a last resort."[116]

Bush's actions in invading Iraq have actually rendered the doctrine of preemption obsolete. Even given reforms in the intelligence apparatus of this country, it is extremely doubtful that our intelligence will be of such a nature that it will be beyond a reasonable doubt and that the public will believe an administration that justifies another so-called preemptive war on the basis of that intelligence. The credibility gap that has resulted from the failure to find weapons of mass destruction in Iraq means that a second application of the Bush doctrine will be more problemmatical.[117] People will hopefully be more skeptical of statements about "irrefutable evidence" if they are made again in relation to some other country. Bush cried wolf once too often in this case, and future statements made about Iran or North Korea would, I hope, not be taken at face value.

According to Zbigniew Brzezinski, the national security advisor under former President Carter, the notion of total national security is now a myth. Total security and total defense in the age of globalization are not attainable. The real issue is, according to him, with how much insecurity can America live while promoting its interests in an increasingly interdependent world? This insecurity we all feel to some degree has to be politically manageable.[118] The Bush doctrine of hegemony, preemption, and unilateralism only creates more insecurity for the citizens of the country.

... a policy of unilateral compulsion would breed an international state of mind in which the surreptitious acquisition of WMD would become a high priority for states unwilling to be intimidated. Such states would then have an additional incentive to assist terrorist groups, which, fueled by a thirst for revenge, would be even more likely to anonymously unleash weapons of mass destruction against America. Survival of the fittest, always inherent to some degree in international politics (although gradually mitigated by international convention guiding the conduct of states), would thereby become the law of the global jungle. In the long run, that could prove to be the fatal undoing of America's national security.[119]

Harping on terrorism, as this administration has done, distorts the public's vision of the world and poses the risk that America will be seen abroad as being self-absorbed and it helps anti-American ideology gain international credibility by labeling the United States a self-appointed vigilante.[120] Instead, according to Brzezinski, the United States needs to encourage the evolution of interstate relations into an informal international governance structure based on an awareness of the common destiny of mankind.[121] Striking a balance between an existential sovereign hegemony and an emerging global community, between the values of democracy and the imperatives of global power, will be America's major dilemma for the foreseeable future.[122]

Fareed Zakaria argues that above all the United States must make the world comfortable with its power by leading through consensus. America's role in the world must be based on not just its strength, but on a global faith that its power is legitimate. If this faith is squandered, the American century will be lonely, brutish, and short.[123] Unilateralism will not do as one nation on its own cannot deal with the menace of terrorism. It will take a concerted effort on the part of all peace-loving nations to confront this menace and devise new rules to govern relations between nations. These countries need to forge new alliances and upgrade multilateral institutions such as the United Nations to deal with the new age of terrorism.

If Iraq does get its act together and becomes a force for democracy in the Middle East, something that seems increasingly remote but is still possible, history will probably go easy on Bush and judge him as having the foresight and courage to force changes in the Middle East that were necessary for world peace in the new age of terror. Perhaps many believe that the end justifies the means and, along with Bush, defend the war as the right thing to do no matter what the reason. People in this country seem already to have forgotten how all this happened and that the existence of weapons of mass destruction were our primary reason for an unprovoked, supposedly preemptive war in which we attacked a country that had done us no harm. The question of what Iraq had ever done to us is still unanswered and, until a satisfactory reason is given for this war that can be defended as morally legitimate, it remains a war that has no moral justification and the world will continue to consider us a rouge nation that uses its power arbitrarily.

As I look again at the Project for a New American Century that may have provided in large measure the motivation for this war, it increasingly appears that this is an imperialistic doctrine by design. It talks about America's responsibility to create a new world order consistent with our interests. Iraq was the first test case for these ideas about American power and world leadership and provided the first opportunity for the new American century.[124] If this is what this war is primarily about, America will suffer the fate of other empires throughout history as it overreaches and overextends itself. What is called for is an idealism tempered by realism, an idealism that recognizes the responsibilities of this nation to better the lives of people throughout the world, tempered with a realistic and humble assessment of America's role in the world and the limitations of our power. The words of John F. Kennedy are instructive in this regard:

> We must face the fact that the United States is neither omnipotent or ommiscient—that we are only 6 percent of the world's population—that we cannot impose our will upon the other 94 percent of mankind—that we cannot right every wrong or reverse each adversity—and that therefore there cannot be an American solution to every problem.[125]

This administration operated on the basis of a theology that viewed human nature in the abstract apart from the restraints provided by history and institutions. Remove the Iraqi people from the tyranny they had lived under for decades and democracy would flourish because people everywhere want freedom. There was no postwar plan because we intended to leave Iraq soon after Saddam was removed from power and leave it to the exiles to clean up any messes we left behind. After this hope proved to be in vain, all that mattered was our will and determination to stay the course. But people are never free from their past experiences or their culture and all the will in the world is not going to overcome the sordid history of the Iraqi people. In the words of David M. Kennedy, a history professor at Stanford University:

> The real purpose for invading Iraq was the extravagant ambition to transform the political culture of the entire Middle East. The Bush Administration bet American might and good intentions against the accumulated weight of centuries of religious rivalry, tribal tensions, wanton bloodletting and authoritarian rule. Even American hyperpower as proved no match for the burden of all that sorry history.[126]

Our hope now is to train enough Iraqi security forces and turn responsibility for the security of their country to them and begin to withdraw our forces. But this strategy has its own problems as we find ourselves in the midst of a growing civil conflict. Creating security forces in Iraq makes sense if the conflict is with insurgents who are trying to overthrow a legitimate government. But if the conflict is sectarian in nature with the police and Army dominated by one group this strategy could only add to the conflict. Most of the Iraq police and military come from the Shiites and Kurds which the Sunnis see as a Shiite-Kurdish milita on steroids, according to a Senior Fellow in Defense Policy at the Council on Foreign Relations.[127] Thus much of the violence is directed at the police and the military, a situation that is likely to continue.

Hopefully the American people are beginning to see through the lies, the deceptions, the bogus claim to be liberating people by getting them killed and to be exporting democracy at the point of a gun and hold this administration accountable for their mistakes. And we need to hold Congress accountable for its role in this mess and make them think through what fighting terrorism really means and whether a doctrine of preemption can be the basis for the use of our military power. There are too many unanswered questions about this war that nobody wants to deal with and too many attempts to make this war seem noble and in the interests of freedom for the Iraqi people when it may have been motivated by something quite different.

Meanwhile this administration continues its assult on cherished American values, including the right of American citizens to a lawyer and a trial by jury, fairness in our tax system, and conservation of our natural resources and protection of the environment. There are definitely weapons of mass destruction in Washington D.C. and they have still not been held accountable. Regime change is more necessary than ever in this country. We need leadership that can formulate and carry out a realistic and effective plan of attack that is in the best interests of this nation and reflects the best this country has to offer the rest of the world.

NOTES

1. Ron Suskind, *The Price of Loyalty: George W. Bush, the White House, and the Education of Paul O'Neill* (New York: Simon & Schuster, 2004), 70–86.

2. "Home Page," *Project for the New American Century*, 1997, www.newamericancentury.org. (4 May, 2005).

3. "Statement of Principles," Project for the New American Century, 1997, www.newamericancentury.org. (4 May, 2005).

4. *Project for the New American Century*, 1997.

5. Suskind, *Loyalty*, 86. According to Ron Suskind in his later book, "The primary impetus for invading Iraq . . . was to make an example of Hussein, to create a demonstration model to guide the behavior of anyone with the temerity to acquire destructive weapons or, in any way, flout the authority of the United States." Ron Suskind, *The One Percent Doctrine* (New York: Simon & Schuster, 2006), 123.

6. Richard A. Clarke, *Against All Enemies: Inside America's War on Terror* (New York: Free Press, 2004), 32.

7. In a book by Anonymous, who turned out to be Michael Scheuer, a senior intelligence official, the author criticizes the Bush administration for being unprepared to strike targets in Afghanistan the day after 9/11 and deliver a crippling blow to al Qaeda forces. The more-than-three-week delay allowed them to disperse their personnel, military stores, and funds within the country and across its borders. Anonymous claims America lost the war against al Qaeda because of its uprepardness to strike immediately. Anonymous, *Imperial Hubris: Why The West Is Losing the War on Terror* (Washington, D.C.: Brassey's Inc. 2004), 22–27.

8. Arthur M. Schlesinger, Jr. *War and the American Presidency* (New York: W. W. Norton, 2004), 34.

9. Schlesinger, *War and the American Presidency*, 34.

10. E.J. Dionne, "Promoting a climate of fear," *Denver Post*, 7 October 2004, p. 7(B). As it turned out, the tubes were a precise fit for Iraq's conventional weapons. See Dafna Linzer and Barton Gellman, "Doubts on Weapons Were Dismissed," *Washington Post*, 1 April 2005, p. A(01).

11. Bob Woodward, *Plan of Attack* (New York: Simon & Schuster, 2004), 249. According to another account, Tenent made this statement in response to a question from a Western Union executive as to whether he thought we would be invading Iraq, not in response to whether Iraq had weapons of mass destruction. See Ron Suskind, *The One Percent Doctrine* (New York: Simon & Schuster, 2006), 211.

12. While the war on Iraq has usually been referred to as a preemptive war, it is more accurately described as a preventive war. The Department of Defense Manual refers to a preemptive war as "an attack initiated on the basis of incontrovertible evidence that an enemy attack is imminent." A preventive war, on the other hand, refers to a potential future attack, and is therefore much more problemmatical and speculative. Even if Saddam had possessed weapons of mass destruction, he had no missiles capable of delivering them to the United States and no known links to al Qaeda. Under these conditions he still would have posed no imminent threat to the United States justifying a preemptive strike. See Schlesinger, *War And The American Presidency*, 23.

13. See Kevin Whitelaw, "Missed Clues, Dropped Balls," *U.S. News & World Report*, 19 July/16 July 2004, 22–23; Kevin Whitelaw, "Getting It 'Dead Wrong'," *U.S. News & World Report*, 11 April 2005, 32–33; and "WMD report: In search of accountability," *The Week*, 15 April 2005, 18.

14. In April 2005 a report commissioned by the president officially stated that the work of the UN inspectors who had extraordinary access during their three months in Iraq was routinely dismissed by the Bush administration and the intelligence community during the run-up to the war. Every new charge made by the administration, including secret purchases of uranium from Africa, biological weapons manufactured

in mobile laboratories, and pilotless planes that could disperse anthrax or sarin gas above U.S. cities, had been tested and disproved by the UN inspectors. See Dafna Linzer, "Critical intel report brings call for more use of U.N. inspectors," *Denver Post*, 4 April, 2005, 12(A).

15. Suskind, *Loyalty*, 72–73.

16. John Prados, *Hoodwinked* (New York: The New Press, 2004), 176–198.

17. See R. Jeffrey Smith, "Libby: Bush gave OK to leaks," *Denver Post*, 7 April 2006, 1(A); Tom Raum, "Leak flap erodes Bush's credibility," *Rocky Mountain News*, 8 April, 2006, 27(A); Pete Yost, "Why CIA-leak news is bad for White House," *Denver Post*, 9 April, 2006, 3(A); and "Bush: When the 'leak' comes from the top," The Week, 21 April, 2006, 4.

18. Paul R. Pillar, "Intelligence, Policy, and the War in Iraq," *Foreign Affairs* 85, no. 2 (March/April 2006): 15–27.

19. James Risen, *State of War: The Secret History of the CIA and the Bush Administration* (New York: Free Press, 2006).

20. In May 2005 a highly classified British memo was leaked during the election campaign there which indicated that President Bush had already decided to overthrow Saddam by the summer of 2002 and was determined that U.S. intelligence data support this decision. The memo quotes British Foreign Secretary Jack Straw, a close colleague of then U.S. Secretary of State Collin Powell, as saying that "Bush had made up his mind to take military action." This memo was written while the Bush administration was still maintaining that no decision had been made to go to war and before the case for war was made to the United Nations. See Warren P. Strobel and John Walcott, "Memo:Bush wanted Hussein out in '02," *Denver Post*, 10 May 2005, 14(A); Douglas Jehl, "British memo rouses Bush critics," *Denver Post*, 20 May 2005, 24(A). See also Eugene Robinson, "Downing Street's smoking gun," *Denver Post*, 17 June 2005, 7(B) and "The Downing Street memo: Was Bush hellbent on war?" *The Week*, 24 June 2005, 16.

21. The words of Secretary of State John Quincy Adams, spoken to the House of Representatives on July 4, 1821, are instructive in this regard. "America does not go abroad in search of monsters to destroy. She is the well-wisher to freedom and independence of all. She is the champion and vindicator only of her own. She will recommend the general cause by the countenance of her voice, and the benign sympathy of her own example. She well knows that by once enlisting under banners other than her own, were they even the banners of foreign independence, she would involve herself beyond the power of extrication, in all the wars of interest and intrigue, of individual avarice, envy, ambition, which assumed the colors and usurped the standards of freedom. The fundamental maxims of her policy would insensibly change from liberty to force. . . . She might become the dictatress of the world. She would no longer be the ruler of her own spirit." Quoted at www.thisnation.com/library/jqadams.html. (10 August 2005).

22. Peter Singer, *The President of Good and Evil: The Ethics of George W. Bush* (New York: Dutton, 2004), 155–162.

23. Robert W. Tucker and David C. Hendrickson, "The Sources of American Legitimacy," *Foreign Affairs* 83, no. 6 (November/December 2004): 20.

24. Tucker and Hendrickson, "Sources," 20.

25. "Democracy won't work under the gun," *The Week*, May 13, 2005, 18. See also H. D. S. Greenway, "As Iraq's stepsister, Afghanistan suffers from 'salutary neglect'," *Rocky Mountain News*, March 26, 2005, 9(C); Fareed Zakaria, "Warlords, Drugs and Votes," *Newsweek*, 9 August 2004, 39; and Pamela Constable, "Assignment Afghanistan," *Smithsonian*, February 2005, 108–123.

26. Schlesinger, *War And The American Presidency*, 24.

27. A 16-member panel of former world leaders appointed by Secretary-General of the UN Kofi Annan said that the United Nations must accept the need for preemptive or preventive global military action under certain circumstances. The report stated that "the international community does have to be concerned about nightmare scenarios . . . which may conceivably justify the use of force, not just reactively but preventively." But the document also warned about unilateral strikes and made it clear that even the world's most powerful nation cannot on its own fight threats to international security. Edith M. Lederer, "Panel urges U.N. to accept need for pre-emptive action," *Times-Picayune*, 1 December 2004, A(1). While the group did write a definition of terrorism, it did not specify any criteria for justifying a preemptive strike. On March 16, 2006, the Bush administration's new national security strategy was unveiled. While the document tones down unilateral action it still legitimizes preemptive or preventive war as a pivotal point without specifying any criteria for such action. See Ved Nanda, "Security strategy hopeful," *Denver Post*, 26 March 2006, 5(E).

28. Statement by David Kay on the Interim Progress Report on the Activities of the Iraq Survey Group (ISG) Before the House Permanent Select Committee on Intelligence, the House Committee on Appropriations, Subcommittee on Defense, and the Senate Select Committee on Intelligence, 2 October 2003. www.cia.gov/cia/public_affairs/speeches/2003/david_kay_10022003.html. (7 April 2006).

29. Philip Shenon, "Ex-arms inspector rips Bush advisers," *Denver Post*, 19 August 2004, 6(A); Fred Kaplan, "The Art of Camouflage," 26 January 2004. www.slate.msn.com/id/2094415/. (1 June 2005).

30. Douglas Jehl, "Report: No illicit Iraq arms," *Denver Post*, 7 October 2004, 1(A).

31. Johanna McGeary, "What Saddam Was Really Thinking," *Time*, 18 October 2004, 50–52.

32. Douglas Jehl, "Report: Iraq intended to make WMDs," Denver *Post*, 17 September, 2004, 23(A).

33. See "Iraq's missing weapons: Was the war a mistake?" *The Week*, 22 October 2004, 18; and Mortimer B. Zuckerman, "The real truth about Iraq," *U.S. News & World Report*, 1 November 2004, 80.

34. "The world at a glance" *The Week*, 6 May 2005, p. 9.

35. Walter Pincus and Dana Milbank, "Commission: No Iraq tie to al-Qaeda evident," *Denver Post*, 17 June 2004, 1(A). In September 2006, a bipartisan Senate Intelligence Committee report based on captured documents and prisoner interrogations came to the same conclusion. See "No Saddam-al Qaida link," *The Week*, 22 September 2006, 5.

36. Pincus and Milbank, "No Iraq tie" 1(A).

37. Terrance Hunt, "War rationale battered again," *Denver Post*, 17 June 2004, p. 15(A).
38. Pincus and Milbank, "No Iraq tie," 1(A).
39. Pincus and Milbank, "No Iraq tie," 1(A). In its final report the 9/11 commission did find evidence that Iran had more suspicious ties to al Qaeda than did Iraq. See Michael Isikoff and Michael Hirsh, "9/11: The Iran Factor," *Newsweek*, 26 July 2004, 24–27. In a Harris poll released in July 2006, 50 percent of respondents in the U.S. stated they believe Iraq had WMDs when it was attacked. This finding was up from 36 percent the previous year. This result shows the effectiveness of the administration's propaganda campaign and leads some to despair about the public's ability to base its conclusions on sound evidence. See Charles J. Hanley, "Poll finds half of Americans believe Hussein had WMDs," *Denver Post*, 7 August 2006, 2(A). In another CNN poll released in September 2006, 43 percent of Americans still believed Saddam was "personally involved" in the 9/11 attacks. See Eric Effron, "The Week," *The Week*, 29 September 2006, 3.
40. Walter Pincus and Dana Milbank, "Bush stands firm on link between Iraq and al-Qaeda," *Denver Post*, 18 June 2004, 17(A).
41. Steven R. Weisman, "Iraq war just, Bush tells U.N." *Denver Post*, 22 September 2004, 1(A).
42. Even U.S. Administrator Paul Bremer finally admitted after he had left Iraq that we never had enough troops on the ground and he should have insisted that more were needed. These troops were also not allowed to do police work, which explains why they did nothing to stop widespread looting after we had taken the country and did not secure ammunition dumps and other critical sites. See Fareed Zakaria, "How to Win the 'Netwar' in Iraq," *Newsweek*, 18 October 2004, 45. See also Ambassador L. Paul Bremer III, *My Year in Iraq* (New York: Simon & Schuster, 2006).
43. Sam Harris states that if democracy were to take root in Middle Eastern countries, it would be little more than a gangplank to theocracy. See Sam Harris, *The End of Faith* (New York: W.W. Norton, 2004), 132. Robert J. Barro in a Business Week editorial predicts that the probability is 96 percent that a state religion will emerge in Iraq. See Robert J. Barro, "Iraq: One Nation Under Allah," *Business Week*, May 9, 2005, 30. See also Stanley Reed, "Mosque and State: Just How Close?" *Business Week*, 21 February 2005, 48–49.
44. Ibrahim Kazerooni, "Iraq kudos misplaced," *Denver Post*, 3 January 2005, 7(B).
45. Thomas Friedman, "A better future for Iraq?" *Denver Post*, 5 May 2005, 7(B).
46. Michael Ware, "Meet The New Jihad," *Time*, 5 July 2004, 24–29.
47. Douglas Jehl and David E. Sanger, "Prewar report foretold costly invasion results," *Denver Post*, 28 September 2004, 10(A).
48. See John Daniszewski, "British study foresees civil war in Iraq," *Denver Post*, 2 September 2004, 18(A). See also Stan Crock, "A Time for Realism and Reaching Out," *Business Week*, 15 November 2004, 52–54.
49. "Iraq teeters at the brink," *The Week*, 10 March 2006, 4.
50. George Will, "Worsening Iraq situation shows no signs of reversal," *Denver Post*, 19 March 2006, 7(E).

51. Paul Garwood, "Attacks on Iraqi civilians raising fears of civil war," *Denver Post*, 17 May 2005, 12(A). Life in Iraq has become a game of Russian roulette. Life goes on, but one has to hope that he or she is not at the wrong place at the wrong time and becomes the victim of terrorist activity. See Ilana Qzernoy, "Learning to Live with the Bomb," *U.S. News & World Report*, 23 May 2005, 33. See also Derrick Jackson, "The victims we don't even count," *The Week*, 21 January 2005, 14; Jonathan Finer and Omar Fekeiki, "Iraqis paying price for war," *Times Picayune*, 5 June 2005, A(19); and Aparisim Ghosh, "When Hate Lives Next Door," *Time*, 13 March 2006, 33–35.; Aparisim Ghosh, "Baghdad Diary, *Time*, 14 August 2006, 24–34. In 2005, the Bush administration estimated civilian casualties at 30,000, but a study released in 2006 by Johns Hopkins University and backed by Human Rights Watch put the count at 601,027 since the invasion. See Julian E. Barnes, "Report puts Iraqi deaths far higher than previous ones," *Denver Post*, 11 October 2006, 18(A).

52. The two sects are separated by doctrinal differences that have a long history. When the Prophet Mohammud died in A.D. 632, he had no surviving sons, so there was disagreement on who should succeed him. Some believed leadership should pass to Mohammud's father-in-law, Abu Bakr. Others wanted it to pass to Ali, the husband of Mohammed's daughter Fatima. The Shiat Ali, or Partisans of Ali, came to be known as Shia, or Shites. Abu Bakr, on the other hand, started a line of caliphs who called themselves Ahl al-Sunnah wal-Jamaah, or simply Sunnis. Even though they are a minority in Iraq, the Sunnis account for about 85 percent of the world's one billion Muslims. "The Shiites and the Sunnis," *The Week*, 4 March 2005, 11. Michael Scott Doran, an Assistant Professor of Near Eastern Studies at Princeton University, writing in Foreign Affairs, states that "Radical Sunni Islamists hate Shiites more than any other group, including Jews and Christians." Michael Scott Doran, "The Saudi Paradox," *Foreign Affairs* 83, no. 1 (January/February 2004), 35–51.

53. Anonymous, *Imperial Hubris*, 213.

54. One commentator thinks the United States has essentially stopped trying to build a democratic order in Iraq and is simply trying to gain some stability and legitimacy. America is spending billions of dollars in Iraq and getting very little for it either in terms of actual improvements on the ground or in winning the good will of the people. Iraq is on track, he believes, to become another corrupt, oil-rich quasi-democracy. See Fareed Zakaria, "Elections Are Not Democracy," *Newsweek*, 7 February 2005, 30. For an article that warns corruption in Iraq is out of control see Michael Hirsh, "Follow The Money," *Newsweek*, 4 April 2005, 34–35.

55. Henry A. Kissinger, "America's Assignment," *Newsweek*, 8 November 2004, 34.

56. Anonymous, *Imperial Hubris*, 200–207.

57. Anonymous, *Imperial Hubris*, 205. As the war dragged on, some supporters admitted they had not taken the culture of Iraq seriously enough. See Andrew Sullivan, "What I Got Wrong About the War," *Time*, 13 March 2006, 72.

58. Joshua Mitchell, "Not All Yearn to Be Free," *Washington Post*, August 10, 2003, B(7), as quoted in Anonymous, *Imperial Hubris*, 203–204.

59. Salama Na'mat, "The foreigners who want Iraq to fail," *The Week*, 27 May 2005, 14.

60. Edward T. Pound, "Seeds of Chaos," *U.S. News & World Report*, 20 December 2004, 20–26. For the story of how U.S. mistakes, misjudgments, and intelligence failures allowed the insurgency to develop see Joe Klein, "Saddam's Revenge," *Time*, 26 September 2005, 45–52.

61. Scott Johnson and John Barry, "A Deadly Guessing Game," *Newsweek*, 16 May 2005, 28–29. See also Dan Eggen and Scott Wilson, "Suicide Bombs Potent Tools of Terrorists," *Washington Post*, 17 July 2005, A(01). After three years of fighting the insurgents, many public services in Iraq are still not up to the level they were before the invasion. See Charles J. Hanley, "lofty goals of rebuilding Iraq run into harsh reality," *Denver Post*, 9 April 2006, 1(A). On September 20, 2001, Bush declared before a joint session of Congress that "Our war on terror begins with al Qaeda, but it does not end there. It will not end until every terrorist group of global reach had been found, stopped and defeated." It seems obvious from this statement that the war on terror will go on forever. See Ron Suskind, *The One Percent Doctrine* (New York: Simon & Schuster, 2006), 19.

62. Already in early 2005, support for the war began to wane as some polls showed that the majority of Americans began to feel that the war had not been worth the cost. See "Iraq: Two years later, was it worth it?" *The Week*, 1 April 2005, 8; and Dan Balz and Richard Morin, "U.S. conflicted: Most believe Iraq better off: war a mistake," *Denver Post*, 16 March 2005, p. 17(A). The war is also depleting military manpower and gear faster than they can be fully replaced. Recruitments are down for both the regular military and the National Guard, and recruits have been enticed to sign up with some very questionable practices. See Ann Scott Tyson, "Two Years Later, Iraq War Drains Military," *Washington Post*, 19 March 2005, A(01).

63. Joe Klein, "The Danger of Yellow Ribbon Patriotism," *Time*, 29 August 2005, 23. See also Reggie Rivers, "You call this support?" *Denver Post*, 13 January 2006, 7(B). See also Marie Cocco, "America detached from war in Iraq," *Denver Post*, 26 May 2006, 7(B).

64. In February 2006 the Bush administration planned to request an additional $65.3 billion from congress to fight the wars in Afghanistan and Iraq after they had just approved $50 billion in December. This amount was expected to last through September 30, 2006. By that time the two wars had already cost over $500 billion since the fighting started, with the bulk of this money going to fight the war in Iraq. The Congressional Budget Office projects additional costs of $266 billion for Iraq assuming our involvement for another decade. Some studies that take into account indirect costs such as veteran's benefits and the effect on oil prices suggest the bill for Iraq could be as high as $2.2 trillion. This is enough money to buy General Motors Corporation stock about 175 times at current prices. Contrast this with Defense Secretary Donald Rumsfeld's estimate of $50 billion in 2003, and Paul Wolfowitz's hope that Iraq's vast oil reserves would help defray the costs of an extended stay. See Andrew Taylor, "Bush requests additional $65 billion for war in Iraq," *Denver Post*, 17 February 2006, 15(A); Mark Mazzetti and Joel Havemann, "Bush will seek extra $70 billion for wars," *Denver Post*, 3 February 2006, 2(A); Kevin G. Hall, "Studies: War could cost $2 trillion," *Denver Post*, 15 January 2006, 23(A); Abraham Lustgarten,

"The Price of Iraq," *Fortune*, April 3, 2006, 22; Matthew Yglesias, "$1.27 Trillion," *The American Prospect*, July/August 2006, 28–32; and Drew Brown, "War costs near $549 billion," *Denver Post*, 28 September 2006, 31(A).

65. See Center for Constitutional Rights, *Articles of Impeachment Against George W. Bush* (Hoboken, NJ: Melville House Publishing, 2006).

66. On the assumption that a picture is worth a thousand words, I would recommend that everyone look at a picture in Time magazine entitled the "Three Amigos" that shows Cheney, Bush, and Rumsfeld in interesting poses on a visit to the President's ranch. Bush is obviously ready to draw his guns (he doesn't have any), a stance that may say everything that needs to be said about how Bush views himself. These three should consider making a Western movie once they are done with their governmental careers. See Nancy Gibbs and John F. Dickerson, "Inside the Mind of George W. Bush," *Time*, 6 September 2004, 27. The picture was taken by Christopher Morris.

67. Timothy Noah, "Elizabeth Cheney, Deferment Baby: How Dick Cheney dodged the Vietnam draft," *Chatterbox*, 18 March 2004. www.slate.msn.com. (27 April 2004).

68. See James Rainey, Stephen Braun, and Ralph Vartabedian, "Guard data show gung-ho Bush lost interest," *Denver Post*, 1 October 2004, 25(A); Edward T. Pound, "The Service Question," *U.S. News & World Report*, 20 September 2004, 24; and "Bush's Guard records reveal lapses," *Denver Post*, 8 September 2004, p. 1(A).

69. William Raspberry, "Reasons for war seem to multiply," *Times-Picayune*, 29 May 2004, B(7).

70. Raspberry, "Reasons," B(7).

71. Catherine Taylor, "Taliban-style group grows in Iraq," *The Christian Science Monitor*, 15 March 2002, 1.

72. Susan B. Classer, "'Martyrs' in Iraq Mostly Saudis," *Washington Post*, 14 May 2005, p. A(01).

73. See Craig Unger, *House of Bush, House of Saud* (New York: Scribner, 2004), for an extensive discussion of the relationship between George W. Bush and the rulers of Saudi Arabia. The jacket photograph on that book shows George W. Bush holding hands with Crown Prince Abdullah at the G8 Summit in Evian, France, on June 1, 2003, the same as he did at his Crawford ranch in the spring of 2005.

74. Some argue that Bush became a Wilsonian and argued that the invasion was necessary to end Saddam's violations of human rights and democratize the Middle East only after the failure to find weapons of mass destruction. See Ivan Eland, *The Empire Has No Clothes* (Oakland, CA: The Independent Institute, 2004), 126.

75. In addition to the books quoted below, see Rashid Khalidi, *Resurrecting Empire: Western Footprints and America's Perilous Path in the Middle East* (Boston: Beacon Press, 2004), and George Soros, *The Bubble of American Supremacy: Correcting the Misuse of American Power* (New York: Public Affairs, 2004).

76. Anonymous, *Imperial Hubris*, 198.

77. Ivan Eland, *The Empire Has No Clothes* (Oakland, CA: The Independent Institute, 2004), 67.

78. Eland, *Empire*, 68.

79. Eland, *Empire*, 12.

80. Eland, *Empire*, 614.
81. Eland, *Empire*, 29.
82. Eland, *Empire*, 51–52.
83. Eland, *Empire*, 104–105.
84. Eland, *Empire*, 112.
85. Eland, *Empire*, 200.
86. Eland, *Empire*, 115, 200–201.
87. Eland, *Empire*, 203.
88. Eland, *Empire*, 204.
89. Eland, *Empire*, 220.
90. Eland, *Empire*, 252.
91. Eland, *Empire*, 194.
92. Andrew J. Bacevich, "The Real World War IV," *The Wilson Quarterly* XXIX, no. 1 (Winter 2005): 43.
93. Bacevich, "World War," 43.
94. Bacevich, "World War," 45.
95. Bacevich, "World War," 58.
96. Bacevich, "World War," 60.
97. Bacevich, "World War," 62.
98. Eland, *Empire*, 252.
99. Eland, *Empire*, 251–52.
100. See Justin Blum, "Oil crews chase dwindling U.S. Supply," *Denver Post*, 10 June 2005, 21(A) for an assessment of the ability of the U.S. to attain energy independence. Some analysts in this article say that barring the development of alternative sources of energy or a significant decline in consumption, the United States will become increasingly dependent on imported oil. See also Kenneth S. Deffeyes, *Beyond Oil: The View From Hubbert's Peak* (New York: Hill & Wang, 2005, for an assessment of the world oil supply.
101. Unger, *House of Bush, House of Saud*, 277.
102. Dana Priest, "Iraq New Terror Breeding Ground," *Washington Post*, 14 January 2005, p. A(01). In September 2006, a Senate report disclosed a CIA assessment that Iraq did not have a relationship with al Qaeda before the war. Saddam did not trust al Qaeda and saw Islamic extermists as a threat to his regime. Jim Abrams, "Saddam no friend of al-Qaida," *Rocky Mountain News*, 9 September 2006, p. 30(A). This report was apparently never passed on to the White House. Walter Pincus, "CIA mum on Iraq intel, panelists say," *Denver Post*, 15 December 2006, 2(A).
103. Priest, "Breeding Ground, A(01). See also Daniel Benjamin, "Why Iraq Has Made Us Less Safe. . . . " *Time*, 18 July 2005, 48. In September 2006, a National Intelligence Estimate completed in April 2006 representing a consensus view of 16 disparate spy services in the U.S. government was reported by the New York Times. This report found that the invasion of Iraq had spawned a new generation of Islamic radicals and since the 9/11 attacks the overall terrorist threat has grown. This was the first formal appraisal of the threat of terrorism since the Iraq war began. The Bush administration contested this account stating that the media accounts described only part of the conclusions and thus distorted the findings. They then declassified portions of the

report so that everybody could draw their own conclusions. See Mark Mazzetti, "Spy agencies say Iraq war fueling terror," *Denver Post*, 24 September 2006, 1(A); Katherine Shrader, "U.S.: Iraq was grooming new terrorists," *Denver Post*, 26 September 2006, 8(A); Greg Miller, "Bush bares intel report," *Denver Post*, 27 September 2006, 1(A).

104. See "How they see us: A sore loser in the war on terror," *The Week*, 6 May 2005, 16.

105. Susan B. Glasser, "Review May Shift Terror Policies," *Washington Post*, 29 May 2005, p. A(01). See also Linda Robinson, "Plan Of Attack," *U.S. News & World Report*, 1 August 2005, 27–34.

106. David E. Kaplan, "Hearts, Minds, and Dollars," *U.S. News & World Report*, 25 April 2005, 24–33. In March 2006 Defense Secretary Donald Rumsfeld stated that the U.S. was faring poorly in the battle of ideas and had not found the "formula" for countering the ideological support for terrorism. See "Rumsfeld: U.S. losing hearts and minds," *Denver Post*, 28 March 2006, 14(A).

107. For the perils of withdrawing our troops too soon see Mortimer B Zukerman, "Seeing the Job Through," *U.S. News & World Report*, 12 December 2005, 80; Fareed Zakaria, "Panic Is Not The Solution," *Newsweek*, 5 December 2005, 35; and Joe Klein, "Think Twice About a Pullout," *Time*, 28 November 2005, 29.

108. See "Bush: No end in sight in Iraq," *The Week*, 31 March 2006, 6; and Julian E. Barnes, "Putting More Time On The Iraq Clock," *U.S. News & World Report*, 3 Arpil 2006, 33–34. It certainly seems like we are in Iraq for the long haul and are planning to maintain a significant presence there for many years to come. Four superbases are being built in Iraq where the Pentagon plans to consolidate U.S. forces after they have left the front lines. And we are building a $592 million embassy, the largest we have ever built anywhere, in the heart of Baghdad's's international zone. The embassy takes up 104 acres which is six times larger than the United Nations compound in New York City. See Michael Hirsh, "Stuck in the Hot Zone," *Newsweek*, 1 May 2006, 32–35; and Charles J. Hanley, "Massive U.S. Embassy rivals Vatican in size," *Rocky Mountain News*, 15 April 2006, 25(A).

109. Schlesinger, *War and the American Presidency*, 33.

110. Schlesinger, *War and the American Presidency*, 32. This quote comes from a memoir written by George H.W. Bush and Brent Scowcroft, his National Security Advisor entitled *A World Transformed* (New York: Knopf, 1998).

111. Cathy Booth Thomas, "Finding the Way Home: The `Gunslingers' of Bradford, Ark." *Time*, 6 June 2005, 26–29.

112. Robert Burns, "Army might not meet its full-year recruiting goals," *Denver Post*, 9 June 2005, 9(A). In response to these declining numbers, some recruiters apparently were using questionable practices to enlist people. To deal with this problem the Army suspended recruiting activities for one day so its recruiters could attend what was called an all-day "values stand-down" on ethical recruiting. See "Recruiting: When the Army falls short," *The Week*, 10 June 2005, 20. See also David Kiley, "Uncle Sam Wants You In The Worst Way," *Business Week*, 22/29 August 2005, 40.

113. See Martin Walker, "The Revenge of the Shia," *The Wilson Quarterly*, XXX, no. 4 (Autumn 2006): 16–20.

114. Kissinger, "America's Assignment," 34.
115. Fareed Zakaria, "Terrorists Don't Need States," *Newsweek*, April 5, 2004, 37.
116. Kissinger, "America's Assignment," 35.
117. Schlesinger, *War and the American Presidency*, xiii. Seymour M. Hersh has written that the U.S. has intensified planning for a possible air attack against Iran's nuclear facilities. These plans even involve the use of bunker-buster tactical nuclear weapons to destroy underground facilities. The administration, of course, denies any such plans. See Seymour M. Hersh, "The Iran Plans," *The New New Yorker*, 17 April 2006, 30–37. Meanwhile, a senior official of of the UN nuclear watchdog agency sharply criticized a House committee's report that tried to make a case that Iran's program is greared towards making nuclear weapons, calling it "outrageous and dishonest." In his opinion, Iran has produced weapons-grade material only in small quantities far below the level that can be used in nuclear weapons. George Jahn, "U.N. nuclear watchdog says report on Iran `outrageous,'" *Denver Post*, 15 September 2006, 2(A).
118. Zbigniew Brzezinski, *The Choice: Global Domination or Global Leadership* (New York: Basic Books, 2004), 17.
119. Brzezinski, *The Choice*, 34.
120. Brzezinski, *The Choice*, 215.
121. Brzezinski, *The Choice*, 218.
122. Brzezinski, *The Choice*, 227.
123. Fareed Zakaria, "The Arrogant Empire," *Newsweek*, 24 March 2003, 20–33.
124. George Packer, *The Assassins' Gate: American In Iraq* (New York: Farrar, Straus and Giroux, 2005, 36.
125. Schlesinger, *War and the American Presidency*, 44.
126. Nancy Gibbs, "Was It Worth It?" *Time*, 27 March 2006, 27–31. See also Laura Secor, "Big Think Central," *The American Prospect*, May 2005, 22–26 for more skeptical comments about making the Middle East more democratic.
127. Stephen Biddle, "Seeing Baghdad, Thinking Saigon," *Foreign Affairs* 85, no. 2 (March/April 2006): 2–14.

Chapter Two

Freedom

There is a tremendous amount of talk about freedom from the Bush administration, particularly in regard to Iraq and the freedom we have supposedly given to that country. Spreading democracy and freedom in the Middle East is the major thrust of our foreign policy in that area and we invaded Iraq as liberators bringing freedom and democracy to that country. As President Bush said in an address to Congress nine days after the terrorist attacks of September 11, "The advance of human freedom—the great achievement of our time and the great hope of our time—now depends on us. Our nation—this generation—will lift a dark threat of violence from our people and our future. We will rally the world to this cause by our efforts, by our courage."[1] A year and a half later we unleashed our "shock and awe" bombing campaign against Iraq in the name of freedom.

After no weapons of mass destruction were found in Iraq, freeing the Iraqi people from the oppression and tyranny of Saddam Hussein became the major justification for our invasion of that country. The best way to fight Islamic terrorism, so believed the president, was to see freedom and democracy spread throughout that region of the world. In Bush's second inaugural address the expansion of liberty became the purpose of foreign policy all over the world. He enunciated an ambitious goal of bringing democracy to the entire world. "The best hope for peace in our world is the expansion of freedom in all the world," he said. "It is the policy of the United States to seek and support the growth of democratic movements and institutions in every nation and culture, with the ultimate goal of ending tyranny in our world."[2]

Freedom is an abstraction everyone rallies around, but it can mean many different things in practice. With regard to Iraq, perhaps George Soros was right when he accused Bush of doublespeak. When Bush asserts that "freedom will prevail," as he did fairly often with respect to Iraq, what he really meant is that America will prevail. In a free and open society, as Soros points out, people are supposed to decide for themselves what they mean by freedom and democracy.[3] Now that elections have been held, time will tell how much freedom the United States will tolerate in Iraq, particularly if they choose to go down a different path than we would like and form some kind of an Islamic state. Once real freedom is unleashed, it is impossible to control. One has only to ask the former leaders of the now extinct Soviet Union.

In any event it seems abundantly clear now that we have had five years of this administration what freedom means to Bush and Company. It means they should be free to do whatever they want and whatever they deem is in the interests of the nation or the world without any accountability whatsoever. They are free from any accountability to the UN when it come to the use of force, they do not adhere to any international attempts to restrict their freedom on issues like global warming, and they do not recognize the existence of any international agreements such as the Treaty of Westphalia that respected the sovereignty of nations. They do not believe that the Geneva conventions apply to handling prisoners in Iraq or in Guantanamo Bay and call them enemy combantants with no rights whatsoever.

At home the Bush administration wants the freedom to devise an energy policy for the country that it deems best without having to disclose the members of the board that designed that policy. They want to shut out any citizen participation in decisions that affect the environment. This has been the most secretive administration in years, refusing to respond to Freedom of Information requests and other attempts of citizens to obtain information about government actions. And perhaps worst of all they want the freedom to call anyone they want a terrorist and deny them the most basic rights most countries recognize when it comes to interning people—the right to confront your accuser and to have legal representation. They want this freedom even in regard to American citizens. And they want the freedom to spy on American citizens and monitor their overseas communications.

THE PATRIOT ACT

The so-called Patriot Act is the worst piece of legislation Congress has passed in years. It allows for secret military tribunals for people suspected of being terrorists, isolated detention of people suspected of crimes, and secret searches of homes and offices of people who may come under suspicion of governmental authorities. This act has nothing to do with patriotism and everything to do with eroding the rights of people in a free nation. It was hurried through

Congress after 9/11 as a response to the attacks against the country. Apparently no one, including the Democrats, gave much thought to the long-term implications of this act and how it would be applied. Some of the specific provisions of this act when first passed included the following:

1. The government is given expanded authority to run "sneak and peek" searches without notifying the person being searched, including investigations of American citizens in cases having nothing to do with terrorism.
2. Police agents are permitted to investigate you without showing probable cause, simply by designating their investigations as being for "intelligence purposes."
3. Federal agents are given shortcuts around court review of their requests for wiretapping our phones and entering anyone's computer. Instead of a "request," which had required agents to show some reason for snooping, the new law allows agents merely to "certify" that the intrusion is relevant to an ongoing investigation. The judge must issue the order, even if the certification appears to be nonsense.
4. The FBI is empowered to force libraries and bookstores to cough up lists of books we have borrowed or bought.[4]

Most people in this country probably believe that these provisions apply only to foreigners suspected of being terrorists. But every citizen of this country should take note that most of the provisions of this act apply equally to U.S. citizens and are available for the police to use in any and all federal investigations. And who is a terrorist? The act defines domestic terrorism as acts that "appear to be intended to influence the policy of a government by intimidations or coercion."[5] It doesn't take any stretch of imagination to realize that peace protestors, abortion activists, union strikers, and demonstrators for environmental or other causes could be labeled as terrorists.

In response to criticisms of this act, the Bush administration called for amending the act to strengthen some of its provisions by authorizing secret arrests for the first time in the nation's history, taking citizenship away from people who belong to or even support disfavored groups, and giving more power to government agents to search our homes and personal records.[6] All this was advocated as necessary to protect our freedom. In other words ordinary citizens can be investigated, detained, interrogated, tried, and punished secretly by the government with no legal protections so the terrorists won't erode our rights and freedoms.

It seems clear, as said at the outset, that what freedom means in this context is that the Bush administration wants the freedom to do as they darn well please with no accountability to any other branch of government. What would the founding fathers think of this act and its relation to the Bill of Rights, which they believed was necessary to protect the rights of individual citizens? They would roll over in their graves and say something like,"NEVER, NEVER, NEVER give the executive or any branch of government this kind of arbitrary authority without any checks and balances on how this authority is going to be used." What in the world was Congress thinking when this act was passed?

Critics of the act saw it as an assult on personal privacy and individual liberty. Five states and 377 separate communities passed resolutions condemming its provisions.[7] In March 2006 President Bush signed a renewal a day before sixteen provisions of the old law were set to expire. Congress had to extend the expiration date twice because of political battles, but finally agreed on a compromise. The new law does contain some curbs on the powers granted under the old act. People who receive subpoenas granted under the Foreign Intelligence Surveillance Act for library, medical, computer and other records can challenge a gag order in court. But most of the expiring provisions of the original act were renewed including one that lets federal officials obtain "tangible items" such as business records from libraries and bookstores if done in connection with foreign intelligence and international terrorism investigations.[8]

DETAINEES

The way this act was going to be used became apparent soon after it passed. Prisoners from the war in Afghanistan began arriving at Guantanamo Bay designated by the government as "unlawful enemy combatants." As such they were detained for two years without access to attorneys and had no recourse to U.S. courts to challenge their detentions. They were not charged with any specific crimes against the nation and were held incommunicado. The U.S. Court of Appeals for the D.C. Circuit upheld this practice with the ingenious argument that foreign nationals held outside the U.S. do not have the "privilege of litigation" before American courts. While a 1903 lease gave the United States "complete jurisdiction and control" over Guantanamo Bay, the court ruled that it is not a formal U.S. "sovereign" territory. Noncitizens have the right to challenge detention only if they are within the borders of the United States.[9]

What was created here, it appears, is an island that was completely outside any law where the detainees had no rights whatsoever. They could be detained and held without charges until the government declared an end to its war on terrorism. America's allies as well as its enemies began to wonder what protections their citizens had against the world's most powerful military. Presumably the United States government had the authority to snatch people off the streets in foreign countries and detain them indefinitely without any charges and any right to counsel. And we have been so quick to charge other countries like China with human rights violations.

Even worse from the standpoint of the rights of American citizens was the detention of two other people who were citizens of this country. One was a native of Baton Rouge, Louisiana, a man named Yaser Esam Hamdi, who was captured in Afghanistan as a Taliban fighter. He was initially taken to Guantanamo Bay and later transferred to a U.S. Navy brig in Charleston, South Carolina, where he was held for two years without access to counsel. The government designated him an "enemy combatant" without having to prove its case in an American court, arguing that the allegations against Hamdi should be sufficient to justify his detention. An appeals court agreed, ruling that a U.S. citizen when "captured in a zone of active combat operations in a foreign country" loses his standing to challenge the facts underlying his detention.[10]

The second case involved a Brooklyn-born U.S. citizen named Jose Padilla, who was arrested at Chicago's O'Hare airport on allegations that he had knowledge of an al Qaeda plan to explode a "dirty bomb" somewhere in the country. He was initially flown to New York City as a "material witness" but a month later was designated an "enemy combatant" and transferred to the same brig in Charleston with Hamdi. The government justified his detention on the basis of six pages of charges against him which the government claimed could not be challenged. In this case an appeals court challenged the government and argued that the president "lacks inherent constitutional authority . . . to detain American citizens on American soil outside a zone of combat."[11]

In both these cases the Justice Department argued that the President, as commander in chief, has the power to detain indefinitely anyone he designates an "enemy combatant" in the war on terror. This interpretation of Article II of the Constitution should give every American citizen cause for grave concern. If this power were upheld, anyone the administration opposed or disliked for whatever reason could be so designated and thrown into jail and denied his or her right to due process, which includes the right to legal counsel to challenge the detention. No administration, no matter how moral and just, should have this kind of absolute power over the citizens of the country.

Fortunately for the country the Supreme Court played its role effectively and acted as a check and balance against this kind of grab for power. The court disagreed with the president's assertion that he had unfettered executive power to lock up suspected al Qaeda and Taliban operatives indefinitely without their being charged. Only one of the nine justices upheld the Bush administration's claim of unilateral freedom to do what it wants with suspected terrorists. This was a remarkable action given the court's conservative makeup, but in the end they argued that the United States should not abandon constitutional principles of freedom as its leaders try to protect the nation from another terrorist attack.[12]

By an 8-1 vote the justices said that a U.S. citizen was entitled to counsel and due process in a federal court even if suspected of being a terrorist. And in a 6-3 decision the court also ruled that the more than 600 foreigners held at Guantanamo Bay also had access to court to challenge their confinement. As a legal matter, the court said, there was no difference between being held in Guantanamo Bay and being held in the United States itself. As Associate Justice Sandra Day O'Connor said, "It is during our most challenging and uncertain moments that our nation's commitment to due process is most severely tested."[13] She also said that "war is not a blank check for the president."[14] In agreeing with the majority on the first decision, Justice Antonin Scalia wrote that "the very core of liberty secured by our Anglo-Saxon system of separated powers has been freedom from indefinite imprisonment at the will of the executive."[15]

In February 2005 a U.S. district judge ruled that suspects held at Guantanamo Bay could challenge their confinement in U.S. courts because military tribunals did not protect their rights. The government had argued that military tribunals met the Supreme Court's demand for legal protection for the detainees. But the ruling stated that these tribunals violated the U.S. Constitution and in some cases the Geneva Convention governing the treatment of prisoners. This conflicted with another ruling which held that the Supreme Court ruling did not provide these detainees the legal basis to seek their freedom in U.S. courts. These conflicting rulings were expected eventually to reach the Supreme Court for clarification of its previous decision with respect to the Guantanamo Bay detainees.[16]

Such a case did reach the Supreme Court in 2006 when Osama bin Laden's personal driver who was captured in Afghanistan and shipped to Guantanamo Bay challenged the legality of Bush's tribunals.[17] The Administration wanted to try Salim Hamdan before a military tribunal where the rules permitted only a cusory defense. Under the rules for these tribunals, the plantiff could have been excluded from his own trial, evidence based on hearsay and torture would have admissible, and his conviction could have been based on evidence that neither the plantiff nor his civilian lawyer could have examined.

In a 5-3 ruling, the Supreme Court issued a stunning rebuke to this procedure, ruling that these tribunals were not acceptable because Congress had passed no law authorizing them or regulating their procedures. The tribunals violated both the Geneva Conventions and U.S. law. Associate Justice John Paul Stevens wrote in support of the decision that even suspected terrorists were entitled to due process "by a regularly constituted court" and were entitled to the basic protections of the Geneva Conventions.[18] This ruling reminded Bush that he is not above the law and does not have unlimited powers as commander in chief in a time of war. Almost immediately, however, the administration began trying to work it way around this decision, and it was not expected to be of immediate help to the 450 detainees at Guantanamo who may continue to sit in prison indefinitely.[19]

In September, 2006, Bush acknowledged what had long been suspected, that foreign-based CIA prisons existed where inmates where subjected to treatment that most people, with the exception of Bush himself, would call torture. Bush also said that 14 of the top terrorism suspects held in these prisons had been transferred to Guantanomo Bay where he wants to put them on trial. Since there were approximately 100 prisoners cycled through this system, that left the fate of the rest in question. Bush also demanded that Congress approve his plan for military tribunals without key legal safeguards for suspects, legalize the CIA's detention program, and shield U.S. officials from war-crimes prosecution.[20]

Several senators balked at this demand, and argued that the Geneva conventions should not be tampered with in this way because it would invite future enemies to do the same to any Americans that they capture. Even former Secretary of State Colin Powell opposed the administration's proposal warning that "the world is beginning to doubt the moral basis of our fight against terrorism."[21] The White House and the dissident senators reached a compromise that would allow the CIA's program to continue and and the trials of suspected terrorists to begin and at the same time preserve the prohibition against mistreating prisoners that are an essential part of the Geneva Conventions.

However the final bill that passsed Congress stripped the 14,000 detainees held by the U.S. in Iraq, Afghanistan, and Guantanamo of their right to challenge their detention in court, a provision that challenged Supreme Court rulings. While they can get partial access to evidence brought against them, evidence that has been obtained through coercion is admissable which in effect legitimizes torture as a means of obtaining information. The president also has the power to decide which interrogation techniques constitute a breach of the Geneva Conventions, and to determine the criteria of exactly who is an enemy combatant. For all the huffing and puffing, the president got practically all of what he wanted.[22] Some of this, of course, was election year politics as the Republicans wanted to maintain their image as the best guardians of the nation's security.

In April 2006 the U.S. government provided the most extensive accounting ever of the hundreds of people held at Guantanamo Bay in response to a Freedom of Information lawsuit filed by the Associated Press. Nearly all of these 558 people had been labeled enemy combatants and were among the first to be swept up in the U.S. global war on terrorism. Many had been held for more than four years and only a handful faced formal charges. The detainees came from 41 countries with the largest numbers from Saudi Arabia, Afghanistan, and Yemen. The names of many of these detainees were disclosed publicly for the first time on March 3 when the Pentagon released about 5,000 pages of transcripts.[23]

With respect to Jose Padilla, in March 2005 a federal judge ordered the Bush administration to either charge him with a crime or release him after more than two and a half years in custody.[24] Finally in November, the administration brought terrorism charges against Padilla in a civilian criminal court. He was charged with being part of a "North American support cell" that had worked to support violent jihad campaigns in Afghanistan and elsewhere, but made no mention of any plans to detonate a "dirty bomb" of which he was initially accused.[25] This action circumvented a Supreme Court case that had been filed by Padilla's lawyers challenging the president's power to seize an American citizen on U.S. soil and hold him indefinitely without being charged or having a criminal trial.[26]

TORTURE

The nation and the world were shocked by photographs of the practices used to torture prisoners held at the Abu Ghraib prison in Iraq. As the evidence mounted, it appeared that hundreds of prisoners had been abused in this scandal terrorized with snarling dogs, subjected to electric shocks and sexual torture. The photographs of Lynndie England gleefully pointing to a group of naked Iraqi prisoners and leading a crawling Iraqi detainnee around by a leash tied to his neck came to symbolize the worst of the abuses. The actions captured by these pictures undermined America's standing before the world.[27]

Court transcripts show that an Iraqi general was punched, slapped, and beaten with a hose by CIA and special-forces soldiers. He was placed in a sleeping bag which was wrapped with an electrical cord while another soldier sat on his chest and blocked his airways. He died a few days later and while an armed forces medical-examiner did not believe he died because of the beating, the examiner did find bruising over his back and five broken ribs that were likely broken a day or two before his death.[28] There are countless other stories like this that could be told about the abuses taking place at this prison.

The scandal led to 10 investigations, dozens of courts-martial, and sworn statements from 37 high-level officials. Lower-level military like England were held accountable, but no evidence was produced that directly supported allegations the abuses were inspired or condoned by superiors higher up the chain of command. Yet people in the While House, the Pentagon, and top military officials all gave the green light to use interrogation methods that violated the Geneva Conventions regarding the treatment of prisoners. Does anyone really believe that these actions were simply the result of a few lower-level people gone astray? Or is it more reasonable to believe that higher-ups created the climate in which such practices were encouraged?[29]

Article 17 of the Third Geneva Convention of 1949 states that "no physical or mental torture, nor any other form of coercion, may be inflicted on prisoners of war." Yet on January 22, 2002, the Justice Department said in a memo to the While House that Geneva would not apply to "the detention conditions of al Qaeda prisoners" and "customary international law has no binding legal effect on either the President of the military because it is not federal law as recognized by the U.S. Constitution." On January 25, 2002, then While House counsel Alberto Gonzales advised the president that portions of the Geneva Conventions are "quaint" and "obsolete" and that adherence would restrict the country's interrogation methods in the "new kind of war." Then on February 7, 2002, the president issued a directive asserting that the Geneva Conventions do not apply to al Qaeda suspects captured in Afghanistan and that neither they nor the Taliban would be eligible for POW status.[30] Do not these statements reflect an administration that wants a completely free hand to treat prisoners any way they want free from any kind of accountability?[31]

Then came stories of abuses of the detainees being held at Guantanamo Bay as allegations were made that the U.S. had sanctioned interrogation techniques that violated the UN Convention Against Torture. Amnesty International called Guantanamo the "gulag of our time" referring to the prison camps of the former Soviet Union that were designed to hold political prisoners. Amnesty accused the U.S. of shirking its responsibility to set the bar for human-rights protections and urged that the facility be closed. In response, White House spokesman Scott McClellan said these allegations were "ridiculous and unsupported by the facts."[32]

A draft UN report concluded that the treatment of the detainees at Guantanamo violated their right to physical and mental health, and, in some cases, constitutes torture. This report was complied by five special envoys to the UN who interviewed U.S. officials, former prisoners, and the detainee's lawyers and families. Violent force-feeding of hunger strikers, incidents of excessive violence used in transporting prisoners and combinations of interrogations techniques "must be assessed as amounting to torture," the report stated. The report urged that the facility be closed and the captives be brought to trial on U.S. territory charging that continued detention is a distortion of international law.[33]

As evidence of abuses at Guantanamo mounted, other information surfaced related to the treatment of these prisoners.[34] In November 2005, a top aide to former Secretary of State Colin Powell said that wrongheaded ideas about how to handle these detainees arose from While House and Pentagon officials who argued that "the president of the United States if all-powerful" and the Geneva Conventions irrelevant. Former chief of staff to Powell Lawrence Wilkerson also stated that Cheney's office, Rumsfeld aides and others argued "that as commander in chief the president of the United States can do anything he damm well pleases." In the field, the U.S. adhered to the policies of these hard-liners who wanted essentially unchecked ability to detain and harshly interrogate prisoners.[35]

In February 2006 the American Civil Liberties Union (ACLU) obtained memos in a Freedom of Information Act lawsuit that showed the FBI strenuously objected to aggressive interrogation techniques being used at Guantanamo and believed they could be illegal. They repeatedly expressed these concerns to the senior military officer at the base and argued that their less aggressive methods were more effective. ACLU attorney Jameel Jaffer said "Now we can say that the documents show conclusively that abuse and torture at Guantanamo was not the result of rogue elements but was the consequence of policies deliberately adopted by senior military and Pentagon officials." In response a Pentagon spokesman said "Guantanamo remains a safe, humane and professional detention operation."[36]

Congress finally acted to stop these abuses and made clear that the U.S. does not permit the torturing of prisoners. Senator John McCain introduced such legislation into the Senate as as amendment to the defense budget. The While House opposed this legislation and threatened to prevent its passage, incorporate a presidential waiver, or at least exempt the CIA from its provisions. These efforts failed and when the ban passed both houses by veto-proof margins, the president had no choice but to sign the bill into law. Called the Detainee Treatment Act of 2005, the bill states that "No individual in the custody or under physical control of the United States Government . . . shall be subject to cruel, inhuman, or degrading treatment or punishment."[37]

However, when the president signed this bill into law he issued a "signing statement" expressing his opinion that he can disregard the prohibition on cruel, inhuman, or degrading treatment or punishment to prevent "terrorists attacks." In other words, this signing statement proclaims that the president retains the right to ignore the ban whenever he thinks it conflicts with his authority as commander-in-chief to protect the American people. Bush has used these signing statements liberally throughout his presidency. In his first term alone, he more than doubled the number of such statements issued throughout the history of the presidency.[38] The Constitution clearly says that only

Congress is empowered "to make all laws." Yet the president through the use of these signing statements says that he can interpret them to mean whatever he wants them to mean and flout the will of Congress and the people. This president wants the freedom to do whatever he wants as became even more evident in the next issue.

SURVEILLANCE

On December 17, 2005, the president admitted to the nation that the National Security Agency (NSA) had been engaged in a program of widespread warrantless electronic surveillance of telephone calls and emails for over four years. Supposedly the executive order allowing eavesdropping without warrants was limited to the monitoring of international phone and e-mail communications where a suspected foreign terrorist was involved. Besides actually eavesdropping of specific conversations, NSA technicians may also have sifted through huge volumes of phone and internet traffic in search of patterns that might lead to terrorism suspects. The program was described by some officials as a large data-mining operation.[39]

The program was first revealed by the New York Times on its website and apparently was started shortly after the 9/11 attacks.[40] Since that time hundreds of people in the country and people outside the United States have been targets of the program. No one knows exactly how many people have been under surveillance. The data was collected by tapping directly into phone companies' switching systems located in New York and other places where international traffic passes through. With the globalization of the telecommunications industry in recent years, many international-to-international calls are routed through American switches. Thus the volume of data available to the NSA is huge and American telecommunications companies cooperated with the NSA to give them back-door access to streams of domestic and international communications.[41]

Critics of the program argue that it violates both the Constitution's ban on "unreasonable searches and seizures" and a 1978 law that was enacted after revelations that the Nixon administration had been spying on Vietnam War protesters. The Fourth Amendment requires the government to show probable cause and provide evidence supporting the allegation that the target of the search is involved in criminal activity before a judge may issue a warrant. All warrants must meet the "paticularity" requirement in that the government must describe specifically what it is looking for and cannot go on a fishing expedition.[42]

The 1978 law called the Foreign Intelligence Surveillance Act (FISA) allows for retroactive approval of surveillance up to 72 hours after it has begun in emergency situations. This grace period had been extended from 24 hours to 72 hours after after 9/11 to facilitate electronic surveillance recognizing that there are times when the government must act quickly. This law provides a comprehensive statutory framework for conducting electronic surveillance for foreign intelligence or national security purposes. It created a special court called the Foreign Intelligence Surveillance Court to review such requests for surveillance. Very few such requests have been turned down. From 1995 through 2004 the Court received 10,617 requests for electronic surveillance and turned down only four.[43]

The Bush administration maintained that this system does not give them enough speed and flexibility to respond to terrorist threats against the country. Bush claimed that he had the legal authority to ignore the law because of the inherent power of the president under the Constitution. "As president and commander in chief," he said "I have the constitutional responsibility and constitutional authority to protect our country."[44] Attorney General Alberto Gonzales defended the practice by saying that FISA was a "peacetime" statute rendered irrelevant by 9/11 that put us in a state of war where the president's inherent wartime powers took precedent.[45]

If this wasn't enough justification, the administration also argued that Congress gave the president approval for a surveillance program in its September 14, 2001, resolution authorizing the president to use all necessary force against al Qaeda. This resolution authorized the president "to use all necessary and appropriate force against those nations, organizations or persons" who "planned, authorized, committed or aided" the 9/11 attacks. This resolution makes no reference to surveillance or to the president's intelligence-gathering powers but the administration claims it implicitly gives them the authority to establish surveillance programs.[46]

The Attorney General Alberto Gonzales went out of his way to assure Americans that this program did not involve American citizens calling their neighbors, and that one party to the communication had to be outside the country. There also had to be a reasonable basis for suspecting an al-Qaeda connection. This, however, was another lie as in May 2006 it was revealed that the NSA was operating a second giant surveillance program that involved billions of purely domestic calls and tens of millions of American citizens. A report in USA Today disclosed that AT&T, Verizon, and BellSouth had turned over tens of millions of customer phone records to the NSA since the 9/11 attacks. The article stated that the NSA had created a database of all calls made by customers of the three companies in an effort to compile a log of "every call ever made" within the country. Denver based Qwest Communications was the only large Bell company that refused to cooperate in the program.[47]

Bush defended the program by saying that the government was "not mining or trolling through the personal lives of millions of innocent Americans," but that the their "efforts are focused on links to al-Qaeda and the known affiliates."[48]

Supposedly the program did not involve listening to or recording specific conversations, but consisted of an analysis of calling patterns in an effort to detect terrorist activity. Such data mining activity involves going through data from past activities and predicting what is likely to happen in the future based on patterns detected in the data itself. Such programs have been used by private companies for years to discern the shopping habits of American citizens.[49]

Private companies, however, are only trying to sell us their products, they can't arrest us or investigate our records for other criminal activity. And what happens when a alarm goes off because of a suspicious pattern of activity. Will not the specific calls involved have to be examined in detail and the personal lives of Americans examined more closely? Will there not be all kinds of false positives in that the suspicious pattern will turn out to be benign? But to determine this means that the privacy of American phone calls has been invaded as specific conversations will have to be examined to determine their content.[50]

General Michael Hyden who was head of the NSA at the time this program was instituted and supervised it defended it by stating that in his opinion it was lawful and was designed to "preserve the security and liberty of the American people." Since he was the nominee to head the CIA after the resignation of Peter Goss, he was expected to face tough questioning in his Senate confirmation hearings.[51] But most likely some Senators will huff and puff a bit and appear to ask tough questions for public consumption, but the Senate will most likely vote for confirmation. Bush will get his way and the controversy will die down until the next revelation. Because the question is what else the administration is doing that we know nothing about?[52]

These programs were the last straw in a series of actions that extended the powers of the president in an unprecedented fashion and caused what some have called a constitutional crisis. The president and his supporters in the White House have insisted that there can be no limits to the power of the commander in chief in wartime and that laws related to domestic spying and torture of detainees do not apply to his actions. In the interests of national security he can break any law and his authority cannot be checked by Congress or the judiciary. And because the war on terror has no end, these so-called emergency powers can be extended indefinitely at the pleasure of the president.[53]

So now we have a country that detains people indefinitely without charging them claiming that they have no rights, that tortures people in the interests of gathering intelligence, and that conduct surveillance programs that are clearly outside the law. The president has become a law unto himself with his claim that the Constitution grants him the authority to do anything he deems necessary to protect the country. Is this a county that we can be proud of given our tradition of protecting human rights? Are these the values we have come to cherish as making our country unique and different from other countries where the rule of law is not respected? Are these the standards the country now accepts as the way we should conduct ourselves? Have we given up on the separation of powers in our government and condone these actions of the president to create an imperial presidency?[54]

FREEDOM AND SECURITY

Jonathan Turley in the Los Angeles Times argued that the cases involving American citizens should never have reached the Supreme Court. The president swore in his inauguration to uphold the Constitution, which meant not only to protect the nation but also to respect the rights of its citizens. But in the hysteria after 9/11 he insisted he had absolute authority to incarcerate anyone he chose and invade any nation he deemed necessary. Both the Democrats and Republicans in Congress went along by authorizing him to "use all necessary and appropriate force" at home and abroad to protect the nation. The high court finally intervened in this lurch toward tyranny, Turley said, and "we dodged this bullet by a hair's breadth."[55] But the administration keeps firing more bullets and not enough people seem to be upset. Perhaps part of the problem lies in our fear of terrorism.

During times like this, the balance between freedom and security is under question and people seem willing to give up some measure of freedom for security. This may be part of the reason behind the rush to pass the Patriot Act and for the president to assume absolute authority in regards to alleged terrorists. Certainly fear plays a large role in where to strike this balance when the country is under some kind of attack, and the Bush administration has proved adept at tapping into this fear to get its way with regard to the assumption of more and more authority over American lives. It is not unrealistic to portray the Bush administration as a fearmongering administration as it continually uses the threat of terrorist attacks as a way of reminding the nation that the Bush administration alone has the toughness and commitment to combat the war on terror effectively. This could be called the politics of fear and was certainly a major factor during the 2004 election.

The 9/11 attacks are one of those times that will be forever etched in our memories, and like with Pearl Harbor, I will never forget where I was when the attacks took place. When 9/11 happened, my wife and I were in Deer Valley, Utah, where we had been going for several summers to escape the heat of New Orleans, where we lived at the time. We rented a condo that had a great view of the mountains across the street from some friends of ours from New Orleans who owned their own place. Days we didn't hike, we either walked around the area in which we lived or went into Park City, where we had temporary membership in an athletic club that had weight lifting equipment. At our ages, we thought it important to do our best to keep in shape and try and stave off some of the ailments that go with advanced age.

That particular morning it was time to do weights, so we drove down the mountain into Park City to the athletic club. When we entered the front door to check in, we noticed several people sitting in the lounge watching television with more than passing interest. When we inquired as to what as going one, we were told that an airplane had crashed into one of the World Trade Center towers. Like millions of other Americans, we initially thought an airliner must have gone off course and this crash was an accident. The thought that this could be a terrorist attack never even entered our minds. We stopped for a few minutes and watched the tower burn and then went into the weight room to do our exercises.

When we finished, the Tower was still burning and had not as yet collapsed. Nor had the second tower been hit as this happened on our way back to the condo. When we arrived at our condo, we rushed inside and immediately turned on the television and learned that the second tower had been hit and that the Pentagon had been hit as well. It was obvious then that we were under some kind of attack. The rest of the day and on into another day, we sat mesmerized in front of the television watching the towers collapse over and over again. We barely took time to eat and go to the bathroom. The pall that fell over us was not unlike what I experienced in Dallas the day President Kennedy was shot. Since I was going to school at Southern Methodist University, I happened to be in Dallas the day of that tragic event.

After two days of disbelief and a kind of numbness we eventually came up for air and began to make contact with the outside world. After watching television nonstop for two days, it finally began to sink in that what we saw on the screen had actually happened. We contacted our friends across the street and found that they had done pretty much the same thing. We called friends and family in New Orleans and shared our disbelief and wondered what was going to happen next. It seemed like a new kind of world where some kind of innocence had been lost. We felt vulnerable and knew that the government was going to make some kind of response, but the question was what could be done to deal with this new kind of threat?

Of course the threat wasn't entirely new as the World Trade Center had been under attack before and the Oklahoma City bombing was still very much in our memory. What seemed to be new however was the scope of the attack and the devastating consequences. Whether the terrorists knew the towers might collapse is not clear, but that they did collapse lives on in our memories. The sophistication of the attacks was also new as even a moment's reflection made one realize the coordination and planning involved in pulling this off. This was no "fly by night" effort. Somebody hated us enough to go to all this effort and sacrifice their own lives in the process. The symbolism gradually dawned on me: that the terrorists had attacked the World Trade Center as the symbol of global capitalism, the Pentagon as the symbol of our military might, and apparently the fourth plane was headed for either the White House or the Capitol, the political centers of our nation. This was a well-orchestrated and thought out attack, which made it all the more frightening.

The 9/11 attacks seemed to be a watershed for the nation in that the attacks proved that we were not insulated from terrorist attacks. After these attacks there is a fear in the nation that it can happen again. The problem with such attacks is their sheer randomness, that innocent people going about their daily routines can be victims without any warning whatsoever. This is certainly a new experience for most of the American people, and fear is a justifiable response. But such fear can become overblown and generate responses that are not justified. We can never become totally secure against terrorism and must not give up more freedom than is necessary in an elusive search for security. Those of us who are older need to learn from younger generations what 9/11 and subsequent terrorists threats mean to them and how they are perceived, but younger generations can also learn from us and the perspective we bring to the situation.

Perhaps those of us who lived through the Second World War can offer a needed balance to the threats posed in this new age of terrorism. While I was only nine years old on Pearl Harbor Day, I remember the events of World War II quite vividly and followed the war in great detail. Given that I loved airplanes, I could name every warplane the U.S. had and provide most of its specifications. And I followed every battle as best I could. We did not have television in those days and where I lived most people did not even get a daily newspaper. But my uncle got the Milwaukee Journal and I made an arrangement with him to go over to his house a half-block away and get it when he was finished. We also got information from the news on the radio and from newsreels when we went to the movies.

From this background it always seemed to me that too much has been made of the 9/11 attacks. Please do not misunderstand what I am saying because I do not want to make light of the almost 3,000 people who lost their lives in the World Trade Center attacks. Those lives were precious to their families and friends, and a life is a life regardless of how and when it is ended. But there were 50-60 million people killed during World War II including the 7 million Jews who were put to death in the concentration camps, the millions of Russian soldiers and civilians who were killed, the millions of Germans and Japanese, the hundreds of thousands of our allies in Western Europe including military personnel and civilians in England, and the hundreds of thousands of our own military who were killed in both the European and Pacific theaters. That works out to about 25,000 killed per day on average. And whole cities or major parts of them were destroyed, like Dresden, Berlin, Tokoyo, and others, not just a few buildings.

Given this perspective, the attacks on 9/11 pale in comparison. Granted this was the first foreign attack on American soil, but did we think we were isolated from what was going on in the rest of the world? There had already been one attempt to bomb the World Trade Center. And we had already experienced one bombing of a federal building in Oklahoma City. According to the 9/11 Commission we had ample warning of some kind of attack, and if we had been able to look at all the pieces at one time and in one place, we may have been able to determine what was planned and prevent it from happening.[56] Apparently we lived with a false confidence that a major terrorist attack could not happen here. While this attack certainly stunned the nation and the world, it hardly compares to Pearl Harbor and subsequent events.

While the killing of nearly 3,000 citizens may have altered and defined the Bush presidency, as Woodward states, it was not in my opinion the Pearl Harbor of the 21st century. Woodward goes on to say, "In some respects the attacks were more devastating. Instead of 1942 Hawaii, which was not then a state, the targets were the power centers of the homeland."[57] But Woodward misses an important point. The 9/11 attacks did not affect our military capability. Much of our fleet was destroyed at Pearl Harbor, and if our carriers had been there and also destroyed or if the battle of Midway had gone the other way and we had lost our carriers instead of the Japanese theirs, we would have been in big trouble. The whole West Coast would have been open to attack by the Japanese if not outright invasion, and we would have had a hard time defending ourselves without that naval capability.

World War II went on for years, not just a few days, and the outcome was always in doubt. Would we be able to mobilize our resources in time to push back the Germans and Japanese and protect our shores? German submarines were off the Atlantic Coast and in the Gulf of Mexico and Japan sent balloons across the Pacific to start forest fires in Western states. Then came rumors of jet planes the Germans were developing, and rockets striking London and other parts of England. And then came the atomic bomb and all the horrors of the unknown destruction that might be unleashed in an uncontrollable chain reaction. This was pretty scary to a little kid growing up in a small midwestern town and gives one a much different perspective from which to view the terrorist attacks.

It seems ludicrous to hear all the talk about the nation being at war as what impact has the war on Iraq or the war on terror made on the average citizen?

The only people to have paid a price in this war are those who lost their lives along with their friends and loved ones. The rest of us were told to go shopping in order to keep the economy going. In World War II however most of the nation's resources were spent in the war effort. Certain consumer goods, such as cars, were not available. The automobile companies were making tanks and had to skip several model years. Rationing was the order of the day, and people were issued coupons for meat and other consumer goods and had to get a gasoline sticker based on need for transportation. Everyone felt the effects and young men were drafted from every community in the country. Most important of all were the stars that appeared in windows of houses around the country. Even a small community like mine had its share of young men who were not going to come back to take over their dad's business or the family farm.

In this so-called war people are given tax breaks and the cost of the war in Iraq is placed off budget for other generations to worry about. To hear Bush call himself a war president as if to compare himself with Roosevelt or Churchill is insulting. This is no war like other wars. There is no enemy trying to invade the country, no enemy forces massed to attack our nation, and no missles aimed at our country that could annihilate it in less than an hour. For the average person terrorism is like a tornado. All one can do is hope you are not in the wrong place at the wrong time and have ample warning either to get out of harm's way or protect yourself as best you can from a terrorist attack. Hopefully we will be less naive and more prepared for another terrorist attack, but given the Homeland Security Department's response to Hurricane Katrina, I have my doubts.

As far as the government is concerned, it should do all it can to protect citizens rather than trying to do the impossible in countries like Iraq. Maybe the best defense is a good offense, and we should take the fight to the enemy, but we need to fight the real enemy, not a country that had done us no harm and was hemmed in on all sides as described in the first chapter. Self-interest should guide our actions, not some far-fetched notions about bringing democracy and freedom to the Middle East. The war in Iraq was a war of choice; it was not a necessity to protect our country. Instead of reducing the threat of terrorism, it may instead have increased the threat, as numerous people have said, including top national security officials.[58]

In any event the so-called war on terror needs to be kept in perspective and the nation needs to be on guard against getting swept up in war hysteria. This administration should not be given absolute authority to fight terrorism any way it deems necessary. The prisoner abuse scandals in Iraq shows what can happen when people have absolute authority over others with no guidelines or commitment to international conventions as a check on their behavior.

American citizens need to get over their fears about terrorism and look at the situation more realistically. We do not need to give up our rights in the interests of fighting terrorism. Everything we stand for should not go down the drain because of a few people bent on destruction. As Roosevelt said during the Great Depression, "the only thing we have to fear is fear itself."

THE ROOTS OF TERRORISM

Perhaps it would help us deal with terrorism if we had a better understanding of what it is and why it seems so prevalent in the modern world. There is no universally accepted definition of "terrorism," and throughout history there have been few common threads beyond a willingness to use violence to achieve political ends of one sort or another. Terrorism has been in existence since the beginning of human life and will continue as long as there are conflicts in the world. What makes terrorism so frightening in the modern world however is the technology available to terrorist groups and the lack of inhibitions they have to do whatever is necessary to achieve their goals.

Two major trends in the world today provide a framework for understanding terrorism in the modern world and what it is about. This framework is particularly useful for understanding Islamic terrorism and what is going on in the Middle East that breeds terrorist activity. One is the trend towards global assimilation that is destroying much of the world's cultural diversity through the creation of a truly world market. The other is a counter to this assimilation as ethnic, religious, and other cultural groups militantly define themselves in opposition. This was the theme of the popular book, The Lexus and the Olive Tree. These are symbols of the post-Cold War era of globalization representing two different forces operative in the world today.[59]

As described by Thomas Friedman, half the world emerged from the Cold War intent on building a better Lexus, meaning they were dedicated to modernizing, streamlining, and privitizing their economies in order to prosper in the era of globalization. The other half of the world, which was sometimes half of the same country or even half of the same person, was caught up in the fight over who owns which olive tree. Fights over the olive tree are so intense because the olive tree represents everything that roots us, identifies us, and locates us in this world, whether it be a tribe, nation, religion, or a place called home. Olive trees provide the feelings of self-esteem and belonging that are essential for human survival. Without a sense of home and belonging, life becomes barren and rootless.[60]

During the Cold War the most likely threat to your olive tree was another olive tree as countries threatened each other with annihilation. The biggest threat to olive trees today, according to the author, is from the Lexus, from all the anonymous, transnational, homogenizing, and standardizing market forces and technologies that are part of economic globalization. The Lexus can be so powerful it can overrun every olive tree in sight, but other things about the Lexus can empower communities to use the new technologies and markets actually to preserve their olive trees. How this conflict plays out in the different olive trees is critical for the future of globalization.[61]

Terrorist activities can be seen as a part of this conflict, particularly those activities in the Middle East, where one man, Osama bin Laden, stood as a symbol for everything terrorism represented. After the events of September 11 people all over the country asked why we were so hated in the Arab world and why they wanted to provoke us into a military conflict they could not win, given America's overwhelming military and technological superiority. What may be misunderstood however is that this action was really part of a struggle over olive trees.

In the imagery of bin Laden and his associates, American culture is regarded as a form of idolatry in its materialistic approach to life that is based on secularism. Western civilization is a form of evil being spread around the world through trade between nations, and the World Trade Center was a potent symbol of the Lexus that is influencing Arab nations. Equally galling to these terrorists is the presence of the American military on the Arabian peninsula, so striking the Pentagon was striking at the heart of American military might. But the issue is not the United States as such and our way of life, it is the Arab states that are being influenced by American values.

Countries like Saudi Arabia and Egypt in particular are regarded as idol worshippers, cowering behind the United States and adopting its values to too great an extent. The leaders of these countries are regarded as hypocrites in having largely abandoned true Islamic values. The attacks of September 11 were designed to force these governments to choose between aligning themselves with the idol-worshipping enemies of God or with the true believers. In the Muslim world economic globalization and the international balance of power both come with an American face. Osama bin Laden's rhetoric divides the world into two camps, the United States and its puppet regimes versus the true believers.[62]

This attempt to polarize the Islamic world was expected to help bin Laden and his followers further the cause of Islamic revolution within the Muslim world itself. They consider themselves an island of true believers surrounded by a sea of iniquity and think that the future of Islamic religion, and therefore the world, depends on them and their battle against idol worship. They are motivated to martyr themselves because they believe they are locked in a life and death struggle with the forces of unbelief.[63] They are motivated by the Islamic tradition of jihad, or holy war, to defend the faith against nonbelievers and are engaged in a global struggle against a corrupt and oppressive enemy.

Thus there is a struggle for power going on in these countries, a battle over olive trees, and the attacks can be seen as a response to the failure of extremist movements in the Muslim world in recent years to topple the leadership of Muslim countries. Revolutions in Egypt, Syria, and Algeria have largely failed and the governments in these countries have managed to crush or marginalize the radicals. The Lexus seems to be winning even in much of the Arab world, but the battle over the olive trees will continue as people struggle with the threats globalization poses to their identity and self-understanding. The issue is not primarily one of poverty or lack of education but strikes at the heart of what it means to be a human being with a unique identity.

When American companies export goods and services to foreign countries or transfer technologies to these countries, they are not just selling products or installing technology; they are also promoting a way of life that involves changes that many of these countries find difficult to accept. This way of life reflects the values of Western industrialized societies, values that relate to a materialistic life style and a secular approach to everyday living. These values are often resisted by foreign countries, as mentioned previously, who find themselves faced with tension and conflict over what kind of society they are and want to become. While many of these countries may be attracted to the increased standard of living that goods and services can produce, they do not necessarily like the values that go along with the life style that accompanies this change.

Neither trend, the engulfment of diverse cultures by globalism or isolationist "tribalism," can produce a true global community. And it is the creation of a global community that is going to work for the benefit of everyone involved in the process of globalization. It is difficult to conduct business where there is conflict and the unleashing of self-destructive forces in people who are willing to sacrifice their own lives for what they believe is a just cause. A truly global community must have a way of accommodating diversity and must recognize that while there may be values that all people hold in common, these values do not exist in abstract form but are embedded in a diversity of traditions, cultures, and ways of living represented by different countries. A nation or culture cannot be expected to accept values that require a suicide of itself through the mutilation of its own history and context of meaningful existence.

We must learn to take people like bin Laden at their word and not buy into all the rhetoric coming out of Washington about bin Laden and other terrorists wanting to destroy our freedoms and liberties. Only we can do this if our reaction to these threats is to give up these freedoms for a false sense of security. The Islamic terrorists want us to quit meddling in their countries for whatever reason, whether it be for oil at cheap prices, to create regimes favorable to our interests, or to extend our empire around the world. In his tape released just before the election, bin Laden expressed disbelief that he had failed to make his point with the American people after everything that had happened in recent years.[64]

Indeed those who have examined his speeches over the years have found a remarkably consistent message. He believes that Americans have repeatedly humiliated Muslim countries with a foreign policy that has propped up corrupt governments in the region who have not remained true to Islamic faith and have perpetuated conflict throughout the region. Thus he justifies terrorism as a logical response to what he sees as U.S.-aggression against Islamic countries. One of his biggest grievances is continued U.S. support of the Saudi royal family, which he regards as corrupt and beholden to outside interests. Other grievances include the U.S.-led sanctions on Iraq after the Gulf War which he claims resulted in "the greatest mass slaughter of children mankind has ever known."[65]

Thus bin Laden and other terrorists believe that oppression and intentional killing of Muslim women and children is a deliberate part of American foreign policy towards Muslim nations. And in his eyes no American is innocent as he holds every citizen accountable for electing this nation's leadership and thus indirectly for shaping U.S. policy towards the Islamic world. Therefore in this latest tape he addressed the American public directly and said the future of terrorists attacks on this country is in our hands and depends on what we do with regard to Islamic countries.[66] We must begin to understand this if we ever hope to come to grips with terrorism.

According to the CIA, there are some 68 countries in which al Qaeda or affiliated groups are operating.[67] We can't hope to eliminate them all, if that is what winning the war on terrorism means. They are more than thugs who kill simply for the sake of killing. They see themselves as engaged in a global struggle against a corrupt and oppressive enemy. Islamic terrorism is a struggle for power within Islamic countries themselves, a struggle where religion is at the center of concern. It is ironic that these countries face the same problem we face here in the United States, the problem of what role religion shall play in the life of society and the government. As Iraq forms a new government, this is the most critical question they have to answer as they write their constitution and decide what influence Islamic law shall have in the society.

In any event people in this country need to get over their paranoia in thinking that others are always out to get them because they do not like the freedoms we have in this country. We need to look at the world through their eyes and put ourselves in their shoes and begin to understand how they see us and our actions in their countries. They do not necessarily like our values and do not like the way their countries are changing in response to American influences. We must learn to respect their values and cultures as we respect our own and not try to make them into societies like ours so that we can live in peace with them. We cannot impose our values at the point of a gun. To do so only invites more hostility and will increase the threat of terrorism and destroy freedom in this country.

NOTES

1. George Soros, *The Bubble of American Supremacy: Correcting the Misuse of American Power* (New York: Public Affairs, 2004), 12.
2. Michael Barone, "Revolutionary president," *U.S. News & World Report*, 31 January, 7 February 2005, 16.
3. Soros, *American Supremacy*, 11–12.
4. Jim Hightower, *Thieves in High Places* (New York: Viking, 2003), 91–92.
5. Hightower, *Thieves*, 92.
6. Hightower, *Thieves*, 92.
7. "The Patriot Act: Finding the middle ground," *The Week*, 22 April 2005, 16.
8. Nedra Pickler, "Bush renews Patriot Act provisions," *Denver Post*, 10 March 2006, 2(A).
9. Chitra Ragavan, "Law in a New Sort of War," *U.S. News & World Report*, 26 April 2004, 34–36.
10. Ragavan, "Law," 34–36.
11. Ragavan, "Law," 34–36.
12. Joan Biskupic, "High court protected liberties by limiting presidential power," *USA Today*, 2 July 2004, 4(A).
13. Biskupic, "High court," 4(A).
14. "'Enemy combatants': Getting their day in court," *The Week*, 16 July 2004, 6.
15. William Safire, "Rights of Suspects," *Times Digest*, 5 July 2004, 8. In October 2005 Hamdi was released from a naval brig and allowed to return to Saudi Arabia. Rather than give him a trial, the Justice Department decided he was no longer a threat. In return for his freedom, Hamdi gave up his American citizenship and agreed to stay out of the U.S. for 10 years and never to visit Afghanistan, Iraq, Israel, Pakistan, or Syria. He also renounced "terrorism and violent jihad" and pledged to notify Saudi officials if he became aware of any plans of terrorist groups. "The world at a glance," *The Week*, 8 October 2004, 7.
16. Esther Schrader, "Foreign terror suspects may fight confinement," *Denver Post*, 1 February 2005, p. 2(A).
17. Liz Halloran, "Rules For An Unruly New War," *U.S. News & World Report*, 27 March 2006, 32–33. Justice Antonin Scalia commented about some of the issues in this case before it reached the court, dismissing the idea that detainees have rights under the U.S. Constitution or international conventions. These comments provoked an

uproar and some said these comments were grounds for recusal. See Michael Isikoff, "Detainees' Rights: Scalia Speaks His Mind," *Newsweek*, 3 April 2006, 6.

18. "Enemy combatants: Getting their day in court," *The Week*, 21 July 2006, 4.

19. Kristine A. Huskey, "Complete Sentence," *The American Prospect*, September 2006, 9.

20. "Terrorists and 'torture': An abstract debate becomes concrete," *The Week*, 22 September 2006, 18; Ron Hutcheson and Margaret Talev, "Secret CIA prisons divulged," *Denver Post*, 7 September 2006, 1(A); Mark Hosenball and Michael Isikoff, "Out From The Shadows," *Newsweek*, 18 September 2006, 32–33.

21. Karen Tumulty and Perry Bacon Jr., "Leading a Rebellion," *Time*, 25 September 2006, 47–48; Michael Hrish and Mark Hosenball, "The Politics of Torture," *Newsweek*, 25 September 2006, 32–33.

22. Michael Duffy, "Letting The President Say," *Time*, 9 October 2006, 29; "New rules for terror suspects," *The Week*, 13 October 2006, 3; Charles Babington and Jonathan Weisman, "Senate passes landmark bill limiting rights of detainees," *Denver Post*, 29 September 2006, p. 1(A).

23. "Government releases list of Guantanamo detainees," *Denver Post*, 20 April 2006, p. 2(A).

24. Mark Sherman, "Judge: Charge Padilla or set him free," *Denver Post*, 1 March 2005, 5(A).

25. Eric Lichtblau, "U.S. terror suspect charged," *Denver Post*, 23 November 2005, 1(A). See also Mark Sherman, "Padilla's alleged terror cell not too potent," *Times-Picayune*, 24 November 2005, A(12).

26. Adam Liptak, "Detainee strategy still not uniform," *Denver Post*, 23 November 2005, 19(A); and Marie Cocco, "Supreme Court diminished itself," *Denver Post*, 7 April 2006, 7(B).

27. See "How they see us: Iraq was betrayed," *The Week*, 28 May 2004, 14.

28. Arthur Kane, Iraqi general beaten 2 days before death," *Denver Post*, 5 April 2005, p. 1(A).

29. "Abu Ghraib: Has justice been done?" *The Week*, 13 May 2005, 20.

30. Evan Thomas and Michael Hirsh, "The Debate Over Torture," *Newsweek*, 21 November 2005, 27–36.

31. See Jane Mayer, Annals of the Pentagon: The Memo," *The New Yorker*, 27 February 2006, 32–41 for the story of how Alberto J. Mora, the outgoing general counsel of the United States Navy, tried to halt what he saw as a disastrous and unlawful policy of authorizing cruelty toward terror suspects.

32. Paisley Dodds, "Guantanamo the 'gulag of our time'," *Denver Post*, 26 May 2005, 2(A).

33. Maggie Farley, "U.N.: Detainees tortured," *Denver Post*, 13 February 2006, 2(A).

34. See Erik Saar and Viveca Novak, *Inside the Wire* (New York: Penguin Press, 2005); John Freeman, "Nightmare of Guantanamo," *Denver Post*, 9 January 2005, 11(F); and Marie Cocco, "Guantanamo a moral cesspool," *Denver Post*, 21 May 2005, 15(C).

35. Anne Gearan, "Powell aide cites D.C. rift on war," *Denver Post*, 29 November 2005, 5(A).

36. Josh White, "FBI opposed inmate abuse at Guantanamo," *Denver Post*, 24 February 2006, 4(A).
37. Center for Constitutional Rights, *Articles of Impeachment Against George W. Bush* (Hoboken, NJ: Melville House Publishing, 2006), 74. The new Army field manual issued in September 2006 also banned all coercive interrogation tactics.
38. Articles of *Impeachment*, 74–75.
39. Eric Lichblau and James Risen, "Spying effort larger than acknowledged," *Times-Picayune*, 24 December 2005, p. A(3).
40. Bush called the leak about the NSA and its surveillance program "a shameful act" that was "helping the enemy" and hoped that the Justice Department would conduct a full investigation into the disclosure. Seeking to limit such leaks of classified information, the Bush administration launched initiatives targeting journalists and their possible government sources. Dan Eggen, "Bush cracks down on leaks of info," *Denver Post*, 5 March 2006, 16(A).
41. Lichblau and Risen, "Spying effort larger than acknowledged," A(3); and Articles of *Impeachment*, 9.
42. Articles of *Impeachment*, 21.
43. Articles of *Impeachment*, 24–25.
44. Eric Lichtblau and David E. Sanger, "Bush: Law on spying is dated," *Denver Post*, 20 December 2005, 1(A).
45. "Gonzales defends surveillance," *The Week*, 17 February 2006, 5.
46. Barton Gellman, "Bush sought war authority inside U.S., Daschle says," *Times-Picayune*, 23 November 2005, A(5). Several legal challenges have been filed against the program thus the federal courts may become the real forum where the issues is debated and resolved. An adverse verdict against the While House in any one of these cases could put a temporary halt to the program. Chitra Regavan, "Packing Heat," *U.S. News & World Report*, 13 March 2006, 27–28. The efficacy of the program was also called into doubt by a suggestion that al Qaeda undoubtedly has changed its means of communication to avoid such monitoring. Nedra Pickler, "Efficacy of spying program in doubt," Denver Post, 13 February 2006, 8(A). It was also revealed that the Pentagon has its own spying program. See Michael Isikoff, "The Other Big Brother," *Newsweek*, 30 January 2006, 32–34.
47. Eric Lichtblau and Scott Shane," No Mining of Lives, Bush Assures Public," *Denver Post*, 12 May 2006, 1(A). Verizon and BellSouth later denied providing local phone records to the NSA but USA Today stood by its story. And a senior government official confirmed that the NSA had access to the records of most telephone calls in the country. Ken Belson and Matt Richtel, "Verizon denies giving NSA data on local calls," *Denver Post*, 17 May 2006, 1(A).
48. Lichtblau and Shane, "No Mining of Lives, 1(A). See also Mark Hosenball and Evan Thomas, "Hold The Phone," *Newsweek*, 22 May 2006, 22–32.
49. Matthew B. Stannard, "Data-mining methods differ, but goal same," *Denver Post*, 15 May 2006, 6(C).
50. There did not seem to be much concern about this program in the public at large. Some polls showed that 63 percent of Americans saw no problem with this kind of surveillance. One commentator attributed this astounding statistic to the prevailing

American mood of fear, insecurity, and resentment. There is a kind of generalized anxiety in the country after 9/11 that the Bush administration has been able to use to its advantage. See Eugene Robinson, "Not even a whimper of protest," *Denver Post*, 17 May 2006, 7(B).

51. Katherine Shrader, "CIA pick defends spy work," *Rocky Mountain News*, 13 May 2006, 25(A).

52. Also in May 2006 Bush granted John D. Negroponte, the intelligence czar, broad authority to excuse publicly traded companies from certain accounting and securities-disclosure obligations. This was done in the interests of national security to keep secret classified work certain defense contractors were doing for the federal government. This action was taken under a 1977 statute that read "with respect to matters concerning the national security of the United States," the President may exempt companies from certain legal obligations. Not many people knew about his provision and it seems to have never been used before. See Dawn Kopecki, "The Spy Chief's New Financial Power," *Business Week*, 5 June 2006, 30.

53. Joyce Appleby and Gary Hart, "We're in a constitutional crises," *Denver Post*, 28 March 2006, 7(B). See also Chitra Regavan, "Cheney's Guy," *U.S. News & World Report*, 29 May 2006, 32–38.

54. See "The Bush push for an imperial presidency—part 1," *The Hightower Lowdown*, 8, no. 4 (April, 2006): 1–4. See also Paul Starr, "Bush vs. Constitution," *The American Prospect*, March 2006, 3.

55. "Enemy Combatants," *The Week*, 6.

56. According to recent evidence, nearly half of the daily intelligence reports leading up to the 9/11 attacks going to the Federal Aviation Administration (FAA) mentioned Osama bin Laden's terrorist network. The 9/11 Commission stated that the "civil aviation system seems to have been lulled into a false sense of security." Levin and Mimi Hall, "FAA got warnings about al-Qaeda," *USA Today*, 11 February 2005, 3(A).

57. Bob Woodward, *Plan of Attack* (New York: Simon & Schuster, 2004), 24.

58. See Dana Priest and Josh White, "U.S. occupation of Iraq aids terror recruiting, panel told," *Denver Post*, 17 February 2005, 2(A).

59. Thomas L. Friedman, *The Lexus and the Olive Tree* (New York: Farrar, Straus, and Giroux, 1999).

60. Friedman, *Lexus*.

61. Friedman, *Lexus*, 29.

62. Michael Scott Doran, "Somebody Else's Civil War," *Foreign Affairs* 81, no. 1 (January/February 2002): 41.

63. Doran, "Civil War," 26.

64. Craig Whitlock, "Bin Laden speech displays disbelief at unmet demands," *Times-Picayune*, 26 November 2004, A(1). See also Ivan Eland, "It's What We Do," *The American Prospect*, January 2006, 38–42.

65. Whitlock, "Bin Laden," A(1).

66. Whitlock, "Bin Laden," A(1).

67. See Walter Laqueur, "World of Terror," *National Geographic*, November 2004, 72–81 for a list of these groups and what they have done around the world.

Chapter Three

Taxes

The tax cuts that were the centerpiece of the Bush administration's plan for the economy was another policy decided upon prior to taking office. We were going to have tax cuts no matter what the circumstances. And not just any old tax cuts but tax cuts of a certain kind that benefited some groups in society more than others. That tax cuts were of this nature is evident in the shifting rationale advocated in support of the cuts. First, when a surplus was projected to last several years, the cuts were giving money back to the people to whom it belonged. Then when the surplus disappeared and the economy tanked, they were necessary to stimulate the economy. While Bush held firm on the tax cuts themselves, he certainly flip-flopped on the reason they were necessary.

The first proposal for tax cuts was unveiled after only three weeks in office. This proposal was called a tax relief package rather than tax cuts to make it sound better. The package was portrayed as one that would give the average family $1,600 in tax relief, assist middle income Americans in their struggle to better their life style, help millions of low wage earners reach the middle class, save family farms and family-owned businesses, and provide a boost to an already sluggish economy.[1] The administration estimated the cost of the cuts to be $1.6 trillion over 10 years, which would leave a good deal of the surplus, which was then estimated at $3.1 trillion over the same time period, available for other purposes.

Several aspects of this plan were misleading. The president claimed that those at the bottom end of the economic ladder would receive the largest cuts from his tax package in terms of actual percentage. In other words they would get the greatest relief from their tax burden. While it was literally true that a low income taxpayer would see a greater percentage cut than a millionaire, this had to do with the fact that they paid little or no income taxes to begin with. Families who paid only $20 in income taxes would indeed be relieved of having to pay any taxes, a 100-percent reduction, but this relief was less than it appeared as removing these families who paid little in income taxes from the tax roles did not cost the nation very much and was no great boon to low income families.[2]

Focusing on percentage reductions helped divert attention from the fact that the tax package was skewed toward the upper classes of society. An analysis done by the Citizens for Tax Justice showed that the top 1 percent, those with incomes above $373,000, would receive 45 percent of the tax cuts; the top 5 percent, those with incomes over $147,000, would pocket almost 53 percent; and the top 20 percent, those with incomes over $72,000, would get almost 72 percent of the total relief package. Meanwhile the bottom fifth of wage earners, $15,000 and below, would get only 0.8 percent of the total package; the bottom 40 percent, $27,000 and less, would get only 4.3 percent; and the middle fifth, $27,000 to $44,000 would get 8.4 percent. The Center on Budget and Policy Priorities estimated that more than 12 million families, almost a third of all families, would not get any tax relief from the package because they had no income tax liability.[3]

Bush also touted the elimination of the so-called "death tax," a eupemism designed to appeal to people's emotions rather than their reason. Repeal of the estate tax was proposed as a way to save family farms and businesses that sometimes had to be sold to pay the tax; thus the estate tax was driving farmers off the land and small business had to be liquidated. But the Center on Budget and Policy Priorities estimated that the estate tax covered a mere 1.9 percent of estates because the tax applied only to estates valued above $675,000, a cutoff amount that was already scheduled to rise to $1 million by 2006. Estates of any size could be passed on to a spouse free of taxes, and a couple could bequeath an estate worth $1.35 million to an heir without paying any taxes to the government. Further analysis failed to find a single instance where a family farm had been lost because of estate taxes.[4]

Eliminating the estate tax amounted to 20 percent of the entire tax package and was estimated to cost $300 billion. It benefited the richest 2 percent of the population, those small number of wealthy Americans of whom only a few had a family-owned business to worry about. If the administration had been concerned about family farms and businesses, the package could have raised the exemption for these enterprises or developed new rules to cover the small percentage of estates that involved a family-owned business. Dumping the entire tax to favor the very rich had to be disguised with the emphasis on saving family farms and businesses.[5]

Only three months after the tax cuts were enacted by Congress, the surplus disappeared. In August 2001 the Congressional Budget Office (CBO) released numbers showing that the federal government would run a deficit of $9 billion in 2001 and would have to tap into the Social Security surplus to cover the shortfall. The CBO analysis estimated that two-thirds of the lost surplus was a result of the final tax package. The other third was said to be the result of a weak economy. Thus almost overnight the nation had gone from a surplus situation to a deficit situation where Bush had to backtrack from his promises to cause no deficits, to enact an affordable tax package, to preserve a contingency fund for unknown problems, and to honor a pledge not to use the Social Security surplus to cover a deficit.[6]

At the beginning of 2003 the economy was in trouble. Growth was anemic, more than 2 million jobs had been lost, and the unemployment rate was approaching six percent. Something had to be done, and again the answer was tax cuts, this time to stimulate the economy. The initial proposal was big and bold, $726 billion over a 10 year period. The proposal included speeding the tax cuts passed in the first package that were scheduled for 2004 and 2006, accelerating the planned expansion of the child tax credit, and a new item that called for eliminating most taxes on stock dividends. This idea had been batted around for some time as many had argued for the elimination of double taxation of dividends, first as corporate income and then as personal income. Now this idea's time had come, and it began to be taken seriously. The main argument for the package was that it would immediately stimulate the economy, yet many analysts argued that it seemed to be advancing a long-term agenda of reducing taxes even further and increasing the possibility for future growth of the economy.[7]

Again the package was portrayed as a great benefit to the middle class, who would keep an average of $1,083 more of their own money. However averages do not tell the real story, since the great majority of the tax cuts would again go to upper income Americans. The large dollar amounts these people would get skewed the average. It was like saying that together Bill Gates and I have an average of $20 billion in assets. Does this say anything about the true nature of my assets? The Tax Policy Center found that nearly 80 percent of tax filers would receive less than $1,083 and almost half would receive less than $100. Those in the middle income range would receive on average only $265. Using the overall average as Bush did only hid the true nature of the tax cuts and who benefited.[8]

Eliminating the dividend taxes was touted as a great benefit for the elderly as they would supposedly get more money from their investments. But this benefit flies in the face of the fact that almost two-thirds of all stock is owned by households that earn over $100,000 a year, meaning that most of the relief would go to wealthy seniors. Fully 40 percent of the cuts, according to the Tax Policy Center, would benefit the wealthiest 2.5 percent of the elderly, those with incomes above $200,000, and almost three-quarters would go to the top one-fifth, those with incomes of $75,000 and above. Seniors who have to struggle to make ends meet would get little or nothing from the elimination of the taxes on dividends.[9]

Considering the entire population, not just seniors, nearly 60 percent of these cuts would wind up benefiting the top 10 percent of taxpayers, people with incomes above $100,000, and two-thirds of this amount would go to the top 5 percent. Citizens for Tax Justice figured that people earning between $16,000 and $29,000 a year would get about $99 from this cut, those making over $374,000 would receive $30,127, while those with incomes over a million dollars would receive about $90,000 in benefits. Thus the gains from eliminating double taxation of dividends would definitely favor higher income taxpayers.[10]

These tax cuts were supposed to pay for themselves by promoting growth of the economy and thus resulting in greater revenues for the government. This was a return of supply side economics, the idea that lower tax rates will yield more revenues. But Congress did not completely buy into this scenario as budget deficits were of concern. The CBO estimated that if the tax cuts were passed as proposed, the deficit would hit $287 billion in 2003 and $338 billion in 2004 and would continue through 2013. The final package was reduced to $320 billion and restructured differently from the original proposal. Most dividends and capital gains would be taxed at 15 percent, and this provision amounted to about half the package. Income tax rate reductions would be accelerated and the child credit was expanded so that middle income families would get a $400 check for each child. The marriage penalty would be reduced and businesses would be able to write off more expenses. But even with these changes it was estimated that taxpayers with incomes over a million dollars would receive $93,500 in tax relief in 2003 while half of U.S. households would get $100 or less.[11]

This tax cut package was the third largest in the history of the nation, behind Reagan's cut in the 1980s and Bush's first round of tax cuts, which were the largest in history. The combined effect of these cuts are only now becoming apparent. According to an analysis in Newsweek, if Bush gets all he wants from Congress, the income tax will become a misnomer. By favoring investment income over salary, the taxes people pay to the federal government every year are really more of a salary tax as almost all income taxes would come from paychecks. This salary tax would come from 80 percent of income for most families and less than half the income from the top 1 percent of taxpayers. Taxpayers who get dividends, interest, and capital gains from their investments would have a much lighter burden than salary earners.[12]

If the total tax people pay is considered, the situation is even worse. About 75 percent of families pay more in Social Security and Medicare taxes than they do in income taxes. The combined Social Security and Medicare tax is 15.3 percent on the first $87,900 of salary (or other earned income) and 2.9 percent of the rest.[13] Then there is the Alternative Minimum Tax (AMT), which is hitting more and more middle income people. However, according to Newsweek, dividends and capital gains are not AMT items and are taxed at only a maximum of 15 percent rather than the 35 percent maximum for salaries. This means that middle income people pay for Social Security and Medicare at the low end and can be hit by the AMT at the high end. Again salaries are hit much harder than investment income.[14]

Bush made a big point that his tax cuts would greatly benefit the average American family who were married with two children and were earning $40,000 of income. This four-person family is average but not typical, comprising only about 25 percent of households. While this average family would get a 98-percent cut on income taxes, it would get only a 24–percent cut in total taxes when payments for Social Security and Medicare are taken into account. Other than for this bracket, the more money people made, the greater percentage cut they received. The upshot is, according to Newsweek, that higher income people get larger percentage cuts in the total tax burden than lower income people. This is the exact opposite of how a progressive tax system is supposed to impact the tax burden.[15]

Meanwhile the taxes corporations pay have been greatly reduced over the years, down to 7.4 percent of overall federal receipts from 20.3 percent 40 years ago. During the boom years of 1996–2000 some 60 percent of American companies having nearly $2.5 trillion in gross income paid no income taxes. There are so many loopholes and credits corporations can take that the actual rate is only about a third of the official rate of 35 percent. One problem is that the IRS has had its funding cut so that fewer and fewer corporate tax returns are audited. Another problem is the explosion in offshore companies. In 1983 these tax havens held only $200 billion. Now it is estimated that $5 trillion is held offshore. Companies can also allocate profits between their U.S.-based operations and foreign subsidiaries to jurisdictions that have a lower tax rate than the U.S. or perhaps no taxes at all. This puts a greater burden on wages and salaries to pay a disproportionate share of federal taxes and, in the words of one commentator, perpetuates a gross injustice on the vast majority of the American people.[16]

The administration argues that when taxes are reduced on capital, the result is greater investment, making workers more productive and resulting in higher wages. Thus over time more and more of the benefit goes to workers. However the Bush tax cuts make it harder and harder for people who start out with nothing to work their way up the economic ladder because so much of their income goes to pay taxes. Currently more than 28 million people, or about a quarter of the workforce between the ages of 18 and 64, earn less than $9.04 an hour. This works out to a full-time salary of $18,800 a year, which marks the federal poverty line for a four-person family. Thus many families are struggling to make it from day to day, and as more and more income and wealth go into the hands of the few at the top of the income ladder, the initiative of those at the lower end is destroyed.[17]

One other item needs to be considered in assessing the effects of the Bush administration's tax policy, and that is the elimination of the estate tax. What this does is allow a class of people at the top to inherit billions of tax-free dollars, invest it and watch it grow largely free from taxes, and then pass it on tax free to their heirs. The net effect is to create a class of landed aristocrats who have a disproportionate share of the wealth of society and can through campaign donations make the political system work in their favor. All in all the elimination of a progressive tax system, the creation of an aristocratic class, and the control of the political system by the privileged are destroying traditional American values of equality and opportunity. This is something the American people had better wake up about before they are completely alienated from the country in which they live and hope to improve their lot in life.

The job of government in our society is to deal with some of the raw edges of capitalism that has a natural tendency towards inequality and provide opportunities for everyone to get ahead, not to exacerbate those inequalities with a tax system that favors the rich and ignores those who are most vulnerable. Indeed inequalities in our society have increased greatly over the past several decades. According to Kevin Phillips writing in *Wealth and Democracy*, the one thing of which we can be certain in all the studies relating to income and wealth is that the portion of U.S. personal income going to the top 1 percent of Americans steadily increased during the 1980s and 1990s. In 1981 the top 1 percent received 9.3 percent of all income in the U.S. including capital gains. In 1997 this share stood at 15.8 percent, an increase of 6.5 percent in absolute terms, or almost 70 percent in terms of relative percentage increase.[18]

The same trend emerges when income is considered by quintiles. In 1997 the top one-fifth of American households earned 44.2 percent of all income; by 1999 this share had increased to 50.4 percent. Meanwhile the bottom one-fifth saw their share decline from 5.7 percent to 5.2 percent over this same time period, a decrease in estimated after-tax income of 12 percent from $10,000 to $8,800. The middle one-fifth experienced a decline of 3.1 percent in after-tax income from $32,400 to $31,400, and a decline in their share of income from 16.4 percent in 1977 to 21.3 percent in 1999.[19] The lion's share of this income increase for the top brackets came from capital gains earned in the stock market boom of the nineties. Between 1980 and 1999 tax-reportable capital gains jumped from around $75 billion to $507 billion, an increase of 576 percent. These increases in capital gains during the nineties were so great they were largely responsible for eliminating the federal deficit.[20]

The same situation exists with respect to concentration of wealth. The top 1 percent of households held 19.9 percent of all the nation's wealth in 1976, the low point of some 75 years of analyzing such data. By 1997 this share had increased to 40.1 percent, almost reaching the record of 44.2 percent set in 1929 before the stock market crash.[21] The result of this concentration is that the United States, the land of opportunity, became home to greater economic inequality than any other major Western nation, including France and Britain, so-called aristocratic nations. By the turn of the century the United States had not only become the world's richest nation, but also the West's citadel of inherited wealth. According to Kevin Phillips again, "aristocracy was a cultural and economic fact, if not a statutory one."[22]

These trends in income and wealth have been exacerbated by the tax cuts of the Bush administration. According to a report by the nonpartisan Congressional Budget Office, one-third of Bush's tax cuts went to people in the top 1 percent of income recipients, people who earned an average of $1.2 million annually. These households received an average cut of $78,460 while households in the middle 20 percent of earnings, about $57,000 a year, received a cut of $1,090 on average. About two-thirds of the benefits from the tax cuts went to households in the top fifth earnings bracket with an income of $203,740 on average.[23]

According to Laura D'Andrea Tyson, a former chair of the Council of Economic Advisers, currently the top 1 percent of households receives more pretax income than the bottom 40 percent and owns nearly 40 percent of total household wealth, which is more than the bottom 90 percent combined. They also earn more than half of all capital income. Bush's tax cuts increased the after-tax incomes of these households by 10 percent compared with a 2.3 percent increase for middle income families and only a 1.6 percent increase for the 20 percent of families at the bottom who have incomes of less than $17,000 on average. The share of federal taxes paid by the bottom 80 percent of taxpayers has increased while the share paid by this top 1 percent has dropped. If these tax cuts are made permanent, the Bush tax cuts will be the most regressive in the history of the country.[24]

It seems as if all the Republicans know is to push for more and more tax relief for the wealthy. In 2004 the House voted to extend the child tax credits so they would not expire the next year. This action would be fine except that the bill would also have expanded the credit's coverage by more than doubling the amount a couple could earn to $250,000 and still claim the full benefit, as if this group was in dire need of financial help.[25] Tax policy seems to be all about helping the rich get richer by any means that can be devised, not about helping those at the bottom of the ladder enjoy some of the benefits of living in America. These are not the values of the country I grew up in and prospered in by getting an education that allowed me to get better and better job opportunities.

Many of us could not have gotten that education without help from the government in the form of the G.I Bill and additional school loans from state and federal sources, yet these benefits are not providing the help they did when previous generations went to school. According to a task force of the American Political Science Association, "the educational and training benefits for America's all-volunteer military are modest compared with those in the original GI Bill and, consequently, have made less impact in boosting the schooling of veterans to the level of non-veterans." With respect to these non veterans, the task force states "rising tuition, the declining value of individual Pell Grants and state budget cuts have made higher education less affordable to non-veterans at a time when its economic value has risen."[26] It is getting more and more difficult for those without economic means to get the education that many believe is the way to get ahead.

Given these trends in inequality and the Bush administration's blatant effort to favor the rich, it seems clear that we are becoming a nation of the rich, for the rich, and by the rich. In the last election no matter who we voted for, we were going to have a President who was a millionaire, educated at Yale University, and a member of the Skull and Bones Society. Our lawmakers in Congress are also hardly representative of the society at large. There are few blue collar workers in the House, and about a third of representatives are lawyers. About 30 percent of congressmen are millionaires while fewer than 1 percent of the population can claim this status. None of them lives in poverty, as do 36 million people in the country at large. None of them has to worry about his or her job being shipped overseas. Nor do any of them have to worry about retirement because of generous pension benefits.[27]

Ordinary people are losing out in every respect. The privileged are more likely to be politically active and organized to press their demands on government. And increasingly our public officials seem to be much more responsive to these privileged groups than to average citizens and the least affluent. Perhaps this is because our elected officials are themselves for the most part members of this privileged group. And if they are not rich themselves, they are beholden to the rich for contributions to their campaigns. Some 95 percent of the donors who made substantial contributions to the 2000 election came from American households with incomes of more than $100,000, a group that represents only 12 percent of the population.[28]

Bush and the Republicans have a good thing going. Cut taxes for the rich and for corporations, and those people in turn increase their contributions to the Republican party and the Bush war chest to keep them in power. Bush collected record amounts of money for his 2004 campaign, money that gave him the opportunity to put scads of ads on the air blasting his opponent. These ads have proven to be effective as unfortunately most of the American public get the majority of their information about candidates from television ads. The whole process of voting has become commercialized as the candidates sell themselves just like companies sell products. In the process the privileged control the situation and see that those who get elected are going to benefit them at the expense of everyone else in the country.

During the 2004 campaign Bush came up with a novel argument to support his tax cuts. He stated that there is no sense in trying to raise taxes on the rich as Kerry was advocating. According to Bush, the rich will just hire more "lawyers and accountants" and ordinary folks will end up paying the bill for them. As he put it in Lima, Ohio, "The rich dodge, and you get stuck with the bill."[29] This logic was supposed to put him on the side of ordinary people, I guess, in that he was opposed to the rich being able to dodge taxes, so much so that we might as well cut their tax bill to begin with so they would not have to spend so much of their money finding ways to get around paying their fair share of taxes. That way they would have more money to invest to make the economy grow so everyone could be more prosperous.

In a book entitled *Neoconomy*, Daniel Altman places the tax cuts in a perspective that involves changing how we think about the economy and the role of savings and investment. Abolishing taxes on savings (dividends, interest, capital gains, and estates) is part of a long-term strategy for the economy that involves a major change in how the tax burden should be distributed. After these kinds of taxes are abolished, the nation's savings rate would rise and the economy would get larger as companies turned these savings into productive capital. Such a larger economy would mean there would be more income to be shared by the nation as a whole. Never mind that the rich got richer, the whole country would benefit from such tax changes so that nobody would gripe about inequalities.[30]

Talk about stimulating the economy through tax cuts was simply a smoke screen for the longer term goal of restructuring the tax system to put more of the burden on wages and salaries and less on investment income. It was a "bait and switch" tactic. While tax cuts would provide some stimulus to the economy in the short-term, they contributed far more towards building the neoconomy. If the goal had been short-term stimulus, more of the cuts should have gone to lower income people who would spend it, not to upper income people who saved more than they spent.

In addition to making such tax cuts permanent, Bush also wants to reform the tax code to be more in line with this kind of thinking. One possibility would be to replace the progressive income tax entirely with something like a flat tax, where everyone would be taxed at the same rate, probably something like 20 to 25 percent. Another possibility is to abolish income taxes altogether and go with a national sales or value-added tax at various levels of the production process, or perhaps some kind of an explicit consumption tax. Such moves would further shift the burden of taxation off wealth and onto wages and salaries since lower and middle income people spend a much higher proportion of their income than do the wealthy. There has also been talk about allowing people to invest large sums of money into savings accounts with tax-free interest or dividends. Over some period of time, this plan would shelter most investment income from taxation, leaving taxes mainly on wage and salary income.[31]

Any of these changes would mean more and more of the economic pie going to increase the wealth of those already at the top of the heap, with those at the bottom footing more and more of the bill for the federal government. The gap between rich and poor would widen as asset owners get richer and many wage earners are left behind.[32] Alan Greenspan who at the time was Chairman of the Federal Reserve Board, noted this is not a very desirable thing to have happen in a democratic society.[33] Would the neoconomy eventually make up for this through increased economic growth for everyone? Or is this another one of the neo-conservative fantasies much like the situation in Iraq where the people were expected to welcome us as liberators and a democratic society would magically emerge out of the rubble?

The tax policies of the Bush administration have saddled us with debt farther than the eye can see. The nation has taken a huge gamble with its future, a gamble that could turn out to be beneficial for everyone or a nightmare for those who are less than well off financially. Those at the upper end of income and wealth can afford to take this gamble, but is it fair for those at the bottom end of the ladder? Is the middle class being destroyed in the process by being asked to take on more and more of the burden?

By 2006, the effect of these changes in the tax structure became apparent. Studies showed that those taxpayers who had incomes above $10 million had a reduction of about $500,000 on average on their investment tax bill for 2003, and their total tax savings on the two tax cuts on compensation nearly doubled to a little more than $1 million. Because of the lowered tax rates, taxpayers with an average income of $26 million paid about the same share of their income in taxes as those making $200,000 to $500,000 a year. Those with annual incomes of $1 million or more which represent about one-tenth of 1 percent all taxpayers, received 43 percent of all the savings on investment taxes.

These savings on investment income were expected to be larger in the coming years because of gains from a rising stock market.[34]

Another commentator pointed out that the two tax cuts, the income tax rate cuts of 2001 and the capital gains and dividend cuts of 2003, lowered the average tax rate for the richest one-tenth of 1 percent of taxpayers by 3.8 percent while the bottom 20 percent received a reduction of only .03 percent. More than 70 percent of the tax savings on investment went to the top 20 percent of taxpayers. Only 14 percent of the 90 percent of taxpayers who make less that $100,000 a year benefited from the dividend-tax cut and only 5 percent from the capital-gains tax cut. Many people in this group hold stocks in retirement accounts which are ineligible for the investment tax cuts, but when these investments are used for retirement income it is taxed at the higher rate applied to wage earnings.[35]

The tax burden on the richest taxpayers has been reduced to where those how earn more than $10 million in income pay taxes at a lower rate that those who earn between $500,000 and $1 million. Thus the share of income to the top 1 percent of taxpayers jumped from 9 percent to 14 percent of our national income. This is an increase of 50 percent.[36] Given these figures it seem clear that Bush's tax cuts favored the rich at the expense of the middle and lower classes and have created a budget deficit that is larger than anything we have seem before and is putting the future of the nation in jeopardy.

Meanwhile, the incomes of most U.S. households has fallen in recent years. The Federal Reserve Board reported in early 2006 that average incomes adjusted for inflation actually fell from 2001 to 2004 and the growth in net worth was the weakest in a decade. Average family incomes fell 2.3 percent compared with 2001 to $70,700 in 2004 which was the weakest showing since the 1989–1992 period. The top 10 percent of households experienced a rise of 6.1 percent in their net worth to an average of 3.11 million while the bottom 25 percent saw a decline. In 2001 this group had assets equal to their liabilities while in 2004 they owed $1,400 more than their total assets.[37] So much for the American dream of financial security.

What are the long-term implications of all these changes for democracy? Is the elimination of a progressive tax system good for democracy? What will happen to the middle class which a progressive tax system has long supported? Have we become an aristocratic nation or are we headed in that direction? Are people happy with current trends in concentration of income and wealth?[38] Does the average American feel that the American Dream, whatever that means for them, is slipping away? People must take a long, hard look at the trends in income and wealth, what effect the tax cuts and other policies are having on these trends, and what they mean for their own lives and the lives of their children.

NOTES

1. David Corn, *The Lies of George W. Bush: Mastering The Politics of Deception* (New York: Crown Publishers, 2003), 79.
2. Corn, *Lies*, 81.
3. Corn, *Lies*, 80–81.
4. Corn, *Lies*, 84–85.
5. Corn, *Lies*, 84.85. In 2005, the House voted to repeal the estate tax altogether and the Senate moved toward a significant reduction. That year the tax was collected only on assets of more than $1.5 million. This represents about 18,800 people which is less than 1 percent of the 2.5 million people likely to die annually. Of this 18,800, only 440 had estates with assets that could primarily be attributed to family farms of family-owned businesses. The House bill would cost the nation about $745 billion from 2012–2021, and considering the interest on the money borrowed to make up for the lost revenue the cost could be as large as a trillion. See Mortimer B. Zuckerman, "So the Rich Get Richer," *U.S. News & World Report*, 2 May 2005, 72.
6. Corn, *Lies*, 91.
7. Corn, *Lies*, 241–244.
8. Corn, *Lies*, 244–245.
9. Corn, *Lies*, 245–246.
10. Corn, *Lies*, 246.
11. Corn, *Lies*, 259.
12. Allan Sloan, "Why Your Tax Cut Doesn't Add Up," *Newsweek*, 12 April 2004, 42.
13. Sloan, "Tax Cut," 43.
14. Sloan, "Tax Cut," 44
15. Sloan, "Tax Cut," 44.
16. Mortimer B. Zuckerman, "An intolerable free ride," *U.S. News & World Report*, 17 May 2004, 80. See also Robert S. McIntyre, "It's Your Money They're Wasting," *The American Prospect*, November 2004, 16; and Reggie Rivers, "Sharing the tax burden," Denver Post, 15 April 2005, 7B. In October 2004 Congress passed a bill that was called the most sweeping corporate tax legislation in almost two decades. Ostensibly it was passed to close an export subsidy that the World Trade Organization had ruled illegal, but it also included $137 billion worth of tax breaks for business, including lower tax rates for manufacturers, lower taxes on foreign profits for multinationals, and other such provisions. See Howard Gleckman, "All That Lard Could Clog Tax Reform," *Business Week*, 25 October 2004, 55; and "Will the corporate tax bill help business?" *The Week*, 22 October 2004, 46.
17. Michelle Conlin and Aaron Bernstein, "Working and Poor", *Business Week*, 31 May 2004, 61.
18. Kevin Phillips, *Wealth and Democracy* (New York: Broadway Books, 2002), 121.
19. Phillips, *Wealth and Democracy*, 129.
20. Phillips, *Wealth and Democracy*, 130.
21. Phillips, *Wealth and Democracy*, 122–123.
22. Phillips, *Wealth and Democracy*, 123–124.

23. Edmund L. Andrews, "Report says tax cuts favor the wealthy," *Denver Post*, 13 August 2004, 7A. Because of the tax cuts Bush saved some $27,000 on an adjusted income of $822,000 in 2003, and Cheney saved 9 percent or $124,000 on an income of $1.3 million. We should all have been so fortunate. "Can the U.S. tax code be saved," *The Week*, 30 April 2004, 38.

24. Laura D'Andrea Tyson, "How Bush Widened the Wealth Gap," *Business Week*, 1 November 2004, 32.

25. Mary Dalrymple, "House votes to extend, renew child tax credit," The Associated Press, 20 May 2004, 1. See also Paul Krugman, "Tax-cut zombies," *Times-Picayune*, 24 December 2005, B(7). Krugman says the Republicans cannot remember why they originally wanted to cut taxes and can't come up with a plan to make up for the lost revenue from tax cuts. They have become tax-cut zombies that keep stumbling forward following the same path towards disaster.

26. E.J. Dionne, "Politics for the privileged," *Denver Post*, 13 June 2004, p. 5(E). See also "Bad time for cuts in federal Pell Grants," *Denver Post*, 3 January 2005, 7(B).

27. Lou Dobbs, "The people's representatives?" *U.S. News & World Report*," 8 November 2004, 44.

28. Dionne, "Politics," 5(E).

29. Jodie T. Allen, "More dough for the rich?" *U.S. News & World Report*, 18 October 2004, 63.

30. Daniel Altman, *Neoconomy: George Bush's Revolutionary Gamble with America's Future* (New York: Public Affairs, 2004), 28.

31. Robert Kuttner, "The Latest Bush Plan—Consumption Taxes," Business Week, 13 September 2004, 26. See also Shawn Tully, "Trashing The Tax Code," *Fortune*, 29 November 2004, 41–44; Scott Greiner, "Consumption levy isn't the right solution for simplifying the system," *Rocky Mountain News*, 16 April 2005, 2(C); Froma Harrop, "VAT is looking better all the time," *Denver Post*, 15 April 2005, 78; and Bruce Bartlett, "Requiem for a tax-reform heavyweight," *Fortune*, 21 March 2005, 60.

32. Michael J. Mandel, "Where Wealth Lives," *Business Week*, 19 April 2004, 34–37.

33. Allen, "More dough for the rich?", 63.

34. David Kay Johnston, "Richest save $1 million in tax cuts," *Denver Post*, 5 April 2006, 6(A).

35. Mortimer B. Zuckerman, "Playing Fair on Taxes," *U.S. News & World Report*, 1 May 2006, 64.

36. Zuckerman, "Playing Fair on Taxes," 64.

37. Martin Crutsinger, "U.S. households pinched as incomes take a dusting," *Denver Post*, 24 February 2006, 2(A).

38. See Arlie Hochschild, "The Chauffeur's Dilemma," *The American Prospect*, July 2005, 51–53 for an analysis of how Bush turns his assult on the middle-class into winning politics.

Chapter Four

Environment

The environment was of crucial importance in my own upbringing which gives me a strong motivation to preserve as much of it as possible. My childhood was spent in central Wisconsin, a place with many woods and wilderness areas in which to wander and explore. It was an area of great natural beauty and during the summer in particular I spent the majority of my time outdoors. Hunting and fishing were sports in which almost everyone engaged and, since our property bordered on a lake, I could fish off our pier anytime I wanted. In the fall I could grab my shotgun and within five minutes be in a marsh hunting pheasants. Even in the winter when it was bitter cold, we spent a great deal of time outdoors skating and sledding.

So the environment came to be an integral part of my life and was not something apart from my immediate experience. It was a place where I could go to get away from people and be alone with my own thoughts. Many kids do not have that experience today and grow up in an environment that is largely controlled and manipulated. What the concept of wildness means is only an abstraction to them. This is unfortunate, I think, and their lives are missing something in my opinion. Growing up in a concrete and asphalt world with maybe a park here and there is simply not the same as growing up in intimate contact with the natural environment.

Living in Denver gives me many of those same opportunities. We can see the front range from Pikes Peak all the way to Longs Peak from our eleventh-floor windows and, on days when the sky is clear, it is a stunning view. Within an hour we can be cross-country skiing in winter and hiking in summer. Rocky Mountain National Park is only an hour and a half away and has some spectacular hiking. And the city itself with all its trees and parks has a great deal of natural beauty. Thus to some extent I have the same connection with the natural environment I had in my childhood.

Given what nature means to me and how important it was in my childhood and now during my retirement years, I have had a great deal of difficulty dealing with the Bush administration's policies towards the natural environment. One thing Bush can do is wage war, and he has waged a war against the environment that is unprecedented in my lifetime. This administration is determined to drill for oil and gas on every square inch of public land and industrialize them if necessary for extraction purposes. It wants to open up our national forests to more logging and allow business organizations to pollute the air and water by rolling back regulations. And it ignores critical problems like global warming that threaten our way of life much more than most terrorist activities.

The natural environment does not seem to matter much to this administration, except for exploitation purposes so that oil and gas companies, logging companies, and mining companies can make more money. The natural environment has no value in and of itself to this administration. And the Democrats are not much more concerned. The environment was not an issue in the 2004 election, and while Kerry has a decent record on the environment, he did not raise this as an issue during the campaign. The environment dropped off the radar screen and was treated as if all was well and thus of no concern. Why this should be so is difficult to understand as our environmental problems are no less important today than they were 10 or 20 years ago when the environment received a great deal more attention.

THE NATURAL ENVIRONMENT: DOES IT MATTER?

Several years ago a very thoughtful book called, The End of Nature, provided a new way of viewing nature that has profound implications for the way we think about our relationship to the natural environment.[1] By "the end of nature" the author did not mean that nature does not matter, but that nature as we have known it in its pure form no longer exists. Human beings have conquered nature as the entire natural world now bears the stamp of humanity and we have left our imprint on nature everywhere. We have made nature a creation of our own and have lost the otherness that once belonged to the natural world. The natural world is so affected by human technology that it is more and more becoming one of our own creations and thus is no longer the autonomous nature in which we sought refuge from human civilization.

What this view suggests is that the world has crossed a threshold with respect to the environment where human activities alter natural processes to a far greater extent than anyone can imagine, and nature has been subjugated and reconfigured according to human needs and desires. Science and technology have given us the ability to alter the natural environment in ways that could have not have been imagined just a few decades ago. We can reshape the landscape to make it suitable for a housing development, tear apart whole mountains for the ore they contain, alter the course of rivers and the amount of water that flows through them, build huge indoor malls with a controlled climate, create cities with millions of people in the middle of a desert where most everything to sustain life has to be imported, drill for oil in water depths that were unthinkable even a few years ago, and may even be altering the world's climate with our industrial activities. This ability gives us a sense of power to manipulate the environment to serve human purposes better, but with it also comes a sense of responsibility to deal with the environment in ways that do not destroy the very foundation of our existence. We simply cannot proceed as we have in the past to exploit nature and not worry about the environmental consequences of our activities.

Taking responsibility for nature involves making conscious and responsible value judgments regarding the kind of planet we want. While science at least attempts to tell us what kind of planet we can have or are likely to have if certain trends continue, albeit with some degree of uncertainty, what we have to make is a value judgment relative to these trends. Value judgments include the answer to such questions as how much species diversity should be maintained? How much of nature should be preserved and what natural resources do we wish to leave for our children? Should the size or growth rate of the human population be curtailed to protect the global environment? How much climate change is acceptable? Science can tell us something about the broad patterns of global transformation taking place, but value questions about the pace and direction of those patterns have to be answered through political and economic systems.

Events of the past few years have accelerated an already growing concern for the environment. Daily news reports give ample evidence of collapsing fisheries, eroding soils, deteriorating rangelands, expanding deserts, disappearing wetlands, falling water tables, more destructive storms, melting glaciers, rising sea levels, and dying coral reefs. The world is said to be losing its biological diversity as plant and animal species are being destroyed faster than new species can evolve. Deforestation continues and shows no sign of slowing as demand mounts for wood and wood products. There is of course a continuing concern with global warming and the effects it is having on the world's climate. And behind all of this, in some sense, is the increase in the world's population that now stands at six billion and counting.

Through a gradual awakening, people need to develop a new perception of humanity's relationship to the earth's natural systems. Such changes are necessary to respond to environmental problems effectively and in time to save the world from irreversible destruction. There is a growing sense of the world's interdependence and connectedness and an understanding that progress is an illusion if it destroys the conditions for life to thrive on earth. These efforts are very often stated in terms of saving the planet or preserving the environment as if the planet and the environment were something separate from human existence. This way of thinking however does not get at the real issue concerning to the environment. The planet will be here for millions of years, insofar as we know at this point, at least until the sun begins to demise and becomes a gas giant that obliterates the inner planets. As long as the earth exists, there will be some kind of natural environment. The real question is whether this earth and its environment can support life, particularly humans, or whether humans will eventually alter the environment so that it can no longer support life as we know it.

THE ETHICAL PROBLEM

As environmental problems impinge on the public mind, attempts are being made to develop new ways of thinking about the environment that overcome the traditional approach that has pervaded industrial societies. The goal of such efforts is to provide alternatives to the split between humans and nature that has undergirded traditional approaches to the environment, approaches in which the environment is seen as something separate from humans to be dominated and manipulated by science and technology for human purposes.

By treating nature in this traditional way and viewing nature in only instrumental terms, the material world has value only to the extent it can serve human purposes. Such an approach promotes an unhealthy separation between humans and the rest of nature and leads to policies and practices that undermine the conditions for supporting human life and activities by destroying the natural world on which we all depend for our existence. This traditional approach was consistent with institutional practices in which environmental impacts were largely ignored with a "nature can take care of itself" attitude.

Humans and their environment, organic and inorganic, are inherently relational, and to speak of them in isolation from each other is never true to the situation. No organism can exist in isolation from an environment, and an environment is what it is in relation to an organism. What we have is interaction between humans and nature, and it is only within such an interactional context that humans can understand nature and their place in the natural world.

Nature cannot be dehumanized, nor can humans be denaturalized. To take the human element out of nature is to make it into a value-free object that can be manipulated and used for human interests without recognizing that value judgments are being made every time nature is altered. An understanding of "human interests" has to be expanded to include the environment in all its richness and complexity. On the other hand nature cannot be taken out of humans by escaping into the realm of the supernatural and locating human consciousness outside natural forces. To do so is to take humans out of their natural context and make them into something that is not dependent on natural processes for their existence, a stance that hardly accords with our experience. While such an abstraction may serve certain spiritual purposes, this does not negate the fact that humans are embedded in nature and are subject to whatever natural forces and processes are part of the natural world.

THE BUSH RECORD

Christine Todd Whitman, the first head of the Environmental Protection Administration under the Bush administration, lists several accomplishments of this administration during her tenure. These include (1) passing the first Brownfields cleanup bill to encourage industrial development, (2) committing to an increase of preserved wetlands in the country, (3) proposing regulations for mercury emissions from power plants, (4) requiring a more than 90-percent reduction in soot emissions and a 99-percent cut in sulfur emissions from nonroad diesel engines, (5) providing more than four billion dollars in tax incentives for renewable energy and hybrid and fuel-cell vehicles, (6) nearly doubling funding for climate-change research, and (7) more than doubling funding for the 2025 Water Initiative to address water quantity and quality problems.[2]

While this list seems impressive, it is more than offset by the overall record of the Bush administration. And some of these items can be questioned. For example many, if not most, scientists say that it is time for action on climate change, not more research. And critics question whether mercury emissions will really be reduced under the new regulations. In any event one can seriously question whether the environment really matters for this administration other than as a source of raw materials and as a place to dispose of waste materials.[3] And one has to wonder about the commitment of the country as a whole to preserve whatever is left of the natural environment.

The complete record of the Bush administration regarding environmental issues from January 2001 through November 2003 can be found in the appendix of a book entitled Strategic Ignorance by Carl Pope, executive director of the Sierra Club, and Paul Rauber, senior editor of Sierra Magazine.[4] The authors of this book claim that in only three years Bush turned the clock back on environmental progress not just by decades but a full century.[5] People haven't paid much attention to Bush's environmental agenda because of the wars in Afghanistan and Iraq and other issues that have received more media coverage, but the environment has been under assault, they claim, and then mention a few specific measures that give some indication of Bush's approach to the environment:

- Approved a plan that subjected many communities to four times more toxic mercury from coal-fired power plants than they would be if the existing Clean Air Act were enforced.
- Exempted more than 16,000 old and dirty power plants, petroleum refineries, chemical factories, and industrial facilities from having to install modern pollution control technologies.
- Filled regulatory agencies with lobbyists and executives from the very industries they are now regulating and suppressed scientific findings from those agencies that ran counter to the administration's ideology.
- Shifted the economic burden of cleaning up toxic waste dumps from polluters to victims, a violation of the "polluter pays" principle.
- Cut by more than a third the value of a human life used in benefit-cost calculations to determine if new regulations can be justified.
- Stripped environmental protections from one-tenth of our nation's surface area, making this area vulnerable to oil and gas development as well as mining activities.[6]

Within the first few months of taking power in 2001, Bush retreated from his promise to regulate carbon dioxide, which is known to be a primary contributor to global warming; announced that he would consider all public lands open for oil and gas drilling; and delayed application of the Roadless Area Conservation Rule, which protected 58 million acres of public land from logging, mining, and development.[7] It became clear early on that the Bush administration was going to favor business interests when it came to the environment and cut back on environmental regulations and protection wherever possible and rely on voluntary compliance.

ARSENIC

One of the first fiascos the Bush administration faced involved arsenic in drinking water. The old standard established in 1942 was 50 parts per billion (ppb), but more recent studies had demonstrated that this level was too low and posed a significant risk of various kinds of cancer. In the final days of the

Clinton administration, a 10 ppb standard was adopted, a standard that the incoming head of the Environmental Protection Agency (EPA), Christine Todd Whitman, former governor of New Jersey, would not implement.[8] Many such executive orders were put on hold for further examination. It is not unusual for an outgoing administration to issue a flurry of such orders, nor it is unusual for the incoming administration to put them on hold for further review.

Arsenic is something people can understand as it has been the poison of choice in many murder mysteries and movies. Thus the Bush administration handed the Democrats and environmentalists an opportunity to exploit for their own purposes. The administration got hammered for its decision to table this standard. The Sierra Club pointed out that the mining industry, which was a major source of arsenic, had given a great deal of money to the Bush campaign, implying that the Bush administration would jeopardize public health because of campaign contributions. Finally a National Academy of Sciences report supported the science behind the 10 ppb standard, and the Bush administration relented and implemented the new standard.[9]

CLIMATE CHANGE

Equally problemmatic is the Bush administration's stance on global warming and its reversal regarding caps on carbon dioxide. Even before the 2000 election Bush had taken a stance against ratification of the Kyoto Protocol, which contained provisions for developed countries to make significant reductions in greenhouse gas emissions in order to slow global warming. According to Christine Todd Whitman, head of the EPA at the time, there was never much support in either party for ratifying this treaty. The major problem was that it did not apply to nations like China and India, which were expected to account for as much as 70 percent of the growth in greenhouse gases in the immediate future. There was also doubt if developed nations could meet the aggressive goals stated in the treaty because of the economic costs involved.[10]

While opposing the treaty, Bush did support a cap on carbon dioxide emissions and argued that the United States should work with other nations to develop new technologies and approaches to reduce harmful emissions. In a meeting in Trieste, Italy, with her G8 counterparts soon after taking over as head of the EPA, Whitman faced considerable skepticism about the administration's intentions regarding global warming. She met this hostility by assuring her counterparts that the Bush administration's commitment to seek a mandatory cap on carbon dioxide emissions was solid and that climate change was seen by them as a serious problem that demanded attention.[11]

While she was on the plane coming back from Italy however, an effort was being launched by Republican members of Congress and executives from the energy industry to persuade the president to reverse himself on this commitment. These efforts bore fruit as the president did reverse himself, arguing that the looming energy crisis, which at that time was hitting California, made it unwise to place any additional burdens on utilities that might seriously disrupt the nation's energy supply. He even stated that carbon dioxide was not a pollutant as defined under the Clean Air Act, which was a strong repudiation of his campaign promise.[12]

This reversal left Whitman hanging out on a limb, and the G8 nations felt deceived and believed that Bush did not care about the health of the global environment. This decision was meant to appeal to the far-right base of the party, many of whom believed that global warming was an incorrect theory advanced by those who wanted to weaken America's competitiveness in the world. It was a victory for American independence from foreign interference, a stance that the United States subsequently took with regard to its invasion of Iraq.[13] This "go it alone" image is now firmly planted in the minds of our European allies as we are now the only major nation that has not signed the Kyoto Treaty. It took effect when Russia finally ratified it after some deliberation.

Meanwhile global warming continues. The Arctic has warmed twice as fast as the rest of the globe, and ocean ice has shrunk by as much as 20 percent, having major effects on ecosystems, wildlife, and people who live in that region.[14] Glaciers are retreating all over the world, particularly in places like Glacier National Park, which may soon be a misnomer. Climate change is already affecting wildlife and plants all across the continent and such impacts are expected to become worse in the future.[15] According to the United Nations, 2004 was the fourth hottest year on record, extending a trend that began more than a decade ago. It was also a year that was the most expensive for the insurance industry in coping with weather-related natural disasters.[16] Business organizations are beginning to recognize the problem and are attempting to limit carbon dioxide emissions in some instances. Many companies are preparing for a carbon-constrained world.[17] Meanwhile the government continues to bury its head in the sand and even blocked efforts at a UN conference on climate change to draw the U.S. back into substantive discussions about ways to mitigate the problem.[18]

CLEAR SKIES

Then came the Clear Skies initiative, in which the EPA was working on a proposal for mandatory controls of certain emissions from utilities. However these efforts were opposed by Vice-President Cheney's Energy Task Force, which laid the blame for America's energy problems on excessive environmental regulations which frustrated the efforts of utilities to increase capacity. This task force focused its concern on a set of regulations called New Source Review (NSR), which required utilities to seek agency review when they made changes to old plants to see if they resulted in new sources of emissions which would require the latest pollution control technology.[19]

The Clinton administration had filed several multimillion-dollar lawsuits against utilities charging that they had violated the intent of NSR regulations. The Bush administration however dropped investigations of 50 of these plants, which some believed was a retroactive waiver of the law's requirements. Then it changed the NSR rules to specify that modernization was required only if 20 percent of the total cost of a plant was spent in upgrading an old facility. This level is almost never reached; thus the effect of the change was to allow the utilities to avoid using the most modern technology, which was also the most expensive, when upgrading their facilities.[20]

The Clear Skies initiative was modeled after the Clean Air Act amendments of 1990, which initiated a cap and trade approach to sulfur dioxide emissions that were responsible for acid rain. It was touted that the plan would cut sulfur dioxide emissions even further, by 73 percent from current levels, nitrogen oxide emissions by 67 percent, and for the first time cap emissions of mercury and cut them by 69 percent.[21] It would have made NSR obsolete as it eliminated the distinctions between new plants, old plants, and modifications to existing plants. All industrial facilities, particularly power plants, would have been required to reduce their emissions in whatever ways worked best for them.[22] While the plan seemed to have some advantageous features, it did not receive enough support from either Republicans or Democrats to pass Congress and resulted in a stalemate.

In September 2004, the inspector general of the EPA itself released a report critical of the agency's regulations of sources emitting thousands of tons of nitrogen oxides and volatile organic compounds which are precursors to ground level ozone. The EPA was accused of repeatedly postponing compliance schedules for cities that failed to meet the federal health standards for ozone, leaving more than 159 million Americans exposed to dangerous levels of the substance. Due to weak EPA oversight and illegal deadline extensions, the report stated that most the nation's smoggiest cities have experienced no significant improvement in smog levels over the past 10 years.[23]

In February 2005 this same inspector general charged that the agency's senior management had instructed staff members to arrive at predetermined conclusions that favored industry when they proposed a rule in 2004 to reduce the amount of mercury emitted from coal-fired power plants. The scientific and technological analysis done by the agency was supposedly "compromised" to keep cleanup costs down for utilities. The goal of management was to allow the agency to say that utilities could do just as well through complying with the Clear Skies initiative as by installing costly equipment that the rule would require. The Clear Skies initiative promised a 70-percent cut in mercury emissions along with cuts in nitrogen oxide and sulfur dioxide emissions but extended the deadline for compliance to 2018, a decade longer than previous legislation.[24]

Meanwhile the debate over the Clear Skies proposal continued. Supporters claimed that the initiative would reduce sulfur dioxide emissions by almost 6 million tons, nitrogen oxides by 3.2 million tons, and mercury by 33 millions tons. These reductions would be permanently capped and allow a trading program to develop that would focus on those reductions that were most necessary and cost effective.[25] Opponents argued that the plan would result in an additional 280 tons of toxic mercury, 20 million tons of sulfur dioxide, and 3 million tons of ozone-forming pollution than would otherwise occur if current laws were implemented. Further it does nothing to reduce carbon dioxide emissions, the major culprit in global warming.[26]

In March 2005 a Senate panel deadlocked 9-9 over approving the plan.[27] The very next day however the EPA itself issued a new rule, called the Clean Air Interstate Rule, that would cap emissions of sulfur dioxide and nitrogen oxide across 28 Eastern states and the District of Columbia. When fully implemented by 2015, the EPA claimed that the new rule would reduce sulfur dioxide emissions by more than 70 percent and nitrogen oxide emissions by more than 60 percent from 2003 levels. These reductions would prevent 17,000 premature deaths and tens of thousands of heart attacks each year in the states covered by the rule and would result in saving of $85 to $100 billion in health benefits annually. The rule sets up a trading system as in the Clear Skies plan, and sets stringent emissions monitoring requirements and penalties for noncompliance. This actions won rare praise for the administration and its new EPA chief, Steve Johnson.[28]

MANAGEMENT OF PUBLIC LANDS

As if this were not enough, the Bush record with respect to management of public lands is even worse in some respects. This includes national forests, wilderness areas, and other areas that are in effect owned by all citizens of the country. These areas are managed by the federal government on our behalf. They are supposed to be managed in such a way that does not overly favor one type of use at the expense of others, a balanced approach so the interests of all concerned are taken into account. Management of these lands is the responsibility of the Department of the Interior and the Department of Agriculture, which includes the Forest Service, the Bureau of Land Management (BLM), and other agencies.

With respect to forests, the Healthy Forests initiative was the Bush administration's answer to the forest fires that flared up across the West because of drought conditions. This initiative was supposed to be focused on clearing out the underbrush that had accumulated over the past several decades as a result of the Forest Service's policy of at least attempting to put out every fire that occurred in our national forests. This meant that dead trees and other debris had collected for some time without being burned off and constituted a fire hazard. In order to deal with this situation, the Bush administration allowed loggers access to our national forests to cut trees for commercial use in exchange for clearing out the underbrush.

The full title of this initiative was the Healthy Forests Restoration Act, and it was signed into law by President Bush in December 2003. The law authorized up to $760 million a year to treat up to 20 million acres of federal forests and grasslands deemed to be at risk of catastrophic fire. At least half of the tree cutting on that land was supposed to be concentrated in areas near homes and communities. The law also limited appeals and environmental reviews of proposed timber sales, making it more difficult for people to challenge them. After the law went into effect, the government won 17 consecutive court cases that favored timber cutting over challenges by environmentalists.[29]

The Forest Service issued new rules in December 2004 that abandoned regulations that had been in force for decades. The National Forest Management Act dating from 1976 required a management plan for each national forest. Before a plan was adopted, the Forest Service had to hold public hearings, gather citizens' comments, and consider effects of the plan on water quality and wildlife. The process involved an environmental impact statement required under the National Environmental Policy Act (NEPA) to review thoroughly all the possible adverse impacts the plan might involve. The new rules had none of these features. Instead they created "categorical exclusions" for the important big-picture problems that do not require environmental review or citizen comments. Critics claimed that the new rules invited industries to pressure the Forest Service to permit logging and oil and gas drilling without consulting the public and allow more roadbuilding, logging, and drilling without having to consider the fate of native fish and wildlife.[30]

The administration's management of wilderness areas was no better. Utah had 4.4 million acres of wilderness-quality land that under the jurisdiction of the Bureau of Land Management. This land did not have legislative protection as an official wilderness area, but the Clinton administration gave it interim administrative protection while Congress was deciding whether to protect it formally as wilderness. These lands were called Wilderness Study Areas and were largely protected from commercial exploitation while awaiting congressional action.[31]

Secretary of the Interior Gale Norton made a secret agreement with then-Governor Levitt of Utah to remove these study areas from protection and open them to oil and gas drilling. Since this settlement, the BLM has leased about 148,000 acres of this land for oil, gas, and coal development.[32] She also withdrew protection of as much as 220 million acres in other states, ending a 25-year practice of the BLM of taking into consideration wilderness qualities of the land under its management before allowing logging, mining, or oil and gas development. She signed a court settlement that in effect promised that neither she or any other interior secretary would ever again protect wilderness areas that had not been officially designated as such by Congress.[33]

It is clear that this administration favors the extractive industries over other uses of our forests and wilderness areas. Our national forests are open to loggers and thousands of acres in wilderness areas are open to leasing by the oil and gas industry. These areas are being industrialized and their value as places in which to hike and fish and enjoy other recreational uses is being destroyed.[34] An editorial in the Denver Post points out that the frenetic pace of drilling for oil and gas in the West is running roughshod over other public goals such as clean air and water and protection of wildlife. And the leases that are currently being granted is creating a backlog of untapped leases that could determine the fate of public lands and forests for decades.[35]

This administration wants to remove all public lands from any kind of protection and eliminate environmental reviews and citizen participation. It regards these areas as their own to be used to reward their friends in business so they can exploit our forests and wilderness areas to make more money. Granted we need energy and wood products, but they can be provided in a responsible manner taking into consideration environmental values and allowing full citizen participation. This administration wants none of these things to stop the plundering of our national resources for private profit.

APPOINTMENT OF PERSONNEL

The Bush administration's values are clear in regard to the personnel it puts in charge of our environmental resources. Apparently this administration knows nothing about conflicts of interest when it makes appointments or does not care about these kinds of ethical conflicts. The most egregious appointment of this nature involves J. Steven Griles, the former deputy secretary and second highest official of the Department of the Interior. Griles was a veteran energy industry lobbyist before being appointed to Interior, where he still continued to receive $284,000 a year from his lobbying firm for value created by bringing in clients. While at Interior, a former client, Advanced Power Technologies Inc., won some $2 million in no-bid contracts from Interior after two people whom Griles supervised pressed the matter. In another incident Griles urged the EPA to drop concerns about opening up eight million acres in Wyoming and Montana to gas drilling by companies that included six of his former clients. All this was after he had promised to remove himself from deliberations involving his former clients. The department's inspector general called Griles tenure an "ethical quagmire."[36]

The secretary herself, Gale Norton, started her career working under James Watt, a former secretary of the interior himself during the Reagan administration, who headed the Mountain States Legal Foundation, the litigating arm of the Wise Use Movement. This was an association of groups that pressed for further exploitation of our natural resources. Norton moved to Washington and also worked in interior under Reagan where she attempted to open up the Arctic National Wildlife Refuge to oil drilling. She also supported the "property rights" movement that sought to expand the taking clause of the Fifth Amendment that would require the government to pay property owners when it imposes new environmental restrictions.[37]

Carl Pope and Paul Rauber writing in Strategic Ignorance have this to say about Bush appointees: "In their view, national forests really ought to be tree farms, rivers are better off dammed to provide reliable irrigation for agribusiness, and, if you want to see wildlife, you can pay your money at an animal farm or game ranch."[38] These are the kinds of people who are stewards of our national resources and are supposed to be managing them in the public interest, not in the interests of oil and gas companies and the logging and mining industries. These people have no apparent appreciation of environmental values and see nature as something to exploit in our own interests.

USES OF SCIENCE

The Bush administration also misuses scientific findings when it comes to environmental matters. It insists its actions are based on "sound science," yet it seems relatively clear to many critics that politics trumps science when deemed necessary by this administration. Eric Schaeffer, former head of regulatory enforcement at the EPA who resigned in protest over the Clear Skies plan, said about the administration's use of science: "'Sound science' is a slogan so manipulated that it has lost its meaning. Sound science ought to mean independent, objective research that leads to informed decisions about how best to protect human health and the natural world. Instead, it has come to mean suppressing data that fails to justify desired outcomes and manufacturing data that does."[39]

Some instances in which science was manipulated for political purposes made the headlines. In 2001 when the Secretary of the Interior Gale Norton encouraged Congress to open the Arctic National Wildlife Refuge to oil and gas drilling, scientists revealed that she had altered data that came from the U.S. Fish and Wildlife Service concerning caribou migration and breeding in the refuge. In 2002 a decision was made to send water from the Klamath River to farmers on the California-Oregon border that overruled the advice of agency biologists and resulted in the death of an estimated 58,000 endangered steelhead and salmon. Finally a decision that removed protection of the greater sage grouse was based in part on a heavily edited scientific review by a political apointee with no background in biology.[40]

In February 2004 some 60 scientists including Nobel laureates, former agency directors, and university professors released a statement that "when scientific knowledge has been found to be in conflict with its political goals, the administration has often manipulated the process through which science enters into its decisions." The statement alleges this is done by (1) placing unqualified people with conflicts of interest in positions of power, (2) by censoring and suppressing information from government scientists, and (3) by failing to seek independent scientific advice. By November 2004 more than 5,000 scientists had signed the statement.[41]

This statement was issued under the auspices of the Union of Concerned Scientists, a nonprofit group devoted to a responsible use of science in environmental policy making. This organization subsequently launched a Restoring Scientific Integrity Campaign, which had two principal goals: (1) restoring integrity to the ways in which science is factored into federal policy decisions and (2) protecting the nation's investment in government scientific expertise, which has brought us sustained economic progress, science-based public health policy, and unequaled scientific leadership within the global community. It accused the Bush administration of being interested in scientific research only to the extent that it conforms to policies that the administration had already chosen and mentioned two examples involving climate change and federal standards to prevent lead poisoning to support this allegation.[42]

WHERE ARE WE HEADED?

The important question to ask is, given the policies of the Bush administration and the apparent attitude of much of the public towards the environment, where are we going and what kind of environment are we creating for ourselves? The answer to this question is critical regarding the kinds of environmental policies we as a society will support and the way in which we personally act with respect to environmental problems. While one can spin many different scenarios in this regard, it seems that the direction in which we are heading is quite clear.

Several years ago there was a movie called Blade Runner, in which the population left after a nuclear holocaust lived in a huge dome where the environment was under total control. The outside world was a forbidden place because of radioactivity and no one was allowed to go outside the dome. Life within the dome was highly regulated so that life inside was sustainable. For example everyone over 30 was exterminated to keep the population at supportable levels. This was done in as humane a fashion as possible but was necessary to keep the population under control. People lived in a totally controlled environment that included the climate and everything else of importance to human existence.

This is an extreme case of environmental destruction, but it can serve as a worst-case scenario of what might happen if we continue to destroy what is left of the "natural" world and industrialize everything in sight for the sake of exploitation for oil and gas and other resources. There will be no wilderness left worth mentioning if we continue down this path, and humans will destroy the habitat for animals and continue the extinction of other species that is currently taking place. We do not seem to realize that extinction of other species will lead to extinction of the human race. We are all in this together. There is no us or them, or it and us, but the environment is the whole of which we are only a part. Yet it seems that we will not be satisfied until we have developed every last square inch of the world, until we have paved over every last square inch of land, until we have exploited every last square inch of earth.

Many millions of people already live in what could be called a controlled environment. They live in climate-controlled houses, drive in climate-controlled cars, work in climate-controlled offices, and shop in climate-controlled shopping malls. The only contact they have with the outdoors is the occasional walk to and from one climate-controlled environment to another. So what difference does it make to them if the outdoors is destroyed? As one friend put it she doesn't care if the environment is trashed to keep her air conditioner running. It is my guess there are millions of people like this in our country who couldn't care less about the natural environment because they never have contact with it anyhow.

So they might as well live in a domed city within a completely controlled environment. Perhaps the nation should be split into those who want to live inside the dome and those who want to live outside in what is left of the natural environment. While the biosphere experiments in Arizona were a failure,

I am confident that in time our technology will allow us to build some kind of a sustainable life within a biosphere that may still have some dependence on the outside environment. But this natural environment will just be used as a source of whatever raw materials are necessary for people to live inside the dome and perhaps to dispose of some kinds of waste material that cannot be recycled or decomposed.

This could be where we are heading, and I think we ought to be aware of the kind of world we are creating. The human need to exploit and develop everything seems to be inexhaustible and is like a bulldozer that cannot be stopped. Sooner or later the Arctic National Wildlife Refuge is going to be opened for oil and gas drilling, and no one can stop it, even though whatever oil is found there is not going to reduce our dependence on oil imports. But it seems inevitable that we eventually are going to exploit every resource available in order to support our life style. The human ego knows no bounds and has no limits. This is a problem because we live in a world that does have limits, and our refusal to live within those limits will surely lead to our demise.

We need to change our notions about the environment and our relationship to the natural environment and all it contains. This is a basic philosophical problem that will require education and discussion, and the question is, can we change our understanding of nature and our place in it in time to save ourselves? To be honest I am not very optimistic about this kind of change, and I only hope that not too many of the mountain areas in Colorado and Utah are destroyed while I am still alive so I can enjoy hiking in them and that not too much redrock country in Utah is opened up to oil and gas drilling so I can still hike and four-wheel in those areas without running into an oil or gas well around very corner.

One major impediment to treating the natural environment in a responsible manner is the way the environment is treated in standard economic theory as this theory in large part dominates the way we behave with respect to the environment. The market does not respond very well to environmental problems and, if left to its own devices, treats the environment as something external to itself. There seems to be no way the value of the environment or any of its services can be determined through a market process since there is nothing to be exchanged. People cannot take a piece of dirty air, for example, and exchange it for a piece of clean air on the market, at least given the current state of technology. The same holds true for other components of the environment.

The competitive system limits the ability of corporations to respond to environmental problems. Some call this inability of market systems to respond to environmental pollution and degradation as market failure, but to use this term is not entirely accurate. Market systems were not designed to factor in environmental costs and it is not fair to blame the system for not doing something for which it was not designed. Property rights are not appropriately assigned as regards the environment and nature often lacks a discrete owner to look after its interests. The rights of nature can be violated by market exchanges, and as a common property resource, nature can be overused and degraded as it is subject to the "tragedy of the commons," a phenomenon that relates to property held in common for everyone.[43]

Market systems evolved to serve human needs and wants; they are not constructed to protect the environment. The environment is treated as a source of raw materials to be used in the production process and as a bottomless sink in which to dispose of waste materials. The environment has no value in and of itself, but it is worth something only as it can be used to serve some human purpose such as enhancing living standards through the creation of more and more economic wealth. The ecological functions of environmental entities have no value as far as the market is concerned. It is only their economic utility or instrumental value that is of importance in a market economy. Thus the market fails to tell the ecological truth as it regularly underprices products and services by failing to incorporate the environmental costs of providing them.[44]

Economic growth comes at the expense of the earth's productive assets—its farmlands, forests, fisheries, aquifers, wetlands, and even from destablizing its climate. The costs of this environmental degradation and pollution are external to normal market processes and are not taken into account in the price mechanism unless these costs are determined through some other process and imposed on the market system. Only then can environmental values be internalized and reflect themselves in market decisions. This is the major task facing business and society; to find some reasonable and acceptable way to factor in environmental costs along with other costs of production.

This task cannot be left to government alone as government is subject to political and ideological pressures that do not allow it to develop a consistent approach to environmental problems. Business must take the lead and work with other elements in society including government to develop an institutional mechanism to figure out these environmental costs and then decide on the best means of imposing these costs on the market, whether it be through standards, taxes, emissions trading systems, or other means. People must be aware of environmental impacts in their own actions. Our political, economic, and social systems must change to take into account environmental interests in every decision.

THE COMMONS AND DEMOCRACY

As part of its transition team, the incoming Bush administration employed the services of Terry Anderson, who headed a Montana think tank called the Political Economy Research Center. Anderson is a libertarian economist who thinks that all public lands ought to be auctioned off to private bidders. All of our public forests and wilderness areas should be partitioned into individual tracts and sold to private interests. This includes our national parks as well, as a divestiture plan should make no exceptions for the Grand Canyon, Yosemite, or other national parks. Conservation of these areas should be left up to the wisdom of the market, which means it would be up to individual owners of the property to decide if they wished to conserve these areas for future generations and indeed if they would allow the public any access at all to enjoy these treasures.[45]

The goal of free market environmentalists such as Anderson is to enclose all common property on the theory that these lands will be better cared for by private property owners than by public stewards. According to Pope and Rauber, this reflects the Bush administration's attitude towards public lands held in common. They cannot stand the idea that such lands belong to everyone to be enjoyed by them and future generations. If they cannot get away with selling them to private interests, then they want at least to allow extractive industries free access to these lands to be exploited for private profit and keep the public out of these decisions as much as possible. For those who see Disneyland as the model for public recreation, the public forests and wilderness areas are a problem.[46]

According to John Balzar, writing in the Los Angeles Times, the ranch that Bush owns in Crawford, Texas, reflects his attitude towards nature. "I've heard cynics describe Bush's sun-scorched ranch as something of a faux cowboy prop that he uses to maintain down-to-earth distance from his old-money East Coast heritage. The truth, I think, is the opposite. These 1,600 acres are not a retreat from elitism, but rather an open-arms embrace of the most uncharitable kind of elitism: the belief that nature belongs to those who can afford it. That nature is a privilege for the privileged. That nature is another free-market commodity for high bidders."[47]

Robert F. Kennedy Jr. argues that one way to measure the effectiveness of a democracy is to look at how much the public is included in community decision making. On this score the Bush administration fails miserably in its attempt to shut out the public from decisions about the use of our public lands. But the most telling aspect of a government, Kennedy says, is how it distributes the goods of the land under its jurisdiction. Does it safeguard the commonwealth in the interests of the public? Or does it allow corporate interests to steal the shared wealth of our communities? Environmental laws were designed to protect the commons—the air we breath, the water we drink, the wildlife we enjoy, the wilderness areas we need to escape from the pressures of urban and city life.[48]

The Bush administration, according to Kennedy, can't seem to see the benefits we have received from investing in our environmental infrastructure, which is a good way to see the environment. It is something akin to roads and bridges, an infrastructure vital to keep in good condition to enable us to live a good and decent life. But all the Bush administration sees are the costs of compliance with environmental regulations for its campaign contributors. It does not care about protecting the commons, those lands it holds in trust for the public at large.[49]

The great majority of us cannot afford 1,600 acres in Texas to escape to in times of stress.[50] We need national parks and wilderness areas in which to get in touch with nature and experience something other than the noise and traffic jams in our cities and urban areas. Turning these areas over to private corporations to exploit for private profit is not necessarily in the public interest. As Kennedy points out, all of us will eventually pay for this travesty with reduced prosperity and quality of life for ourselves and future generations.[51]

If indeed McKibben is right and nature as it once was understood no longer exists, and rather than being an autonomous force that needed to be conquered it is now largely under our control, this means we are shaping the environment in which we and future generations will have to live and move and have our being. Thus we should all have the opportunity to participate in the decisions that shape that environment and those decisions should not be left to energy executives meeting behind closed doors with only their own interests in mind. And science should be respected and used appropriately and not distorted to serve the administration's and corporate interests. The environmental policies and practices of this administration are a threat to cherished American values with respect to the environment.

NOTES

1. Bill McKibben, *The End of Nature* (New York: Random House, 1989).
2. Christine Todd Whitman, *It's My Party Too: The Battle For The Heart Of The GOP And The Future Of America* (New York: Penguin Press, 2005), 195.
3. With regard to toxic wastes, this administration allowed Superfund to expire, meaning that cleanup of hazardous wastes is no longer the responsibility of corporations that dumped there and cleanup of these sites is now paid by taxpayers. They abandoned the "polluter pays" principle. See Carl Pope and Paul Rauber, *Strategic Ignorance: Why the Bush Administration Is Recklessly Destroying a Century of Environmental Progress* (San Francisco: Sierra Club Books, 2004), 197–202.
4. Pope and Rauber, *Strategic Ignorance*, 241–254.
5. Pope and Rauber, *Strategic Ignorance*, 15.
6. Pope and Rauber, *Strategic Ignorance*, 16,24.
7. Pope and Rauber, *Strategic Ignorance*, 46.
8. Pope and Rauber, *Strategic Ignorance*, 65–66.

9. Pope and Rauber, *Strategic Ignorance*, 67. See also Whitman, *It's My Party Too*, 157–161.

10. Whitman, *It's My Party Too*, 169.

11. Whitman, *It's My Party Too*, 170-72.

12. Whitman, *It's My Party Too*, 174–76.

13. Whitman, *It's My Party Too*, 177–78.

14. See Michael D. Lemonick, "Meltdown!" *Time*, 22 November 2004, 72–73; Charles W. Petit, "Arctic Thaw," *U.S. News & World Report*, 8 November 2004, 66–69.

15. Katy Human and Kim McGuire, "Climate-change report states impact evident," *Denver Post*, 16 December 2004, 6(A). In its 3 April 2006 edition, Time magazine ran a special report on global warming, where one author claims the crisis of global warming is already upon us as the climate is changing faster than anyone expected. See Jeffrey Kluger, "By Any Measure, Earth Is at. . . . The Tipping Point," *Time*, 3 April 2006, 34–42. See also Bret Schulte, "Turning Up The Heat," *U.S. News & World Report*, 10 April 2006, 34–37. Even if we were to stop burning fossil fuels tomorrow, the earth would continue to warm for at least 100 more years because climate change is time delayed. See "The global warming we're stuck with," *The Week*, 8 April 2005, 23.

16. Kevin Gray, "2004 is 4th hottest on record, says U.N.," *Denver Post*, 16 December 2004, 10(A).

17. See John Carey, "Global Warming," *Business Week*, 16 August 2004, 60-69.

18. Larry Rohter, "U.S. scuttles effort to set up new climate talks," *Denver Post*, 19 December 2004, 2(A). The U.S. would not even agree to seminars to discuss the issue and initially insisted that "there shall be no written or oral report" from any seminars. All that could be achieved was an agreement to hold a single workshop in 2005 to "exchange information" on climate change.

19. Whitman, *It's My Party Too*, 181–83.

20. Pope and Rauber, *Strategic Ignorance*, 87.

21. Pope and Rauber, *Strategic Ignorance*, 85.

22. Whitman, *It's My Party Too*, 186.

23. Earth Justice, "Internal Report Slams Agency's Enforcement," *In Brief*, Winter 2004, 12–13.

24. Felicity Barringer, "EPA is accused of rigging outcome for mercury rules," *Denver Post*, 4 February 2005, 4(A).

25. Douglas H. Benevento, "Cleanup progress requires new law," *Denver Post*, 27 February 2005, 1(E).

26. Vickie Patton, "Measure would be radical retreat," *Denver Post*, 27 February 2005, 1(E).

27. Jeff Nesmith, "Air-pollution bill stalls in committee," *Denver Post*, 18 March 2005, 6(A).

28. Edwin Chen, "Pollution rule wins rare praise for Bush," *Denver Post*, 11 March 2005, 7(A). The EPA soon issued another rule covering mercury emissions for the rest of the country, which was quickly attacked by critics who argued that Western states would see a spike in toxic mercury emissions from coal-fired power plants. Kim McGuire, "EPA's mercury rule attacked," *Denver Post*, 16 March 2005, 1(B).

29. Matthew Daly, "New law helps Forest Service win 17 cases to allow cutting," *Denver Post*, 21 May 2004, 16(A).

30. "New Forest Service rules silence public," *Denver Post*, 2 January 2005, 6(E); Natural Resources Defense Council, "White House Cuts Down Forest Protections," *Nature's Voice*, March/April 2005, 4. In 2001 the Department of Agriculture rewrote the Roadless Area Conservation Rule, which would have protected 58.5 million acres of national forest.

31. Pope and Rauber, *Strategic Ignorance*, 130.

32. "The Editors Respond," *High Country News*, 21 February 2005, 20-21.

33. Pope and Rauber, *Strategic Ignorance*, 130.

34. For a discussion of the impact industrial facilities make on the natural environment see Brian Hayes, "The Ghosts in the Machines," *Natural History*, September 2005, 36–43.

35. "Oil and gas leasing moving too quickly," *Denver Post*, 12 February 2006, 8(E). See also John Mitchell, "All Fired Up: Tapping the Rockies," *National Geographic*, July 2005, 92–113.

36. Anne C. Mulkern, "When advocates become regulators," *Denver Post*, 23 May 2004, 17(A).

37. Pope and Rauber, *Strategic Ignorance*, 54.

38. Pope and Rauber, *Strategic Ignorance*, 176.

39. Pope and Rauber, *Strategic Ignorance*, 156.

40. Laura Paskus, "Conscientious Objectors," *High Country News*, 20 December 2004, 12. For other examples see this same issue of High Country News and Earth Justice, "The Fine Art of Manipulating Science," In Brief, Winter 2004, 24–25. See also Andrew C. Revkin, "Bush aide massages air data," *Denver Post*, 8 June 2005, 1(A).

41. Paskus, "Conscientious Objectors," 12.

42. Letter from Kevin Knobloch, President, Union of Concerned Scientists, undated.

43. See Garret Hardin, "The Tragedy of the Commons," *Science* 162, no. 1 (December 13, 1968): 1243–1248.

44. See Lester R. Brown, *Plan B: Rescuing a Planet Under Stress and a Civilization in Trouble* (New York: W.W. Norton, 2003), especially 199–222.

45. Pope and Rauber, *Strategic Ignorance*, 117–18. In early 2006 Bush's budget proposal contained a provision to sell more than 300,000 acres of forests and other public land deemed to have little scenic, recreational, or resource value. The proceeds would be used to pay for schools and roads in rural counties hurt by logging cutbacks on federal land. Associated Press, "Bush budget would sell land to raise $1 billion," 13 February 2006, www.msnbc.msn.com/id/11257181/(26 April 2006). This plan proved to be very unpopular as thousands of comments were filed opposing the plan to privatize public land for short-term economic purposes. The plan would have to be approved by Congress and appeared to be "dead on arrival." Steve Lipsher and Mike Soraghan, "Public sees big 'not' in forest plan," *Denver Post*, 26 April 2006, 1(A).

46. Pope and Rauber, *Strategic Ignorance*, 118–19.

47. Pope and Rauber, *Strategic Ignorance*, 114.

48. Robert F. Kennedy, Jr., *Crimes Against Nature: How George W. Bush and His Corporate Pals Are Plundering the Country and Hijacking Our Democracy* (New York: Harper Collins, 2004), 43.

49. Kennedy, *Crimes Against Nature*, 44.

50. Choosing a ranch in the heat of Texas shows the folly of private decision making. It is not the panacea for all our problems that free marketers would have us believe. The decisions of private property holders are oftentimes as stupid and destructive as those of public servants. Private property is no guarantee that property is going to be used more efficiently and taken care of appropriately. We all know people who do not take care of their houses or cars or anything else they own as private property.

51. Kennedy, *Crimes Against Nature*, 198.

Part II

VALUES AND RELIGION

Chapter Five

Fundamentalist Christianity

What do all of these policies and activities of the Bush administration, both foreign and domestic, have to do with religion? What religious elements have influenced these policies and activities? What problems do these religious influences pose for the nation? The assumption is that George W. Bush and many people in his administration are part of the religious right, that they do not just give lip service to Fundamentalist Christianity in trying to win votes, but that they share its outlook on life and its values in a way the elder Bush and his administration did not. The contention here is that this religious worldview shapes their perspective on the world and how they understand their roles in government.

Religion to me has always been a private matter, and I respect the right of people to believe whatever they want as I expect other people to respect my beliefs. If people want to believe in a God who manipulates things in the world, if they want to believe in the resurrection as a physical supernatural event, it they want to believe in the second coming of Jesus, that is their perogative. People can believe in the tooth fairy, if they like, and I have no quarrel. Whatever works to give their lives meaning and purpose and helps them cope with life's trials and tribulations is fine and I have no cause to be upset. Whenever religion enters the public arena however and begins to influence public policy on issues like stem cell research, abortion, the teaching of evolution or intelligent design in public schools, and the appointment of federal judges, it ceases to be a private matter and is fair game for criticism. The way religion has entered public life today makes me very upset, and I think it is very detrimental to the country. And of course it is not just any religion that is of concern relative to these matters, but the Christian religion in its most fundamentalistic interpretation.

Chapter Five

THE CHRISTIAN STORY

Thus we must first of all deal with the kind of world Christianity entails. Every religion has a story to tell that attempts to address some, if not all, of the deepest mysteries of life, such as how the earth was created, what is the meaning of life, and where do we go, if anywhere, after death. The Christian religion has a particular story about the origins of life, the end of times, and everything in between spelled out in a book called the Bible. To fundamentalists this book is the ultimate authority and contains the absolute truth about all these questions. It is looked to for answers about all life's problems and mysteries.

The story in its essence goes something like this. In the beginning God created the world in six days, and rested on the seventh. This world was created out of nothing, or ex nihilo as it is called in theological terms. God looked at his creation and saw that it was good. He (or she) also created man and woman (Adam and Eve) and placed them in a Garden of Eden, a perfect place where all their needs were taken care of. Human beings were created directly by God; they did not evolve from other forms of life. Things went bad for these first humans however as Adam was tempted by Eve to eat the forbidden fruit and thus fell into sin. This sinful condition was then passed on from generation to generation, and so every child born from that time to the present is born into sin and has to be saved from its consequences.

The Old Testament is the story of the Jewish people and their journey from Egypt to the promised land of Israel. Once there they formed a society based on the law as revealed to Moses on Mount Sinai and became the chosen people of God to redeem all nations. Following the law was the way to redeem oneself and win God's favor. However the law eventually became an end in itself, and people began to believe they could attain their own salvation by religiously following the letter of the law. In the process they became rigid and self-righteous and began to lose sight of the intent of the law, which was to free them from sin and death and give them life.

Thus God sent his son, Jesus, into the world to show the proper way to attain eternal life. By his example and teaching he hoped to save mankind from sin and death and offer them hope. He deliberately broke the law in the interests of human compassion and spent the majority of his time with the outcasts and sinners in Jewish society. Jesus performed miracles to heal people and feed them if necessary. He appointed 12 disciples to spread the message of love and forgiveness to all the world. It should be noted that he did not come to abolish the law, but to fulfill the law and reestablish its true intent. Thus the Old and New Testaments are sometimes characterized as law and gospel, the Old Testament being about the law and the New being about the gospel message of love and forgiveness.

Eventually Jesus offended enough people in Jewish society that he was put to death on the cross. But this was not the end of the matter as he overcame death to rise from the grave and ascend into heaven. It is believed that Jesus died for our sins and we can overcome sin and death if we accept Jesus as our Lord and Savior. He became the Christ when he ascended into heaven to be with the father. At the appropriate time he will return to earth and establish his kingdom. At that time the wheat and the chaff will be separated on the great Judgment Day, and those who have acknowledged him as Lord will join him in heaven while all others will descend into hell to burn in the eternal fires. The book of Revelation contains all sorts of details about the Mark of the Beast and other things related to the end of times that I am not going to get into in these pages.[1] But the Christian story goes from the beginning of time to the end of time and in this sense encompasses all of human history.

Surveys show that many people, in some cases the majority of the population, believe in many of the tenets of this religion. They believe in God, in heaven and hell, in angels, in miracles, and other things of this nature.[2] It is my observation however that many members of mainstream religions do not take much of this story too seriously. However, the fundamentalists, so-called because they believe in the infallibility of the Bible in matters of faith, morals, and history, take all of this very seriously. They do not believe in evolution, for example, and want creationism to be taught in our public schools, and if they can't get creationism to be taught exclusively, they are willing to settle for it being taught side by side with evolution for the time being. When it comes to the age of the earth, to cite another example, they reject the findings of geology and hold that the earth is about 5,000 years old because that is what the Bible says. The Bible is taken as the absolute truth because it was literally dictated by God and therefore can contain no errors because God is a perfect being.

FUNDAMENTALIST CHARACTERISTICS

All religions either produce or attract a certain kind of person, and it is not clear whether religion shapes the characteristics and attitudes of its adherents or whether people with certain personalities are attracted to religion. Most likely the influence runs both ways, that a certain kind of person is attracted to religion and thus shapes the nature of that religion and that religion also influences what that person becomes. Fundamentalist Christianity then both attracts a certain kind of personality that is already shaped to some extent and also helps to shape that personality. The religion is what it is because of its adherents, and it also shapes what its adherents become. It is the characteristics of fundamentalist Christians that are important to understand with respect to the Bush administration and its practices.

The intent here is not to suggest that every adherent of fundamentalism displays these characteristics, that one can generalize and find these characteristics in all people who call themselves fundamentalist Christians. Nor do I mean to suggest that non-Christians or even atheists do not have some or all of these characteristics. Fundamentalists do not have a monopoly on these things, but it is argued here that these characteristics are at the core of fundamentalist belief and a key part of the worldview fundamentalism contains. These characteristics pose certain problems that will be mentioned and lend themselves to certain kinds of abuse that will be discussed. In the next chapter the way these characteristics show up in the Bush administration will be considered along with the problems this poses for American society.

Absolutism

Fundamentalism involves an absolutist type of thinking, in which there is only one source of truth and that source is the Bible as the Word of God. This kind of absolutist thinking cannot compromise this knowledge of the truth, cannot enter into an honest discussion about issues, and is not open to knowledge that comes from other sources like science. Compromise is not necessary if one knows the absolute truth, but more than that it is not possible because it is a contradiction. Absolute truth cannot be compromised or it would not be the absolute truth. People who think this way believe they know the absolute truth about the creation of the world, about original sin and the need for salvation, about heaven and hell, and about every other thing that has to do with human existence.

Typical of such an approach are the views of John Stott, rector emeritus at All Souls of Langham Place in London, whom David Brooks, a writer for the New York Times, thinks is more representative of evangelical Christians than either Falwell or Robertson. Stott does not believe that truth is plural and that all faiths are independently valid. Nor does he believe that truth is something humans are working toward. Truth has already been revealed. In the bibical witness to Christ, God's revelation is complete and to add any words of our own to the finished work of God is derogatory to Christ.[3]

There are many problems overlooked by absolutists in viewing the Bible as the final authority in all these matters. For one thing, which translation is the authentic Word of God? There are many translations of the Bible, all of which claim to be superior to the others. Which is the right one? What about contradictions in the Bible? Which creation story is most authentic? The gospels contain different accounts of the life of Jesus; which is the right one?

The absolutist thinker ignores all these questions and simply chooses whatever serves a particular interest and then claims some ultimate authority in these matters. The Bible itself is simply another book written by human beings in a certain time period. Any claims for the ultimate authority of the Bible comes from the absolutists themselves who look to it for the definitive answer to all of life's problems.

Our society is split at this point, and this split is most often referred to as the culture wars, as if we have two cultures with respect to social issues in particular, be it abortion, stem cell research, gay marriage, or other such issues. This split is of course reflected in the way people vote, and in the election of 2004 analysts suggested that these kinds of moral issues were more important than the economy and terrorism. National exit polls showed that 22 percent of voters cited "moral values" as their top issue compared with 20 percent who mentioned the economy, 19 percent terrorism, and 15 percent Iraq. Of those who mentioned moral values as their top concern, 79 percent voted for Bush.[4] The conclusion was that moral values ultimately determined the winner in the presidential election.[5]

The fundamentalists who hold an absolutist position on these issues have a different worldview or different assumptions from people who are in favor of gay marriage, abortion, and the like. They cannot talk to each other because there is nothing to talk about. On the one side are those who believe that moral values lie on something of a continuum between good and bad, right and wrong, and one makes a cut somewhere along this continuum that one thinks will work out the best for everyone involved. This cut could be on one side or the other in favor of gay marriage, for example, depending on how strongly a person holds certain values and on the circumstances surrounding the issue. But the point is that there is not an absolute position here and one can change his or her mind on issues of this nature as more information becomes available.

For the absolutist however there is no continuum; there is only right and wrong, good and evil, and the nature of the choice is black and white. There is not even a slippery slope. Sometimes it is argued, for example, that if gay marriage is allowed, pretty soon polygamy and other forms of unions will be allowed. Where does it stop? If an absolutist allows for any of this he or she will not just start sliding down a slippery slope; they will plunge over a cliff into the abyss. Murder is murder and a society cannot allow any kind of murder, abortion or otherwise, to be legal. Being gay or not is a choice. It is not genetic in any way and it is a choice that goes against the will of God. Thus to allow gay marriage is to invite the wrath of God to be visited on those who support such a practice.

Issues of sexual morality receive disproportionate attention because they are the point where human desires and impulses most powerfully threaten to destabilize conventional family structures. Constituting these structures as divinely ordained, rather than historical accidents, cultural preferences, or the product of negotiation, is thus a way to defend these structures against the challenges of secularism and secure their perpetuation. There is no negotiation or no choice involved when dealing with something divinely ordained. How differences of this nature are ever going to be bridged and how common ground can be found on these issues is beyond my comprehension. Two competing worldviews are in collision and there seem to be no compromises that would allow each side to maintain its integrity.

Thus another way of characterizing the split in society is to refer to it as a split between absolutists and pluralists, between those who believe in one source of truth and those who believe there are multiple sources of truth. Pluralists believe religion has something to say about truth to be sure, but so does science, and so does human experience. Thus if science begins to provide evidence that homosexuality is possibly genetic, this has to be taken into account. If studies show that making abortion illegal means that rich women go to Europe to have an abortion and poor women have to go to back alleys, this is an important factor to take into consideration. If science can indeed help cure some nasty diseases like Alzheimer's through stem cell research, this becomes a major factor in the decision whether to proceed with further research.

There are many sources of knowledge about our world and the human condition, and no one of them can be taken as absolute. Even if there is such a thing as absolute truth, how would we as humans with our finite minds know it when we saw it? It is not that truth is relative as some approaches to the world are better than others; it is that none of us has the absolute truth in our back pocket. But none of these arguments are going to persuade an absolutist. Anyone who believes he or she is getting revealed truth is beyond logical argument and evidence. An absolutist is who he or she is because of this characteristic, and to give up being an absolutist is to give up one's identity. This identity is all tied up with a belief in a God who is all knowing and all powerful and who punishes the unfaithful and rewards the faithful.

Belief in an Anthropomorphic God

This absolutism stems from a belief in an anthropomorphic God, a God who has human attributes. This God gets angry, can be loving and forgiving, is sad at times, and displays many other human characteristics. At the same time this God is all knowing and all powerful, a God who is a personal being who stands above all things and controls the destiny of the world. This God is perfect and unchanging and constitutes absolute truth. Thus anyone who lays claim to a belief in this God lays claim to being in touch with the absolute truth as revealed in God's Word, the word that is preached on Sunday morning in churches around the country. This God pulls the strings and manipulates things; he (or she) is not subject to the laws of nature but stands outside those laws and can intervene in nature at will. This God is prayed to as an acknowledgement of this power and the dependency of humans on his (or her) mercy.

This belief in a personal God who relates directly to people and can intervene on their behalf leads to all kinds of problems, not the least of which is that it opens the door for people to claim God-like powers. It is my contention that some people who believe in this kind of God really don't believe in God at all. What they really believe is that THEY are God and act accordingly. When some people claim to know the will of God, what they really want is for others to follow their lead without question because how can anyone question God's will? When someone believes he or she possesses absolute truth, they are acting like an all-knowing God rather than a finite human being with limited knowledge. While this may not be a teaching of Christianity, the door is open to this kind of abuse.

God is also used to fill in the blanks. Many fundamentalists always have the answer to everything. Is there something we don't understand? Just use God to fill the gaps in our knowledge. Do we know how the universe actually came into being; in other words, do we know what lies behind the Big Bang, which is currently the most popular theory about the beginning of the universe? Of course no one knows. But rather than leave this as an interesting question that warrants further discussion, fundamentalists invoke God as the creator of the universe. End of discussion. Do we really know why people, both young and old, have to die such horrible deaths sometimes or go through so much suffering? Fundamentalists reply that it is God's will or that God is testing their faith or some such thing. End of question.

Two days after the 9/11 attacks Jerry Falwell appeared on Pat Robertson's 700 club. Both Falwell and Robertson explained these attacks as God's displeasure relative to what is happening in American society. This event had a great theological meaning for them and had to be explained in these terms to make sense. Robertson later distanced himself from the remarks of his colleague and made some attempts at apology and explanation and Falwell started to backtrack after realizing that what he had said was not politically correct.[6] Robertson's statement is quoted first, then Falwell's statement which was the most dramatic and most discussed.

> We have allowed rampant secularism and occult, etc. to be broadcast on television. We have permitted somewhere in the neighborhood of 35 to 40 million unborn babies to be slaughtered in our society. We have a court that has essentially

stuck its finger in God's eye and said we're going to legislate you out of the schools. We're going to take your commandments from off the courthouse steps in various states. We're not going to let little children read the commandments of God. We're not going to let the Bible be read, no prayer in our schools. We have insulted God at the highest levels of our government. And then we say, "Why does this happen?" Well, why it is happening is that God Almighty is lifting his protection from us. And once that protection is gone, we all are vulnerable because we're a free society, and we're vulnerable.[7]

And I know that I'll hear from them for this. But throwing God out successfully with the help of the federal court system, throwing God out of the public square, out of the schools. The abortionists have got to bear some burden for this because God will not be mocked. And when we destroy 40 million innocent babies, we make God mad. I really believe that the pagans, and the abortionists, and the feminists, and the gays and the lesbians who are actively trying to make that an alternative lifestyle, the ACLU, People For the American Way, all of them who have tried to secularize America. I point the finger in their face and say: "You helped this happen."[8]

God is the answer to everything, to all of life's problems and mysteries and disasters.[9] Several years ago I was driving around Chicago and went past a church with a big sign that read "Christ is the Answer." Someone had written in these words underneath, "What was the Question," which I thought was most appropriate. For fundamentalists everything has to have an answer. Everything happens for a reason; there is no room for chance or luck, either good or bad. God rewards and punishes, and his (or her) ways are not our ways. We do not always understand what God is up to, but someday it will all become clear as we come to understand God's purpose for the world or for our lives. God is in control and knows what he (or she) is doing. There is no room for error because God is all knowing.

God is also used as an explanation for things that happen that are beyond our control and understanding. Several years ago when I was living in New Orleans, a hurricane named Georges was heading straight for the mouth of the Mississippi, a worst-case scenario for the city where not only would the river back up and overflow its levees, but Lake Pontchatrain would also end up flooding the city, all of which lies below sea level. Predictions indicated that the entire city could end up being under as much as 20 feet of water. Before it reached land however, the hurricane veered to the east and the eye ended up going over Biloxi, about 90 miles to the east of New Orleans. Plenty of damage was still done in New Orleans because of the flooding and overturned trees, but as least the city was spared from disaster. Yet many churchgoers in the city could not help thanking God that the city was spared from the worst-case situation. Instead God in his (or her) infinite wisdom apparently sent the hurricane to hit those sinners in Biloxi with its full fury.[10]

There is a certain arrogance in this attitude as these people apparently believe God favors them over the other poor souls who were hurt or killed or suffered the loss of all their life's possessions. But there is also a certain sadness in other situations of this nature. There was the case of a soldier who was badly shot up in Iraq and may never walk again because of his injuries, yet he thanked God for sparing his life, without blaming God for taking away certain of his important life functions and putting him through so much suffering. Apparently his belief gave him a certain amount of comfort, and he certainly needed something to help him through his ordeal. But he never questioned why he was sent to Iraq in the first place.

God is also used as a crutch to help us through rough times in life. When things get bad and there is no one to care or help us through, it is helpful to believe there is someone like God who cares and who is going to help us get through trying times. We can pray to God and hope that he (or she) will intervene on our behalf. It gives us some comfort to believe that there is help somewhere and that someone understands our plight. In this instance God becomes a projection of our own unmet needs. There are a lot of unloved people in the world, people who feel rightly so that no one cares about them or loves them. People often don't care about each other enough, and God's love is a substitute for the human caring and compassion that is lacking.

Belief in this kind of God also tends to make people ego-centric and believe the world revolves around them. God sent his Son into the world to save them personally, and is concerned about the salvation of their soul. God can break the laws of nature for their sake if necessary. God is on their side if they do the right things and live a righteous life. Football players who thank God after scoring a touchdown are a good example. Does God really care if someone scores a touchdown given all the other more serious problems in the world? The same goes for a team who prays together before a game. Does God really care if they win or not? People pray for all sorts of things that reflect their personal wants and desires. If they can't get these things another way, perhaps God will provide them.[11]

Belief in this kind of God may thus be simply an extension of a person's own ego and gives a person a sense of extraordinary powers. There is no doubt that belief in God can give people courage to do things they would not otherwise think of doing. The suicide bombers are a case in point. How many of us would willingly sacrifice our lives for a belief in some kind of afterlife? Stories about the Mormons and the hardships and suffering they endured to settle in Utah and make a life for themselves are inspirational. Belief in God and his mission for them certainly helped them in their endeavors.

The Supernatural

The Christian faith involves a good many supernatural elements such as the virgin birth, the miracles Jesus is reported to have performed, the resurrection, life after death. The supernatural can be understood as things that lie outside or beyond the natural world, things that lie outside our experience. These things are not part of the natural world we live in every day; they are not things we can touch, feel, see, hear, or in any other way come to understand like we do most of the things we relate to or that govern our everyday lives. Thus to believe in something like the resurrection requires what is called faith, faith that this event actually took place even though there is no direct evidence that it ever literally happened and is something that is quite beyond our everyday experience. Similarly with the belief in an afterlife. The existence of some place called heaven cannot be proven or disproven by ordinary human experience but requires faith in something quite beyond our understanding.

Thus the Christian faith requires just that, faith in something that cannot be proven by ordinary human methods. It requires that people set aside at least part of their intelligence to believe in something that lies beyond human intelligence. What that something is of course comes from the Bible itself which is full of stories about miracles and God acting outside the laws of nature. The fundamentalists consider these stories to be literally true, that if the Bible talks about Jesus rising from the dead, then Jesus actually rose from the dead despite the fact that our human experience gives us no cause to believe this actually happened. There is no symbolic or theological meaning to these stories. They had to have actually happened; otherwise there is no ojbect of faith. If these stories are taken literally, the Christian faith stands or falls on the basis of belief in the supernatural. That's why there have been so many battles with science over the years and why things like evolution have been fought over so bitterly.

A literal interpretation of the Bible fails to see the real theological and, if you will, human meaning of the stories in the Bible. Every one of the miracles has a theological meaning and as such does speak to the conditions in which we humans find ourselves. The resurrection for example is a beautiful story of the possibilities of life after death—not a physical death but the real denigration of the human spirit that often takes place because of depression, low self-esteem, and emotional problems of one sort or another that makes one wish he or she were physically dead. It also speaks to those who are throwing away their lives in the pursuit of false gods or rather in the pursuit of unsatisfying and unfulfilling goals for their lives.

A literal interpretation of the Bible misses all these things. People who believe in supernatural miracles miss all the miracles right in front of them, the miracle of human and animal life, the miracle of a beautiful sunrise or sunset, the miracle of technological devices that make our lives easier and provide us with more opportunities for enjoyable experiences, the miracle of an awesome vista in the mountains or desert country. It is a mystery to me why people have to believe in supernatural miracles when there are so many miracles that take place every day as part of our ordinary lives. These are what make life meaningful, not some supernatural things outside of our everyday experience.

It is my contention that people who put their faith in the supernatural in some literal sense are really escaping their responsibilities as human beings and escaping a world they cannot accept and deal with in a fashion that may lead to something constructive. They hope for some divine intervention that makes things better. As John Dewey, an American philosopher, puts it: "Men have never fully used the powers they possess to advance the good life, because they have waited upon some power external to themselves and to nature to do the work they are responsible for doing. Dependence upon an external power is the counterpart of surrender of human endeavor."[12]

Belief in the supernatural is also a way of insulating oneself from the real demands of the Christian faith, which calls us to care about one another and the world in which we live. But we can go about our business oblivious to the suffering and pain around us by believing Jesus loves us and this is enough to comfort people. We can avoid taking responsibility for the environment by believing the Second Coming of Christ is imminent and thus what we do to our environment does not really matter[13]. We can avoid any sense of social concern that involves support for civil rights or other social causes because the only thing that matters is the state of our souls. The really important thing is to prepare our souls for entry into the blessed state of affairs in the afterlife.

Thus the real meaning of life comes from outside life itself. Our lives have significance only in light of what comes after our existence on earth. Our earthly existence is only some kind of testing period to determine if we are fit for life eternal. What we do here on earth has no meaning in and of itself. Meaning is tied up with the supernatural, the belief that there is more to life than what we experience in our day-to-day existence. What we do in this world is not good enough for fundamentalists as we cannot reach fulfillment of our potential in this world, but only as we reside with God in the hereafter.

Dehumanization

Fundamentalism involves a dehumanization of people and nature. A literal interpretation of the Bible involves viewing its writers as mechanical automatons who were simply recording the Word of God as it was dictated to them. It does not see them as living breathing human beings who were trying to cope with life's mysteries in the context in which they lived, using their imagination and creativity to write a story about things that interested them. And the world they lived in was a mythological world in which there were demons and angels, where the universe was viewed as containing an earth with heaven above and hell below. It is within this mythological worldview that they wrote about things important to them and borrowed from other writings available to make their points. What else could they do as human beings? Anyone who writes today does the same thing.

Granted that sometimes those of us who write get inspired to the point where the words seem to come from somewhere outside ourselves, that doesn't mean those words are coming from God or from some supernatural realm. When words just seem to flow on the page, it simply means we are really into our task and the rest of the world fades in importance. We are even oblivious to ourselves as we can get so wrapped up in our work that time doesn't matter and we miss meals and the like. But the words still come from ourselves, our brains, our experience, our connections with people and the world in which we live. These words do not come from some supernatural world outside our experience, anymore than they did for the writers of the Bible.

The trouble with a literal interpretation of the Bible is that it confuses mythology with the message and in doing so misses the theological intent of the stories in the Bible. The resurrection has actually to have happened or it has no meaning. Literalists are not able to project themselves backward into the worldview of the writers to get at the meaning they were trying to express. We are rooted in a scientific worldview whether we like it or not and understand things from this perspective. But we must set this aside to understand the worldview of the writers of the Bible and demythologize the stories in order to get at the real message. By accepting the mythological worldview as scientific fact, that is to say that the miracles actually happened, is to insulate oneself from the real meaning of the miracles and their impact on our everyday lives.

The Bible is not a book of history; it is not a book of science; it is a book of theology. People who accept it as literal fact however are dehumanizing themselves, and their faith is rooted in some mythological worldview that has nothing to do with their everyday experience. By doing this, they cut themselves off from the world in which they actually live. Rather than accepting the findings of geology and seeing the age of the earth as an interesting question that needs further research and discussion (science does not possess absolute truth either), they dismiss these findings and treat the Bible as a book of fact about the age of the earth. What may be going on here is that people may not be willing to accept their humanity and want to play God and believe they have the ultimate truth about the age of the earth using the Bible as the ultimate authority.

Digital Thinking

We live in a digital world where most everything is represented by 1's and 0's and analog devices have gone by the wayside. These binary digits more accurately reproduce reality as our music is clearer, our TV pictures are sharper, our phone conversations are more understandable. Fundamentalists however could be seen as the first digital people because of the way they treat moral issues. Digital thinking involves what could be called binary logic; the world is divided into 1's and 0's; the world is black and white with no shades of gray in between. With respect to moral issues, there is right and wrong, good and evil, justice and injustice, sinners and saints, the wheat and the chaff. In other words there is a distinct place where one can draw the line between moral and immoral. Binary logic is restrictive and requires this kind of dichotomizing.[14]

The abortion debate provides a good example of binary logic and how it polarizes the debate. One is either pro-life or pro-choice; there is very little in between and the two sides do not try and understand the other's position. Yet there is merit in each position. The pro-lifers have a point about the beginning of human life and whether abortion is really another kind of murder. But by calling it murder the deck is stacked against the pro-choice people and no compromise is possible. If a woman is considering abortion, she obviously doesn't want the child, and rather than being born into a situation where the child is not wanted and not cared for and loved adequately, more counseling and adoption services must be made available.

The pro-choice people also have a point in that abortion eventually boils down to a choice in every situation anyhow. But they need to recognize what kind of decision is involved in the choice to have an abortion. Is a human life being destroyed and can a woman live with that decision? Are there other alternatives that should be considered? This issue has become so dichotomized over the years however that the resolution has become nothing more than a power struggle and no new discussion of the issue has taken place in several years. People have engaged in digital thinking on this issue and do not seek to understand each other's position or search for a reasonable compromise.

Certainty and Uncertainty

The reason for digital thinking may very well be the search for certainty. It seems that fundamentalists cannot tolerate uncertainty and have to have answers for everything. Thus God has a plan for everyone's life and everything that happens, no matter what it is, fits into this plan. If this is so, it seems that God has some pretty awful plans for some people who are born with disabilities or who spend the majority of their life in pain and suffering. But we are not to question God's wisdom although some people do as did those who questioned how God could let 9/11 happen. The question of why bad things happen to good people has plagued religion since the beginning of time. But the answer is to have faith that it will all work out in the end and that there is a silver lining in every cloud. There is no room for random events, for chance, or luck in this kind of scheme.

Yet life is full of accidents, of chance events, and the luck of the draw. Fatal car accidents could have been avoided by just a spit second in some instances. Is this really part of God's plan, that some people should die in a car accident? Others are exposed to chemicals that eventually give them cancer, and they spend a good deal of their lives in pain dealing with this disease. Is this part of God's plan? If one believes in an all-powerful and all-knowing God, and he or she thus allows these kinds of things to happen, this God must be an arbitrary monster. What loving God would let these things to happen if he or she has the power to prevent them.

Fundamentalists seem to be stuck in a Newtonian universe where everything is deterministic. God has this plan and everything fits into it somehow. Yet we live in a quantum world where probabilities are the order of the day and the world is indeterminate and uncertain. It may provide some degree of comfort to believe that everything is under control and going according to plan, but this seems totally unrealistic. We live in an uncertain world and experience this every day, and to deny this part of our experience is to deny part of our humanity. It is again to play God and claim to know things beyond our comprehension and understanding.

There is a paradox here however because of the nature of the God in which fundamentalists believe. This God transcends the laws of nature and can make the sun stand still, part the waters of a sea, raise people from the dead, and perform other such miracles. This belief creates uncertainty as who knows what this God is going to do and what he (or she) may approve or disapprove of at any given moment. This God can act in a totally arbitrary manner and can do things without any accountability. This creates all kinds of uncertainty and has motivated people throughout the ages to make human and animal sacrifices to try and please their God. But how can we ever know for sure what pleases God, and whether some day we are going to do something that really ticks him (or her) off and makes us a target for his (or her) displeasure?

The quest for certainty, for security, according to John Dewey, "translated into a desire not to be disturbed and unsettled, leads to dogmatism, to acceptance of beliefs upon authority, to intolerance and fanaticism on the one side, and to irresponsible dependence and sloth on the other."[15] It involves a certain anti-intellectualism as one does not have to think about moral issues but just follow the rules or dictates of a moral authority. The Bible thus contains all we need to know about how to live in the world, and fundamentalists believe all we have to do is follow these religious precepts and all will be well with us and our future.

Self-Righteousness

Belief that one knows the absolute truth in many cases leads to self-righteousness and people who make this claim believe they are better than others and God favors them because they are believers. This produces arrogance and certitude that may rob people of their humanity and their ability truly to understand the positions of other people who disagree and have a different view of things. If one possesses such certitude, one does not have to learn about other societies and how they function. The goal is to change those societies through missionary efforts to make them over into one's own image.

In this country we tried to destroy the culture of the Native Americans by Christianizing them and making them adhere to the beliefs of the Christian religion and forsake their own religious beliefs and practices. We took their children and put them in schools where they could learn the American way of life and adopt Christian beliefs and practices. We broke treaty after treaty in the interests of manifest destiny when we wanted the land on which they resided. We knew what was right for them and had the power to enforce our will over their existence. We did not try to understand their way of life in a "live and let live" attitude but tried our best to destroy their way of life and make them over into our image.

People can have a self-righteous image not only about themselves, but about their country. Many believe our country is special because it is a Christian nation favored by God. That is why it has been so successful in so many things and why it has so much power and wealth. When something like 9/11 happens, people raise questions as to how God could let this happen, and people like Falwell have to look for theological reasons as to why God failed to protect his people on this occasion. Many fundamentalists believe Americans are the chosen people of God and have the duty to impose our will on other nations to make them over in our image.

Morality and Ethics

It is my observation that moral sensibility and moral concern are at an all-time low in the United States of America, at least at an all-time low for the 73 years I have lived. Things this country has done in the past several years, what its leadership has exemplified, and what significant numbers of people in this country have supported lead me to this conclusion. Apparently a great majority of Americans agree with this observation as a recent Gallup poll shows that, regardless of party preference, Democrats and Republicans agree that morals are going downhill in American society. Fully 80 percent of those polled rated moral values in the United States as only "fair" or "poor."[16] Many examples can be mentioned to support this conclusion.

Let me start with a President who blatantly lies to the American people and points his finger at the television screen to emphasize his assertion that he did not have sex with "that" woman. Then we have a Republican Congress that is more interested in forcing him to vacate the office of the presidency than it is in justice and so spends more than $50 million of taxpayer money in a futile attempt to drive him from office.[17] After that comes scandals in corporate America of an unprecedented scope that resulted in the demise of the seventh largest corporation in the country and what had been previously known as a stalwart Big Five accounting firm. These scandals have shaken trust in corporate America and in notions of justice and fairness as the people most responsible for these transgressions are brought to trial. Then there are the moral problems of the current administration that will be mentioned in subsequent chapters.

Fundamentalists would of course agree with this assessment and would argue that the nation needs to return to its Christian roots to prevent a further lapse into secular debauchery. We must return to the teachings of the Bible in order to find our moral compass and climb out of this immoral morass. The assumption behind this view is that both individuals and nations can be moral only if they adhere to the God of the Christian faith, that moral truth comes from him or her alone, and that following the precepts of this faith is the only way to be moral. Nonbelievers cannot be as moral as believers because they do not believe in the Christian God who is the sole source of truth. They have not accepted Jesus Christ as their savior and have not been saved from their sins in order to live a moral life.

It is interesting to note however that if the country is going to hell in an immoral handbasket, it is happening when church membership is at an all-time high. According to the 2001 New Historical Atlas of Religion in America, church membership has increased in the United States from 25 percent to 65 percent of the total population over the past century and a half.[18] And fundamentalist religions have increased faster than any other denominations. If this is the case, why haven't morals gotten better in this country rather than worse? If more people are going to church and professing a belief in the Christian faith, why are there so many ethical transgressions in business and government?

Perhaps religion is not all it is cracked up to be, and fundamentalism in particular may actually contribute to the problem. While religion may foster in some individuals an extraordinary moral sensibility and concern, religion does not necessarily promote these traits. Religious intolerance among fundamentalists is a particular problem as the belief that one has found absolute moral truth fuels a religious extremism that results in bombing of abortion clinics, denial of gay rights, and other such measures. If people believe they are doing God's will, anything is possible and nothing is forbidden to destroy the infidels who are ruining the country. The ordinary ethics and morality by which the majority of citizens live their lives do not apply. In the name of God, religious people throughout history have sanctioned racism, anti-Semitism, slavery, torture, ethnic cleansing, genocide, and of course war against those who would destroy our way of life.

Far from promoting moral behavior, several studies suggest that religion may actually do the opposite. Already in 1934 for example one researcher found a negative correlation between acceptance of religious beliefs and honesty, i.e., as religiosity increased, honesty decreased.[19] Another study in 1950 found that agnostics and atheists were more likely to express their willingness to aid the poor than those who considered themselves to be deeply religious.[20] Two sociologists reported in 1969 that there were no differences in the self-reported likelihood to commit crimes between children who did not attend church and those who attended church regularly.[21] A 1975 study found that college-age students in religious schools were no less likely to cheat on an exam than their atheist and agnostic counterparts in schools that were nonreligious.[22] Based on these and other studies, Michael Shermer concludes that "not only does religion not necessarily make one more moral, it can lead to greater intolerance, racism, sexism, and the erosion of other values cherished in a free and democratic society."[23]

Some churches have been the last institutions in the country to accept Blacks as members or to ordain women as clergy, and they will also be the last to accept gays as members or as leaders in the church. Gays are opposed because of their threat to the institution of marriage, of course, yet some studies found that born-again Christians are more likely to get divorced than are non-Christians and even atheists are less likely to get divorced than born-again Christians. This same study found that the divorce rate for born-again Christians was 27 percent as compared with 24 percent for non-Christians. This study was done in 1996, but this same researcher found that in 2001 the divorce rate for born-again Christians was 33 percent as compared with a statistically identical rate of 34 percent for non-born again adults.[24]

Thus there are good reasons to question the assumption that morality comes from the Christian conception of God alone. In addition to the intolerance that stems from fundamentalism, there is also something of an exchange mentality operative in its concept of God, an ethics of exchange if you will, the view of ethics as an exchange of one thing for another. Thus if the nation repents for the errors of its ways and changes its behavior, God will once again restore his protection. If we live a righteous life in this world, we will be rewarded with life eternal.

This ethic is like a Santa Claus ethic in that if we are good, Santa will bring us presents. If we pray hard enough, God may give us what we want. It is not a matter of giving of oneself without hope of reward. We bargain with God to get what we want by doing what we think God wants. If we do God's will, we will earn his or her favor and reap whatever rewards he or she has to offer. Such an ethic, however, hardly promotes good relationships between people and the creation of a civil and peaceful society. Instead it promotes competition between people to win God's favor and results in a society where people who have strong religious beliefs are accountable only to God and not to secular authorities or civil society.

Recklessness and Self-Destruction

Fundamentalism is a very self-destructive kind of religion. To be told over and over again that one is a sinner and barely worthy of God's grace certainly does wonders for self-esteem and self-confidence. To be told that your own will is sinful and you must curb your desires to do the will of God certainly does wonders for self-development and creativity. One is not to follow one's own path for life but to seek out the will of God and do what he wants. Of course that is the question. What is the will of God for one's life? It would seem that what God would want for every individual is to live a fulfilled and rich existence, but that is not what most fundamentalists mean as they seek to control lives and impose their will on others. To brand one's own will as sinful is to take away the most fundamental motivating force that enables us to do something interesting and beneficial with our lives and take our place in society.

Fundamentalists can also take a reckless attitude towards the world because the world is a sinful place. While it was created good, man fell into sin and the world is thus an evil place. It is a place where temptations to fall into sin abound, and the goal is to live a righteous life in preparation for the life beyond. Thus environmental problems like global warming and pollution do not matter because when Jesus returns to establish his kingdom, these will no longer be a problem. In the afterlife, the streets will be paved with gold and Jesus will turn stones into bread and water into wine. This belief leads one to view nature as sinful, such that one might as well exploit it to the fullest in a reckless "eat, drink, and be merry kind" of way because tomorrow Jesus is coming.[25]

There is reason to be worried about this attitude because fundamentalists look forward to the end of time when Jesus shall establish his kingdom.[26] There have been numerous predictions about the end of the world throughout history, and none of them has come true. Fundamentalists must be getting tired of waiting and have a desire to hurry things along by promoting armageddon as a self-fulfilling prophecy. There apparently is a great deal of interest in end times, and it is disturbing to think that life is so bad for so many people that they yearn for something different.[27] What is going on here? Is this any different in kind from a suicide bomber who apparently has so little desire to live in this world that he or she willingly sacrifices his or her own life to attain a better life in the afterworld?

Fundamentalism provides a view of the world and an understanding of the human condition that is largely based on mythology, and thus is radically different from the scientific worldview in which we live our everyday lives. People who seriously believe in Christianity must have to live in two different worlds, particularly if they are engineers or doctors who have to do their jobs adhering to scientific principles and laws related to what we know about the physical properties of materials and the working of the human body. To be effective in these kind of professions, they have to live in one kind of world during their working hours and another kind of world when they are in church and worship the God in which they believe.

For some people, getting hooked on fundamentalism is a bit like being on drugs, and while it perhaps is a more constructive approach to their problems, it is nonetheless an escape into a fantasy world. Some people may be so lonely and feel no one really cares about them that the love of God and believing Jesus is their friend gives them comfort and a reason to keep on going. Others may be searching for meaning and purpose to their lives and hope to find it by a belief in the supernatural and a purpose that lies beyond the natural world that we directly experience. Still others may have such a fragile ego that they need to believe there is a God who cares enough about them to have sent his Son into the world to die for their sins.

The sad part of all fundamentalist religion and its interpretation of Christianity is that it misses the real message of Christianity by adopting its mythological framework as the literal truth. The story woven by the writers of the Bible is a wonderful story and contains many insights into the human condition and our place in the world. The concepts of sin, redemption, forgiveness, etc. have a profound meaning for human existence. The concept of God has great meaning when it is understood in such terms as the ground of all being, as Tillich suggests, or as being itself.[28] What this concept means in terms of love and unity is of great importance to every human being. But when understood as a kind of Victorian gentleman up there pulling all the strings, it may be nothing more than an extension of our own desire for power and control and a refusal to accept our own fragile existence in a highly uncertain world.

NOTES

1. There apparently is a great deal of interest in apocalyptic matters these days, as the Left Behind"series of evangelical novels by Tim LaHaye and Jerry B. Jenkins have sold more than 60 million copies worldwide. See David Gates, "The Pop Prophets," *Newsweek*, 24 May 2004, 45–50.

2. For example, one *Newsweek* poll showed that 55 percent of Americans believe that the faithful will be taken up to heaven in the Rapture, and 74 percent believe that Satan exists. Another 17 percent believe that the world will end in their lifetime. Gates, "The Pop Prophets," 48. Another *Newsweek* poll showed that 79 percent of American adults believe in the virgin birth and 67 percent believe that the Christmas story in its entirety is historically accurate. See John Meacham, "The Birth of Jesus," *Newsweek*, 13 December 2004, 51.

3. David Brooks, "Who is John Stott?" *Times-Picayune*, 1 December 2004, B(7).

4. Eric Gorski, "Evangelical Christians Credited in Bush Win," *Denver Post*, 4 November 2004, 1(A).

5. Many of course dispute this conclusion. David Broder, for example, argues that the Republicans did a better job than the Democrats in mobilizing their supporters and getting them to the polls, and that is essentially why they won the election. David Broder, "Keeping the flock intact," *Times-Picayune*, 6 December 2004, B(7).

6. Bruce Lincoln, *Holy Terrors: Thinking About Religion After September 11*. (Chicago: The University of Chicago Press, 2003), 37.

7. Lincoln, *Holy Terrors*, 104. This statement about vulnerability is very revealing. Apparently many people shared the same assumption as they asked questions after 9/11 as to why God could let this happen. The assumption seemed to be that for some reason America was invulnerable to such attacks. They might have happened in Europe and the Middle East, but the United States was different. While we had experienced attacks from internal terrorists as in the Oklahoma City bombing, foreign attacks were something different. But our assumption that we were immune to such attacks is arrogant and totally unrealistic.

8. Lincoln, *Holy Terrors*, 106. Thus the nation has been brought to mortal peril by rampant and immoral secularism. In an odd sort of way bin Laden echoes these com-

ments of Robertson and Falwell. In the opening words of his videotaped address delivered on October 7, 2001, the 9/11 attacks are seen as the visitation of divine vengeance on a sinful nation. "Here is America struck by God Almighty in one of its vital organs, so that its greatest buildings are destroyed. Grace and gratitude to God." Lincoln, Holy Terrors, 102. Apparently for bin Laden this attack also had a significant theological meaning.

9. One has to wonder why some of these fundamentalist leaders did not see the four hurricanes that hit Florida in the summer of 2004 as God's punishment for messing up the 2000 election.

10. See Michael Shermer, *The Science of Good & Evil* (New York: Times Books, 2004), 67–68 for other examples of this nature. When Katrina hit New Orleans, I no longer lived there, but heard stories about people who saw the hurricane as God's punishment of New Orleans for being sin city or as God's punishment of the nation for tolerating gays.

11. See Marianne Szegedy-Maszark, "How We Talk To God," *U.S. News & World Report*, 20 December 2004, 55–62, for some of the things people pray about. One person for example prayed that his hot running car would be fixed. Another prayed that a former best friend and his wife would get divorced because they had played a significant role in the escalation of her marital problems that led to divorce. Still another prayed for the life of her pet chicken.

12. John Dewey, *A Common Faith* (New Haven: Yale University Press, 1934), 46.

13. "For in spite of supernaturalism's reference to something beyond nature, it conceives of this earth as the moral center of the universe and of man as the apex of the whole scheme of things. It regards the drama of sin and redemption enacted within the isolated soul of man as the one thing of ultimate importance. Apart from man, nature is held either accursed or negligible." Dewey, *A Common Faith*, 53.

14. Shermer, *The Science of Good and Evil*, 17.

15. John Dewey, *The Quest for Certainty* (New York: Capricorn Books, 1929, 227.

16. From Scripps Howard New Service as reported in the *Denver Post*, 22 May 2004, 29(A).

17. It has always been my contention that the charges against Clinton should have been postponed until he had left office and thus could be tried as an ordinary citizen. Lying under oath and obstruction of justice are serious offenses but were are not impeachable offenses in Clinton's case because they related to a stupid sexual affair that had no impact on national security, did not affect the economy, and had no impact on anything else I can think of that was of national importance. These transgressions did not constitute high crimes and misdemeanors against the state, and the Senate agreed by acquitting him on both charges of perjury and obstruction of justice. The vote wasn't even close as impeachment proponents did not win a simple majority on either charge, let alone the necessary two-thirds majority for removal from office. The major consequence of this affair was to give the right wing fanatics the opportunity to spend more than $50 million of taxpayer money in a futile attempt to drive him from office. Justice however may not have been served. People have gone to jail for perjury and obstruction of justice, and while Clinton paid a fine and lost his license to practice law, he did not serve any jail time.

18. Edwin S. Gaustad, Philip L. Barlow, and Richard Dishno, eds., *New Historical Atlas of Religion in America* (New York: Oxford University Press, 2001).

19. A. N. Franzblau, "Religious Belief and Character Among Jewish Adolescents," *Teachers College Contributions to Education*, no. 634 (1934), as quoted in Shermer, *The Science of Good and Evil*, 235.

20. Murray G. Ross, *Religious Beliefs of Youth* (New York: Association Press, 1950), as quoted in Shermer, *The Science of Good and Evil*, 235.

21. Travis Hirschi and Rodney Stark, "Hellfire and Delinquency," Social Problems, 17 (1969): 202–13, as quoted in Shermer, *The Science of Good and Evil*, 235.

22. R.E. Smith, G. Wheeler, and E. Diener, "Faith Without Works: Jesus People, Resistance to Temptation and Altruism," *Journal of Applied Social Psychology*, 5 (1975): 320-30, as quoted in Shermer, *The Science of Good and Evil*, 235–36.

23. Shermer, *The Science of Good and Evil*, 236.

24. George Barna, *Index of Leading Spiritual Indicators*, 1996 and 2001, as quoted in Shermer, The Science of Good and Evil, 236. In a study published in the Journal of Religion and Science, Gregory S. Paul found that the more religious a society is the more social problems it has. Within the United States, according to the study, the highest rates of abortion, murder, divorce, and teen pregnancy are not the int blue states, but in the red states where church attendance is highest. Correlations is not causation, however, and it may be that "high levels of social dysfunction fuel religiosity." not that religion causes social problems, according to the researcher. However, the study does suggest that too much religion may be a dangerous thing. See Rosa Brooks, "When faith itself is the problem," *The Week*, 14 October 2005, 16.

25. As a general rule, politicians who espouse fundamentalistic beliefs are also rabidly anti-environment. For example, Senator James Inhofe of Oklahoma, chair of the Senate Environment and Public Works Committee, holds an extreme fundamentalistic perspective and thinks global warming is a myth. Some 178 House members in the 108th Congress allied themselves with the religious right and earned only a 15 percent approval rating from the League of Conservation Voters. See Glenn Scherer, "Religious Wrong," *E Magazine*, May/June 2003, 35–39.

26. Within the fundamentalist worldview, the wreck of the earth can be seen as good news, as it can signify the beginning of the end of the world and the return of Christ. See Scherer, "Religious Wrong," 36.

27. The Left Behind novels, according to some commentators, "gleefully celebrate religious intolerance and violence against infidels." See Nicholas D. Kristof, "Jesus and Jihad," *New York Times*, 17 July 2002, A(25).

28. See Paul Tillich, *Systematic Theology: Volume One* (Chicago: The University of Chicago Press, 1951).

Chapter Six

Fundamentalism in Government

Some have called the Bush presidency the first faith-based presidency in the history of the country.[1] On his very first day in office he called for a day of prayer and cut federal spending on abortion. In no previous administration has the While House hosted so many weekly Bible studies and prayer meetings, and never have religious leaders been more gratefully welcomed.[2] It has been estimated that Bible study and prayer groups involve some 200 of the 500 White House staffers. A BBC correspondent has been quoted as saying "It's not uncommon to see While House functionaries hurrying down corridors carrying Bibles."[3]

To be sure, other presidents spoke openly of religion. John F. Kennedy is reported to have quoted more Scripture in his speeches than any president before his time. Nixon was an ardent Quaker who had a relationship with Billy Graham. Jimmy Carter claimed to be born again and even taught Sunday School during his White House years. Reagan claimed to have a vital Christian faith and sense of mission. And even Bill Clinton claimed to be a Baptist believer and spoke repeatedly of the need for religious values in the life of the nation. Yet rarely, according to one commentator, did these presidents attempt to apply the power of religion to the responsibilities of the federal government.[4]

The connection between the current Bush administration and religious fundamentalism is much different than it was in the senior Bush administration. George H.W. Bush always had difficulty winning the trust of the evangelicals and this may have cost him the 1992 election. While he often said the right things in trying to appeal to them, they always held him suspect and did not feel he really believed what he was saying. And while the elder Bush had lived in Texas, he was deeply embedded in the Eastern Establishment and felt most at home in his summer retreat in Kennebunkport, Maine, where he now spends most of his time.

George W. Bush, however, has his home away from home in Crawford, Texas, in the heart of the Baptist-dominated Bible Belt. He is a real Texan more than anything else and embodies all the virtues of self-reliance, toughness, and independence that go with a cowboy image. More to the point, he is a genuine born-again Christian who has accepted Jesus Christ as his personal savior and regularly reads the Bible and prays to his Lord and Savior.[5] He is attuned to the evangelicals and no one questions his sincerity. He replaced his father's lack of vision by "forging a neo-Reaganite vision that jibed with an evangelical sense of destiny."[6] Kevin Phillips goes so far as to say that George W. Bush is both president of the United States and leader of the Christian right.[7] The policies of this administration reflect the values of the religious right because of this kind of close identification.

What distinguishes the Bush presidency is not just the openness with which he has discussed his personal conversion to Christianity and his spiritual life. Rather he is set apart by his sincerity about religion in that he seems genuinely to believe privately what he says publicly and seeks to integrate his faith with public policy at the most practical level.[8] This is a faith-based presidency, and the political vision of this administration is fueled by faith. Given how fundamentalism permeates this administration, we would expect the characteristics mentioned in the previous chapter to show up in the Bush administration and its policies.

ABSOLUTISM

The Bush administration provides many examples of the absolutist mind at work. With regard to the war in Iraq, most of us believed at the outset that Saddam had weapons of mass destruction. After all, as Bush repeatedly pointed out, he had gassed his own people. Many of us assumed he had not destroyed all these stockpiles after the Gulf War and had probably amassed more such weapons. However, when the UN inspectors had renewed access to the country and could find no shred of evidence to indicate any weapons of mass destruction, some of us changed our minds. Not so the Bush administration. They discredited these inspections and would not let the inspectors finish their job in the rush to war as they did not want more doubt to be sowed in the minds of Congress or the American people. They knew without a doubt that Saddam had weapons of mass destruction and they would be found. Thus the scanty intelligence that this country had was interpreted to support this preconceived conclusion. The best intelligence available was ignored because it did not support this belief.

Bush, Cheney, and Company firmly believed they possessed the absolute truth about this matter, that Saddam had such weapons despite the evidence. And without a doubt they believed they would ultimately be vindicated when these weapons were found, and the nation and the world would thank them for taking preemptive action. When they were not found and Duelfer issued his final report, they had to scramble to find other reasons for the war, reasons that by themselves would never have convinced Congress and the American people the war was justified. The supposed weapons of mass destruction and the threat they posed to the security of this nation were the only reasonable justifications for the invasion of Iraq.

Paul O'Neill, the first Treasury Secretary in the Bush administration, states that he was surprised by the lack of policy discussions in the Bush administration because there were such discussions in all the previous administrations he had served.[9] But the major decisions about invading Iraq and about tax policy, in which he was an expert, were made without any serious discussion. Any discussions he participated in were in the nature of how to implement the decisions that had already been made on the basis of what he called ideology. O'Neill concluded that ideology and an absolutism dictated policy in this administration.[10] The Bush administration came into office with an invasion of Iraq on the agenda and with tax cuts already in mind because it knew in some a priori sense that these were the right things to do and there was no need for discussion. It stuck to these policies despite changing conditions and made a virtue out of its ability to make hard decisions and stick to them.

This absolutism is also evident in Congress. Many moderates have quit Congress because they no longer enjoy the work despite its many benefits. They say Congress has lost the civility it had in the past, and there is no real discussion of issues—but only power politics of the nastiest kind. The result is that policy making has become a struggle for power and compromise is less and less possible. Anything goes with this "take no prisoners attitude" where politics is another kind of warfare, and many want out in order to return to a more civilized existence. Congress is the loser as it becomes more and more polarized just like the rest of the nation.

While the Democrats certainly share in this problem, I do not believe it is unfair to blame the Republicans for most it. When they were in power, they used tactics never before used to get legislation passed or to win elections. And the reason is, I would argue, that the Republican party is dominated by the religious right; this is its base and the majority of its Congressional members share at least some of the characteristics of fundamentalist Christianity. One of these is absolutism. The Republicans believe they have the truth, and thus compromise is not necessary or possible. And since politics at its best is the art of compromise, politics degrades into a power struggle. Civility goes out the window because those who know the truth have a mission to destroy those infidels who do not see the truth and who actually want to engage in an honest discussion of the issues to reach a compromise position. There is nothing to discuss for those who already know the truth.

According to one study, the proportion of all legislation submitted with special rules that prevented floor amendments increased from 15.7 percent in 1975–1976 to 44.6 percent 10 years later. The figure for 2004 was 85 percent. Republicans routinely use procedural tactics like closed votes, legislation drafted in conference, bills dictated entirely by the Republican leadership, floor votes kept open beyond the time limit, rampant secrecy, and barring of Democrats from participation at the committee, floor, and conference levels. This is hardly indicative of a deliberative body.[11]

In an interview with two Time magazine correspondents, John Breaux, a Democratic senator from Louisiana who retired in 2004, mentions that when he was in the House in the 1980s, the minority leader and speaker, who were from different parties, spoke to each other more in one day than the current leaders do in an entire year. He also remembered about the number of joint lunches where Republicans and Democrats would sit down and hear each other out. This doesn't happen anymore, according to Breaux, and he recommends more interaction between the two parties.[12] Perhaps this will start to happen again after the 2006 elections.

BELIEF IN GOD

There is ample evidence that the Bush administration, particularly Bush himself, believes in a God who has a plan for the world. Bush has said he believes God is guiding the affairs of this nation and believes that the United States has an obligation to spread freedom and democracy throughout the world, particularly in the Middle East. It is this belief that allows him to ignore the lessons of history with regard to countries like Iraq and argue that all people around the world yearn for freedom and democracy.[13] Thus when freed from a tyrant like Saddam, the Iraqi people will sit down and reach compromises to establish a working democracy despite a history of ethnic violence and no experience with democracy.

There was no plan to win the peace because there didn't need to be any as the Iraqi people would seize the moment and take charge of their future. They would welcome us as liberators from decades of tryanny and fear and quickly establish some form of democratic government. There is some truth to this view as some Iraqi's did welcome us initially and were glad to see Saddam removed from power. But by not recognizing there would be difficulty in establishing the peace and not providing enough troops to secure the country, we have lost whatever goodwill did exist in some of the people. The average Iraqi citizen probably lives in more fear of his or her life now than they did under Saddam's reign when there was at least some degree of order and stability.[14]

Bush has also referred to his belief that he has been called for this role of spreading freedom and democracy and that he has a higher father, a remark he made to Bob Woodward in response to a question about his earthly father.[15] So there is a good bit of evidence to suggest that Bush believes in the kind of God who controls the world and calls certain people to carry out his (or her) mission. The problem is that this view of God allows Bush to evade his responsibility for where this country is going. By believing he is merely an instrument of God's will, he can admit no wrongs and continue to believe in the rightness of his actions in Iraq despite the fact that the initial assumptions about weapons of mass destruction and links to al Qaeda proved to be wrong. It is belief in this kind of an infallible God that feeds into the absolutism of the Bush administration. Truth is what the Bush administration says it is because their truth comes from God himself or herself.

THE SUPERNATURAL

All the talk about God guiding the affairs of this nation reflects a belief in some supernatural being that is somehow directing the way this nation behaves. Actually it is the Bush administration that is guiding the affairs of this nation, but by invoking God, Bush puts his own responsibility for what this nation does above criticism. If God has a plan for this nation and Bush is following it, how does anyone dare to criticize what God has in mind. By appealing to the supernatural, Bush avoids taking responsibility for what is happening to the country and cannot admit any mistakes with respect to the invasion of Iraq or any other policies he has instituted. To admit a mistake is to admit that God was wrong.

That Bush believes in miracles is also evident in his approach to Iraq. It will indeed be a miracle if any kind of order can be established in Iraq in the near future and the country can avoid sinking into ethnic warfare. Yet Bush continues to insist that he can perform miracles. There is no doubt that Bush has a strong will, but the problem is that he believes he can will democracy into existence in Iraq despite all the evidence to the contrary. He also hopes to perform miracles with respect to a balanced budget and other aspects of the economy. But willing something into existence does not make it so, and Bush is not God and cannot create something out of nothing. He has to work within certain contingencies, but these are largely ignored given the absolutist approach of this administration.

Chapter Six

DEHUMANIZATION

The war itself has been dehumanized. The press mainly covers the number of American troops killed along with the number of insurgents who have been killed or captured in particular incidents. Very little is said about the impact of this war on the Iraqi people as a whole, yet some estimates put the number of Iraqis killed as a result of the invasion at 100,000 and counting. The risk of death by violence is 58 times greater after the war than before. Infant mortality has nearly doubled since the war began. Acute malnutrition among children under five rose from 4 percent before the war to 7.7 percent in 2004. These figures suggest that 400,000 Iraqi children are badly malnourished.[16]

This administration has also prevented pictures being taken of the bodies of American soldiers arriving at Dover Air Force Base and made public—until, that is, some pictures of flag-drapped caskets were accidentally disclosed. The military also put obstacles in the way of family members who wanted to travel to Dover to receive their loved ones who had been killed. One family even asked for media coverage of a burial at Arlington National Cemetery, a request that was denied. The administration doesn't want the public to see the true cost of the war, which might erode public support. Thus we continue to dehumanize these soldiers who have sacrificed their lives and treat them as simply statistics.[17]

Then there was the dehumanization of prisoners at Abu Gharib. When people have complete control over others and there are no rules as seemed to be the case in this situation, the prisoners and their captors became dehumanized. The prisoners were treated as something less than human, and the captors became sadistic in their behavior. Some of the captors seemed gleeful over the things they did to the prisoners and were enjoying seeing them suffer. They apparently had lost all sense of empathy and concern for them as human beings. Such dehumanization is often seen under the pressures of wartime, and those in control must take responsibility for the behavior of people under their command.

Many people still believe that Iraq had weapons of mass destruction and that Saddam Hussein had provided significant support to al Qaeda, and people who believe this tended to support Bush and his policies. People who believe this apparently claim to know more than the people who put together the Duelfer report, which after an exhaustive investigation found that Iraq did not have a significant WMD program, and the 9/11 Commission that could find no cooperation between Iraq and al Qaeda after reviewing all the evidence pertaining to this connection.[18] Such a refusal to accept overwhelming evidence to the contrary can be seen as a kind of dehumanization, an inability to accept what seems to be true about the world in which we live and a desire to live in a world of one's own making.

DIGITAL THINKING

The Bush administration is full of either/or thinking. Regimes are either good or evil, and the Bush administration knows the difference. Countries are either with us or against us, and there is no in between. This kind of approach gives Bush the appearance of being decisive and a strong leader. But are moral issues really this simple? Is not fuzzy logic that sees many shades of gray really more realistic? Granted that a decision maker eventually has to come down on one side relative to most issues of this nature, but should not this decision be made with full recognition that there is another side to the issue that should be taken into consideration? Do we not want leaders who consider the pros and cons of many options and engage in extensive discussion of the issues before making decisions? Bush is a strong person, of that there is no doubt, but do we not also want thoughtful and cautious leaders?

Granted, Kerry seemed to equivocate on many things during the 2004 campaign, even as to whether he owned an SUV or not. Many of his positions seemed to be an attempt to have it both ways. But has not the oversimplification evident in the Bush administration gotten us into all sorts of trouble? The assumption that the Iraq people were going to welcome us with open arms and immediately establish a democracy was ludicrous and meant we did not do adequate planning for rebuilding the country, assuming this can be done to any degree. But Bush knew that every human heart longed for freedom and democracy and that they would emerge automatically once Saddam was removed from power. This kind of simplification makes it easy to make decisions and justify them to oneself. But is this what makes a good leader?

Some people, however, like this kind of simplification and are willing to follow Bush no matter where he leads. They like his strong leadership and his moral certitude. His failings matter less than his motives, and his faith is what is important to them.[19] Given that Bush is a strong leader, does it not matter where he is leading the nation? Would these people have followed Hitler if they had been in Germany in the 1930s as he came to power? Please do not accuse me of comparing Bush to Hitler as I am only using the most extreme example I can think of to make a point. People who follow someone simply because he is a strong and decisive leader or has faith without caring where he is leading them are like sheep going to the slaughter.

CERTAINTY AND UNCERTAINTY

Moral choices in particular are messy, but it helps to simplify them into black and white and reduce the uncertainty. And it definitely helps to believe that one is doing God's will because who can argue with the will of God? But not dealing with uncertainty can get us into all kinds of trouble. The Bush people were certain Saddam had weapons of mass destruction; there was no doubt in the minds of the president and vice-president (their choice of words) that these weapons existed. Thus more than 3,000 American soldiers and thousands of others have sacrificed their lives because of this kind of thinking. Yes, there are other reasons for ousting Saddam from power, but it is my contention that Bush would never have made the case for war to Congress or the American public without this supposed threat to our security.

Kerry was asked a question during the 2004 campaign as to whether, knowing what we know now, he would still support the president's request to Congress to go to war. His answer was that he would. Bad answer. The important question was whether the president, knowing what we know now, would have taken the issue to Congress. Hillary Clinton who responded to the same question by suggesting it was a moot question, because if the administration knew for a fact that Iraq did not have weapons of mass destruction, it would never have been able to make a case for war and thus the request for congressional approval would never have been made.

Then there was the certainty that the Iraqi people would welcome us as liberators much as the French did in World War II and would jump at the chance to establish a democracy and live in peace and harmony forever. Bush is something of an idealist perhaps, and this kind of vision is welcome in our leaders, but it must be tempered by realism. What was going to happen in Iraq after Saddam was removed from power was very uncertain, and we should have planned accordingly. We created a power vacuum, and it still isn't clear who is going to fill it. When our troops finally do pull out of Iraq, what is going to happen to whatever government is in power at the time? Will the country collapse into an ethnic power struggle? Will the Islamic fundamentalists succeed in creating an Islamic state? No one really knows what is going to happen and to claim otherwise is a flight into sheer fantasy.

SELF-RIGHTEOUSNESS

Believing one is certain in regard to moral issues leads to a self-righteousness, the belief that one is right no matter what the consequences and that everyone else is wrong. Thus Bush, when first asked what mistakes he had made, couldn't come up with an answer. When asked a second time, he referred to the "consequences of catastrophic success," meaning that the United States military had been so successful in so quickly conquering Iraq that an enemy who should have surrendered or been destroyed lived to fight another day.[20]

During the debates Bush referred to certain mistakes in regard to appointments. but he did not admit to any mistakes of policy or in assumptions about Iraq and its threat to the United States. The Bush administration interpreted the Duelfer report to their own advantage, saying it proved Saddam was trying to game the sanctions and would rapidly rebuild his weapons programs once the sanctions were removed.[21] If Bush is doing God's will and has been chosen by God to fulfill a certain role in history, how can he make any mistakes? Having such a faith in one's cause without any doubt leads to a self-righteous moral arrogance.[22]

Thus one can believe that he or she has made no mistakes worth mentioning because whatever was done was done for a righteous cause. So maybe there are no weapons of mass destruction in Iraq. What difference does it make anyhow? Removing Saddam from power was a righteous action for whatever reason. He was an evil man and a threat to the Middle East and the world. He had used weapons of mass destruction against his own people. He was firing on American aircraft that were enforcing the sanctions imposed by the United Nations. He invaded his neighbors. He subsidized the families of suicide bombers in Palestine. He was a source of instability in the world's most volatile region. The Iraqis and the world are better off without him in power.

It was our mission to bring freedom to the Iraqi people and free them from this tyrant. Many Americans seem to believe that our intentions in Iraq were noble no matter what the outcome. Bush argued that the war in Iraq is the "ultimate expression of compassionate conservatism," by which he meant bringing freedom to the people of Iraq after years of oppression. Spreading such freedom is also the best and perhaps only way to make America safer. Thus, as Karen Hughes said, "So as we work to make America safer we are also doing something very noble."[23]

This is the nature of self-righteousness, that one's intentions are noble in spite of the consequences. Perhaps it was necessary to ignore the best evidence about weapons of mass destruction to build support for what was seen to be a righteous endeavor. The removal of such an evil from the world cannot be anything but good, and if it was necessary to stretch the truth a bit, as in Bush's reference in his State of the Union address to Saddam's alleged purchase of uranium, so be it if it helped to get the job done.[24] The Iraqis should be thankful they are free of this tyranny and the world should be grateful for the removal of this threat. If tens of thousands of Iraqis lose their lives in the process, so be it.

The firm belief that one is on a righteous mission means that one is accountable only to God, not to the international community, not to Congress, not to the American people. Legitimacy comes from God alone, not from adherence to international law or from the international community. This ties in with the desire of the Bush administration to have the freedom to do whatever it pleases, and who dare question an administration that is doing the will of God? As stated earlier, Bush believes that God is guiding the affairs of this nation, and of course he is the emissary of God to see that his will is carried out in the nation and the world. The intent is not to debate or discuss issues but to carry out the will of God and sidestep anyone who gets in the way of this mission.

MORALS AND ETHICS

This administration is the most morally reprehensible of any administration in my lifetime. At the time I thought the Nixon administration represented the low point of morals in government, but this administration makes Nixon and his aides look like saints. In terms of hardball tactics to get its way in Congress and government agencies, it makes the plumbers look like pikers.[25] It will do anything necessary to win and has no moral scruples to provide limits on its behavior. Senator Edward Kennedy, who has served many administrations, both Republican and Democratic, has this to say: "This is an ideological Administration that's different from Reagan and Bush One, which were very conservative but principled. They wanted to win, but this Administration wants to destroy the opposition."[26]

This president misled Congress and the American public about weapons of mass destruction to get us into a war with Iraq for that has cost thousands of American lives and hundreds of billions of dollars in what will prove to be a futile attempt to "bring" democracy to the country. This same administration lied about the true cost of the Medicare prescription drug plan that is supposed to benefit seniors but will probably end up benefiting only the profits of the pharmaceutical companies. This administration misled the populace about the nature of the tax cuts and who would really benefit. Then they engaged in the same sort of subterfuge over revisions to Social Security.[27] The list could go on and on.

Equally disturbing is the lack of outrage over these practices in the country at large. While a good many books have been written about the Bush administration and some demonstrations have been held in various places throughout the country, these are far too few and far between given the outrageous moral transgressions these actions represent. The protests these days are infrequent and seem to lack the same intensity as those during the Johnson years. During the Vietnam War we protested everything in sight, and it seems as if we were out on the streets almost every day of the year protesting something. Students at Kent State, without knowing it at the time, put their lives on the line for their convictions. These protests had an effect as President Johnson eventually got the message and had the wisdom not to run for a second term.

This president, however, vows to stay the course and awards some of his top officials who were most responsible for the fiasco in Iraq the freedom medal.[28] George Tenant, former director of the CIA, was one of the recipients even though his slam dunk regarding weapons of mass destruction proved to be an air ball. The other recipients—Tommy Franks, who was the architect of the plan that sent too few troops to Iraq to secure the peace, and Paul Bremer, who disbanded the Iraqi army and ousted Baathists from government jobs which contributed to the current chaos in the country—are equally undeserving.[29] One suspects these medals were given for loyalty rather than performance.

Meanwhile, the American people re-elected this administration to another four years, and while it was not an overwhelming victory, the majority of the people apparently like what they are getting. While morals seemed to be a factor in the 2004 election, morality for many people, particularly the religious right, went no further than abortion, stem cell research, and gay rights. It did not extend to the war in Iraq, the environment, human rights violations, growing inequality, poverty, and other social problems. As a bishop put it in a letter to the editors of Newsweek, "The church's failure is shown by the fact that so many supporters of Bush cite moral values as their reason for electing him. What God do these people worship? Do they really think a country stained with the blood of 100,000 dead is a moral improvement over one stained blue dress?"[30] Or as another letter-writer said, "In the years to come, when huge debt is wreaking havoc on our economy, we are wheezing through polluted air and few of us can afford health care, I wonder if all those who voted for Bush will look at their suffering children and say to them, Take heart, honey, at least gays can't marry."[31]

One last thing needs to be said while on the subject of morals and ethics, and that concerns this administration's use, or rather misuse, of science.[32] If God is indeed directing the affairs of this nation and the Bush administration is carrying out God's plan, why pay any attention to scientific findings? The Bush people are not subject to such human concerns and their sense of ethics and morality does not derive from an effort to be honest with what science tells us about issues of concern. Their truth comes from the Almighty and is not subject to question by science. Thus scientific findings can be altered or ignored in the interest of pursuing God's will, which of course is probably nothing more than the will of the Bush administration. This administration, in its infinite wisdom, knows better than the scientific community about things like global warming and other such matters.

RECKLESSNESS AND SELF-DESTRUCTION

Senator Robert Byrd has characterized the Bush administration in the subtitle of his book as reckless and arrogant.[33] To say that the Bush administration has been reckless in their first four years is an understatement. They have squandered our military resources in an totally unnecessary war, gone from record surpluses to record deficits, eroded cherished rights of American citizens, destroyed the environment in a headlong pursuit of corporate profits, and destroyed whatever goodwill we had established in the world after the 9/11 attacks. They have rushed headlong into everything without adequate debate and discussion as if there is no tomorrow and have exploited terrorism to strike fear into the hearts of Americans so they can pursue their agenda without significant opposition.

After eight years of this administration, this country will be in the worst shape it has been in since many of us can remember. What We Have Lost is the title of a book by Graydon Carter written in 2004, but if it were written today, I'm sure it would be at least twice as long.[34] Whether the United States can recover or not is an open question. The American people have always been resilient enough to respond to crises, and hopefully this characteristic is still there in younger generations. But we have to come to grips with what is happening in this country and admit that faith-based policies do not work. Public and foreign policy has to be based on facts, the best scientific evidence available, on self-interest in the best sense of the word, not on the faith of a particular administration that they know what is best for the country and the world because they are carrying out the will of God and thus should not be questioned.

In summary, the Bush administration reflects fundamentalist characteristics in all its behavior. It is self-righteous, it is arrogant, it sees issues in black and white, it is reckless, it believes it is carrying out God's mission for the country and the world. And it is scary for those of us who do not believe in these things. The country has been flirting with this ever since the Reagan administration, and it is too bad the country has to go down such a self-destructive path before people wake up and realize what is happening to democracy. Religion and democracy don't mix, as will be discussed in the next chapter, and the founders of the country realized this when they wrote the Constitution and guaranteed freedom of religion and freedom from religion. What is required for democracy to work properly is antithetical to religious belief of the kind that is professed by many officials in the Bush administration including Bush himself. The relationship between church and state is the most fundamental issue that needs to be examined when one is assessing the Bush administration and its use of political power.

NOTES

1. Arthur Schlesinger, Jr., "Holy War," *Playboy*, November, 2004, 42.
2. Stephen Mansfield, *The Faith of George W. Bush* (New York: Tarcher/Penguin, 2003), xiv.
3. Schlesinger, "Holy War," 42.
4. Mansfield, *Bush*, xviii. "Not since Abraham Lincoln has a sitting president talked so much about God as President George W. Bush. Ronald Reagan and Franklin Roosevelt referred to the Almighty on occasion too, but President Bush broaches spiritual issues with a frankness and conviction that is unprecedented in modern times." Thomas M. Freiling, ed. *George W. Bush On God and Country* (Washington D.C.: Allegiance Press, 2004), 9.
5. Craig Unger, *House of Bush, House of Saud* (New York: Scribner, 2004), 113. See George W. Bush, *A Charge To Keep* (New York: William Morrow and Company, Inc., 1999, 136 for Bush's own description of his conversion experience.
6. Unger, *House of Bush*, 193.
7. Kevin Phillips, *American Dynasty* (New York: Viking, 2004), 223.
8. Mansfield, *Bush*, xviii-xix.
9. Ron Suskind, *The Price of Loyalty: George W. Bush, The White House, and the Education of Paul O'Neill* (New York: Simon & Schuster, 2004), 165–69.
10. Suskind, *The Price of Loyalty*, 292.
11. Sam Rosenfeld, "Then Came the Hammer," *The American Prospect*, December 2004, 53.
12. Michael Duffy and Douglas Waller, "What We'll Miss And What We Won't," *Time*, 29 November 2004, 32–34. The new Congress elected in 2004 was even less likely to reach out to Democrats and was even more divisive. See Alexandra Starr, "In Congress, A Vanishing Center," *Business Week*, 15 November 2004, 46–47.
13. In his acceptance speech at the Republican convention in2004 Bush said, "I believe that America is called to lead the cause of freedom in a new century. I believe that millions in the Middle East plead in silence for their liberty. I believe that given the chance, they will embrace the most honorable form of government ever devised by man. I believe these things because freedom is not America's gift to the world; it is the Almighty God's gift to every man and woman in this world." John Aloysuis Farrell, "President accepts nomination, makes case for second term," *Denver Post*, 3 September 2004, 1(A). The president apparently has not read some of the poll information coming out of Russia, which strongly suggests that after a series of deadly terror attacks, many Russians would agree to significant limitations on their freedoms to ensure security. The results of the poll showed, according to one analyst, that the Russian people are not deeply imbued with liberal and democratic ideals, which is why they are moving toward authoritarianism. Survival and material well-being are much more important than questions of freedom or liberty. See Steve Gutterman, "Russians de-prioritize liberty," *Denver Post*, 7 October 2004, 20(A).
14. See Ilana Ozernoy, "We Might Be Killed," *U.S. News & World Report*, 25 October 2004, 64. See also Borzou Daragahi, "Worries and frustrations mount for ordinary Iraqis," *Times-Picayune*, 25 November 2004, A(24); Bassem Mroue, "Number

of Iraqi dead unknown but large," *Denver Post*, 9 September 2004, 23(A); and Jonathan Finer and Omar Fekeiki, "Iraqis paying price for war," *Times-Picayune*, 5 June 2005, p. A(19).

15. Bob Woodward, *Plan of Attack* (New York: Simon & Schuster, 2004), 421.

16. Nicholas D. Kristof, "Iraqi children depending on us now," *Times-Picayune*, 1 December 2004, B(7).

17. Jonathan Alter, "Yes, We Can Handle the Truth," *Newsweek*, 3 May 2004, 29.

18. *The 9/11 Commission Report: Authorized Edition* (New York: W.W. Norton & Company, 2004), 66. Researchers at the University of Maryland found that 72 percent of Bush supporters continued to believe Iraq had weapons of mass destruction and 75 percent believed that Iraq was providing substantial support to al Qaeda with 63 percent believing that clear evidence for this support had been found. Large majorities of Kerry supporters had exactly opposite perceptions about these issues. Gerard A. Hauser, "Facts or fallacy," *Denver Post*, 19 December 2004, 1(E).

19. Nancy Gibbs, "The Faith Factor," *Time*. 21 June 2004, 33. See also Joe Klein, "The Blink Presidency," *Time*, 28 February 2005, 25.

20. Nancy Gibbs and John F. Dickenson, "I've Gained Strength," *Time*, 6 September 2004, 43.

21. Kevin Whitelaw, "The Vanishing Case For War," *U.S. News & World Report*, 18 October 2004, 38–40.

22. Joe Klein, "The Perils of a Righteous President," *Time*, 17 May 2004, 25. See also "Bush's convictions: Must a president admit his mistakes?" *The Week*, 30 April 2004, 18.

23. Howard Fineman, "In The Driver's Seat," *Newsweek*, 6 September, 2004, 28.

24. John Prados, *Hoodwinked: The Documents That Reveal How Bush Sold Us A War* (New York: The New Press, 2004), 181.

25. The plumbers were a group led by G. Gordon Liddy who did odd jobs for the Nixon administration, like breaking into the Democratic headquarters that led to the Watergate scandal.

26. Nancy Gibbs and John F. Dickerson, "Inside The Mind of George W. Bush," *Time*, 6 September 2004, 31.

27. See Richard Cohen, "The Social Security crisis," *Denver Post*, 21 December 2004, 7(B).

28. Jennifer Loven, "Bush gives freedom medal to 3 key figures in Iraq war," *Denver Post*, 15 December 2003, 10(A).

29. Richard Cohen, "Bush's standard of excellence," *Denver Post*, 16 December 2004, 7(B).

30. The Most Rev. Mark S. Shirilau, "Letters," *Newsweek*, 29 November 2004, 16.

31. Eliza VanCort, "Letters," *Newsweek*, 29 November 2004, 13.

32. See Sheldon Rampton & John Stauber, *Banana Republicans* (New York: Tarcher/Penguin, 2004), 116–120 for several examples about the misuse of science by the Bush administration. This approach to science opens the door for corporations to shape the government's science policies to suit their objectives. See David Michaels, "Doubt Is Their Product," *Scientific American*, 292, no. 6 (June 2005): 96–101.

33. Robert C. Byrd, *Losing America: Confronting A Reckless and Arrogant Presidency* (New York: W.W. Norton, 2004.

34. Graydon Carter, *What We Have Lost* and Giroux, 2004).

Chapter Seven

Church and State

People can believe whatever they want, and the religious freedom we adhere to in this country allows this possibility without fear of persecution in most instances. There are lines that can be crossed, as the Mormons discovered, who had to move to Salt Lake City to practice their beliefs. Even there, the laws of the country forced them to modify some of their practices with regard to marriage. Yet we have an unprecedented amount of religious freedom in this country, and it has led to a great diversity of religious beliefs and practices. This is all to the good, as long as one particular set of religious beliefs does not begin to dominate our public life.

THE FOUNDING FATHERS

The founders of the republic were well aware of the dangers religion posed for a free society. Many of them had watched Europe almost destroy itself over religious wars of one sort or another. Colonial America also had its share of religious controversy like the one over antinomianism in Massachusetts where the Puritans were banished and had to establish a new colony in Rhode Island. As Thomas Jefferson put it, "Millions of innocent men, women, and children, since the introduction of Christianity, have been burnt, tortured, fined, imprisoned; yet we have not advanced one inch towards uniformity. What have been the effects of coercion? To make one half of the world fools, and the other half hypocrites."[1]

Contrary to popular opinion, the founders did not create a Christian nation based on Christian principles. They were products of the Enlightenment whose philosophers had laid the groundwork for a secular political system as free as possible from religious influences. There was to be no established church in this country. The rights and values this country held dear—the right to life, liberty, and the pursuit of happiness—were not grounded in religion or some supernatural force; they were rather part of the natural order of things. They were derived from nature and secured by the consent of the governed, not by the dictates or dogmas of any particular religion.

The only direct reference to God in the Declaration of Independence appears in the very first paragraph, where it invokes the "laws of nature and of nature's god." Even though the final copy capitalizes all four nouns, Jefferson wrote these words without capitalization. This phrase, "nature's god," is said to reflect Jefferson's deism, a belief that he shared with Franklin, in a creator whose divine handiwork is evident in the wonders of nature, a naturalistic conception. They did not believe in a personal God who interceded directly in the daily affairs of mankind.[2]

The Constitution does not even mention God, and in that sense is a godless document. Religion is mentioned only twice, once in the First Amendment's separation of religion and government, and second in Article VI's prohibition of religious tests for public office. There were attempts during the Constitutional Convention to favor recognition of Christianity in the Constitution, but these were rejected.[3] Fundamentalists themselves favored separation of church and state as they rightly feared that if the United States were a Christian nation, the denominations in the majority at that time would gain effective control at their expense, and they remained separationists for some 200 years. It was only in the 1980s, when Ronald Reagan brought them into the Republican tent, that they began to get involved in politics and threaten such a separation.

However, Christian fundamentalists now continue to contend that this is a Christian nation that has lost touch with its Christian origins. But nothing could be more clear than that the founding fathers intended to create a constitutional separation of church and state after careful deliberation and extensive, documented debate. The perpetuation of this myth, however, allows for the promotion and insertion of fundamentalist religion into all aspects of our public life, justified on the basis that all contemporary social ills are the result of the removal of God and religion from the public sphere.[4]

Religious freedom is protected in this country, and the counterpart to the prohibition of a state religion is the prohibition against government interference in how people freely exercise their beliefs. People are free to believe what they want, but this can only be accomplished if religion is separated from government. History is replete with examples showing that where church and state are wedded, individual liberty suffers, especially religious liberty. But it is not only liberty that suffers; it may also be prosperity.

Bernard Lewis, a historian of the Middle East, alleges that the secularization of Western cultures is one of the strongest reasons for their prosperity and progress in science, technology, and culture. It is the lack of separation of church and state in Muslim countries that has driven the Arab world from its medieval apex of human achievement to its current status as a cultural backwater.[5]

FUNDAMENTALISM AND DEMOCRACY

Those people who are unswervingly devoted to fundamentalistic religion have to be hostile to democracy, for democracy not only involves the ability to compromise but also rests on this fundamental value of liberty. But those who are imbued with the absolute certainty of their conclusions because they come from God can never compromise these beliefs nor be persuaded of the importance of liberty. They would like to see everyone adhere to the same set of beliefs as they and would hope to establish a theocracy in this country. In a democracy, government derives its legitimacy from the consent of the governed, not from the will of God or some other religious belief. In a theocracy the authority of government comes from God, and those who claim to speak for God have the ultimate authority in government. The words of Pat Robertson as a presidential candidate in 1988 are instructive:

> When the Christian majority takes over this country, there will be no satanic churches, no more free distribution of pornography, no more abortion on demand and no more talk of rights for homosexuals. After the Christian majority takes control, pluralism will be seen as immoral and evil and the state will not permit anybody to practice it.[6]

Fundamentalists have what has been called a maximalist approach to religion, i.e., the conviction that religion ought to permeate all aspects of a society—its politics, its social policies, indeed all aspects of human existence. They would reconstruct the nation as a Christian entity and develop a Christian state as a political instrument to promote their goal of creating a proper Christian culture. Less militant than al Qaeda, they are equally maximalist. By way of contrast, the minimalist position relegates religion to certain concerns that are mostly metaphysical in nature, protects its rights against state intrusion, but largely restricts its power and influence to a specialized sphere.[7]

According to Michael Shermer, in order to generate greater liberty for more people, we must maintain the separation of church and state and foster the greater secularization of society. Public morality must be legislated only by secular bodies. Private morality can be as religious as the individual prefers, and the members of secular bodies may be as religious as they prefer, but the body itself must remain religiously neutral.[8] In other words people elected to public office also have religious freedom to believe what they prefer, but these beliefs should not unduly influence how they vote on particular issues, how they decide cases as judges, and how they see their role in government.

Church and state issues where religious neutrality has been a concern have taken many forms throughout our history. Many issues have emerged over the use of tax money to support religious activities or institutions, the most recent example being the faith-based initiative program of the Bush administration. Church and state issues are also part of the battle over the teaching of evolution vs creationism in our public schools.[9] They are also involved in posting the Ten Commandments in public buildings, prayer in public schools, the words "Under God" in the pledge of allegiance, and the debate about school vouchers.

Over the past several years the Supreme Court has reversed course in allowing a variety of public subsidies for religious instruction and permitting religious displays in public places. In 2002 the court struck down limitations on state subsidy of educational materials in sectarian schools (Mitchell v. Helms). Also in 2002 the court upheld an Ohio school-voucher program even though 96 percent of the students receiving the vouchers were attending church-affiliated schools. In addition the court has allowed religious groups to operate government-subsidized social services as long as there was no explicit proselytizing in the programs.[10]

The president has moved ahead with his plan to fund faith-based groups. One of the first acts of his presidency was to create a White House Office of Faith-based and Community Initiatives. Such offices have also been established in seven executive agencies including the Department of Justice, the Department of Labor, the Department of Agriculture, and the Department of Health and Human Services. They are to give equal treatment to faith-based programs when providing grants and not hold these organizations to a different standard or deny them grants because they are faith-based. In 2003 more than $1 billion of federal government money was sent to religious organizations for charitable purposes.[11]

The argument is that faith plays an important role in healing and restoration, and therefore faith-based programs can be more effective in dealing with the prison population, the homeless, drug abuse, and other social problems. Bush had to make the case that he was not funding these organizations so they could spread their beliefs. These groups must use the government funds they receive to assist the needy and not try to convert them to a particular faith. But this distinction may not hold up in practice, as the very phrase "faith-based" implies that some kind of faith commitment is integral to the healing process.[12] The president himself has asserted that faith-based programs are effective only because they are based in a particular faith. He also described the Bible as the "handbook" for federally funded childcare programs.[13]

President Bush has said that faith-based initiatives can start with any group "from Muslims, Mormons, and good people with no faith at all." Yet as one author suggests, "Imagine an atheist applying to the Office of Faith-Based Services." The point is that there is no practical way of promoting faith in general without promoting particular faiths.[14] While the fundamentalists may have the upper hand in these efforts at the present time, some believe there is an iron law of religious zealotry. "Breach the church-state wall and a zealot whose beliefs are more dogmatic and dangerous than yours will seize the opening."[15]

FUNDAMENTALISM AND PUBLIC POLICY

This trend towards religious influences dominating public policy is apparent not only in these kinds of issues, but it is showing up all over in many different kinds of issues where it is not usually expected. Elected officials who adhere to fundamentalist beliefs see themselves as having a mission to implement those beliefs in their role as government officials whether as legislators voting on bills, as court judges making decisions about cases before their court, or as members of the executive branch making decisions and implementing policy. They have abandoned a secularist position and in many cases have been quite honest about their avowed mission in government. While this characteristic has been most often called ideology in the popular press, religion is the fuel that keeps ideology burning so intensely.

Perhaps this phenomenon has been made no more explicit than in the statements of James Watt, the first secretary of the interior in the Reagan administration. The secretary became a very controversial figure because of policies he advocated to ease strip mining rules; open up more offshore land to oil and gas exploration over the objection of state and local interests; and "unlock" many acres of onshore federal lands for mining, drilling, timber harvesting, and exploration. Watt became very influential in shaping the overall environmental policy of the Reagan administration.

Watt made no apologies for the fact that the policy changes he advocated were based on very explicit theological assumptions that grew out of his faith as a born-again fundamentalist Christian. He was quoted as saying that his "responsibility is to follow the scriptures which call upon us to occupy the land until Jesus returns." Thus the federal government's role is to use the country's natural resources to ensure that "people are provided for until He does come." Regarding preservation of resources for future generations, Watt remarked, "I do not know how many future generations we can count on before the Lord returns."[16]

One must give Watt credit for being so straightforward, which is in some ways refreshing, but one must also question whether basing public policies on such explicit religious beliefs is a proper course for a public servant. When public policies are so explicitly based on doctrines held by some but not by all people in the society, does this action not violate separation of church and state? If the government adopts policies based on certain religious beliefs regarding the second coming of Christ, is it not favoring some religious groups over others? Is not the implementation of a specific theological doctrine held only by certain churches making an established religion?

One has to respect the right of James Watt and other public servants to hold whatever religious views they desire, and obviously these views, along with a host of other factors, are going to influence their behavior. One does not expect these people to be anything less than human. But basing public policies that affect millions of people and the nation's well-being on explicit religions beliefs that are highly questionable for everyone but fundamentalists is a quite different and very serious matter. One does not desire these public officials to be anything more than human either.

So now we have a president who is attempting to integrate faith as a whole into American public policy at the most practical level. He is using faith-based institutions to solve the nation's problems and transform American social policy.[17] And he apparently believes he is called by God to spread liberty and freedom around the world, in particular to Middle Eastern countries. We had an attorney general who received a 100-percent rating on every Christian Coalition scorecard from the time he entered the U.S. Senate. The ACLU stated that John Ashcroft had steered his "entire political career" in one direction. He has been trying to institute sectarian religious practices and beliefs into United States laws.[18]

Tom DeLay, former House majority leader, has said that "Christianity offers a way to live in response to the realities we find in this world—only Christianity." Further he suggested that the tragic shootings at Columbine High School in Littleton, Colorado, occurred "because our school systems teach our children that they are nothing but glorified apes who have evolutionized out of some primordial mud." Peter Singer states, "DeLay apparently believes that God is using him to promote 'a biblical worldview' in American politics."[19] Rod Paige, secretary of education during Bush's first term, was quoted as saying "that he would prefer to have a child in a Christian school, partly because there were too many different values in the public schools to easily arrive at a value consensus."[20] And finally Supreme Court Justice Antonin Scalia made the following remarks on the subject of the death penalty at the University of Chicago Divinity School:

> This is not the Old Testament, I emphasize, but St. Paul. . . . [T]he core of his message is that government—however you want to limit that concept—derives its moral authority from God. . . . Indeed, it seems to me that the more Christian a country is the less likely it is to regard the death penalty as immoral . . . I attribute that to the fact that, for the believing Christian, death is no big deal. Intentionally killing an innocent person is a big deal: it is a grave sin, which causes one to lose his soul. But losing this life, in exchange for the next? . . . For the nonbeliever, on the other hand, to deprive a man of his life is to end his existence. What a horrible act? . . . The reaction of people of faith to this tendency of democracy to obscure the divine authority behind government should not be resignation to it, but the resolution to combat it as effectively as possible. We have done that in this country (and continental Europe has not) by preserving in our public life many visible reminders that—in the words of a Supreme Court opinion from the 1940s—"we are a religious people, whose institutions pre-suppose a Supreme Being." . . . All this, as I say, is most un-European, and helps explain why our people are more inclined to understand, as St. Paul did, that government carries the sword as "the minister of God," to "execute wrath" upon the evildoer.[21]

Scalia was in line to become chief justice of the Supreme Court when and if Renquist retired. Thus we have in this country, governmental officials in positions of great power, including the president himself, who have no trouble seeing God as guiding the affairs of this nation and letting the Christian religion be the determining factor in their public decisions. They see themselves as promoting religion—and not just religion in general but a particular kind of religion favored by the president and leaders of his party. This means that non-Christians, and those who may be Christians but believe religion should stay out of politics, have no standing and are not equal participants in the public policy process.

FUNDAMENTALISM AND WAR IN THE MIDDLE EAST

There has not been much discussion of the role of religion in the war on Iraq and our policies with respect to the Middle East in particular. Michael Moore's Fahrenheit 9/11 did not even mention religion. Some books describe the war in Iraq as an example of our imperialistic ambitions or our desire for empire, a desire that goes all the way back to the Spanish-American War, according to some authors,[22] but they do not see religion playing a major role either. Yet Bush early on described the war in Iraq as a crusade, a word he immediately dropped because it was not politically correct.[23] Yet slips of this kind oftentimes reveal more accurately someone's real intentions than a more scripted response crafted to be politically correct.

What is this war really about? Is it about fundamentalist Christianity vs fundamentalist Islam? Is it about the clash of two different conceptions of God? Perhaps General Boykins was right, and this war is an attempt to prove that our God is bigger than their God.[24] The fact that this may be in part a religious war needs to be discussed and examined far more than it has been by the press and society at large. Religious wars have been some of the most brutal throughout history, and it should come as no surprise that the war in Iraq may have some religious undertones. And it is fundamentalism that constitutes the major problem in many societies in recent years.[25]

Al Qaeda certainly sees the war in religious terms, as a struggle of the faithful against the infidels, of which America is the prime example. They represent themselves as the most faithful heir to the prophet Mohammed and his original followers, and the enemy of unbelievers in both the Muslim and the Western world.[26] The authority bin Laden claims is religious, that he is acting in the interests of preserving the faith. The goal is to establish a Muslim community that is permeated by a certain brand of Muslim religion and impose that view of ethics on the rest of the society, much as the Taliban did in Afghanistan. All of this sounds strangely familiar as one examines the goal of the fundamentalists in this country.

Yet the Bush administration fails to recognize the role religion plays in al Qaeda and in the insurgent rebellion against American troops in Iraq. Bush defends Islam as a religion of peace and tries to separate the jihadists from the God in whose name they fight. Thus those who oppose us are called thugs, insurgents, and the like, and while they use religious terms to justify their actions, they are not religious people. Perhaps Bush cannot allow the possibility that the enemy is motivated by its understanding of God's will, as some have suggested, lest his critics point out that he believes the same of himself.[27]

Arthur Schlesinger Jr., writing in an article entitled "Holy War," states that Bush is fighting a holy war predicated on his religious convictions, much the same as Osama bin Laden who fights for his interpretation of Islamic religion. He quotes a passage from the book The Bushes: Portrait of a Dynasty in which a family member is reported to have said, "George sees this as a religious war. His view of this is that they are trying to kill Christians. And we Christians will strike back with more force and more ferocity than they will ever know."[28] In describing the Left Behind literature, one commentator notes that the portrayal of a bloody Second Coming in these books reflects a change in a view of Jesus as a sort of gentle Mister Rogers figure to a martial messiah presiding over a sea of blood. As he puts it, "Militant Christianity rises to confront Militant Islam."[29]

Speaking of the end times, Iran offers an even more scary proposition. The President of Iraq, Mahmoud Ahmadinejad, is said to be a fervent believer in the imminent reappearance of what is called the 12th Imam. This is Shiism's version of the Messiah and the President has said in official meetings that the end of history is only two or three years away. The Islamic revolution is to prepare the way for the return of this messiah who will appear in the last days to reign over a just world in which Islam is universally embraced by promoting upheaval worldwide. So we have the prospect of two nations armed with nuclear weapons both of whom have an interest in promoting a nuclear armageddon to prove whose God is bigger.[30]

THE RISE OF THE RELIGIOUS RIGHT

How did fundamentalism come to play such a dominant role in our political life? For much of the nation's history, fundamentalist Christians have concentrated on saving souls rather than electing politicians to represent their beliefs in the political system. This began to change in the 1970s, and perhaps the turning point was the Supreme Court's decision on abortion.[31] Roe vs Wade was decided in 1973, and in 1979 Jerry Falwell formed the Moral Majority, an organization of the religious right that urged Christians to endorse political candidates with conservative religious beliefs. Falwell believed that America had lost its way and mentioned abortion, pornography, homosexuality, divorce, and secular humanism as major evils threatening the country. While Falwell had been critical of ministers who participated in the civil rights movement, he came to change his mind as the following quote indicates:

> I never thought the government would go so far afield, I never thought the politicians would become so untrustworthy, I never thought the courts would go so nuts on the left. We have defaulted by failing to show up for the fight.[32]

The Moral Majority came to an end in 1989 as a result of a flawed strategy. Some have pointed out that Falwell thought he could change America from the top down and, after helping Ronald Reagan to the presidency in 1980, believed the Reagan administration would vigorously pursue the agenda of the organization. This did not happen, but the Moral Majority did play a major role in politicizing religious conservatives and giving them a taste of political power that they apparently found appealing. Thus came the Christian Coalition led by Pat Robertson, an organization that recognized that real change comes from the grass roots and focused on local politics as well as the state and federal levels.[33]

The Christian Coalition has become a dominant force in the Republican Party and Pat Robertson did not hide his goal of wanting to take over the party 100 percent.[34] Fundamentalist Christians have been enormously successful in getting the political system to work for them by getting voters registered, platforms adopted, and candidates elected. They have changed the terms of the political debate in the country as every candidate, Republican or Democrat, has to pay homage to their religious beliefs at some point in their campaign. Religion has taken on an importance in public life unprecedented in my lifetime. Some observers of the political scene have made the following comments regarding the effectiveness of the religious right:

> What gives the religious right its power is a clear vision of the kind of society it wishes to create. In part, because of their effectiveness with the media, the religious right is currently much more organized than the political left. They vote in greater proportion to their numbers and they communicate with their elected representatives . . . fundamentalist leaders often manipulate religion to meet their political ends. They are well versed in political processes and marketing techniques. They seem to thrive because secular modernity seems exhausted of solutions to social problems.[35]

With respect to the Republican Party and what it used to stand for, it seems appropriate to say that the worst thing that happened to the party was to be taken over by the religious right. Many of my friends who happen to be Republican feel in some sense disenfranchised. The Republican Party used to stand for fiscal conservatism, meaning a balanced budget or some semblance of it at least, and fiscal restraint regarding government expenditures. While Republican leaders may give lip service to a balanced budget, since the Reagan administration the Republicans have presided over the largest deficits in the history of the nation, and they are projected to grow even larger under the current administration. Those who are old-line Rockefeller Republicans have nowhere to go to find a fiscally responsible party.

THE THREAT TO DEMOCRACY

Christian fundamentalists apparently find political power attractive because they are not even following the teachings and example of Jesus. He continually refused any political office or title that the Jews wanted him to take, reminding them that his kingdom was not of this world. Render unto Caesar the things that are Caesar's and unto God the things that are God's he is reported to have said. And he spent the majority of his time with the sinners and outcasts of Jewish society, not with the political leaders plotting how to take over the leadership of society. One wishes the fundamentalists would follow his example and get out of politics and respect the wisdom of the founding fathers to keep religion and politics separate.

Yet, the opposite seems to be happening as the Catholic Church is now getting into the act. During the campaign in 2004 some Catholic bishops announced they would refuse communion to candidates running for political office who supported abortion. This put the Democratic candidate, John Kerry, in a bind as he was a practicing Catholic who supported abortion. The bishop of Colorado Springs went even further by suggesting that communion ought to be denied any parishioner who supported a candidate that did not adhere to the position of the church on the issues of abortion, gay marriage, and stem cell research. No mention was made about the war in Iraq, the poor, crime, or other social problems.[36]

One can understand the frustration some church leaders must feel about the things going on in the country. Perhaps the fundamentalists have become tired of waiting for Jesus to return and have taken things into their own hands. There have been numerous predictions throughout history regarding the Second Coming of Christ, none of which has proven true. This must be frustrating, so perhaps they have decided to take action and build the kingdom themselves. And the Catholic Church must be frustrated about issues like abortion and perhaps has decided to get politically involved to change society. Apparently these religious groups have found the love of Christ to be a weak force for change in society and have decided to try and force their beliefs on others through the use of political power.[37] And this is exactly the problem in a democratic society.

> To be sure, Christian fundamentalism is not unique in its "we are right and you are wrong" mentality and its insistence upon a literal reading of invented histories framed in legend and allegory. There is little difference in essence between Christian fundamentalism and Islamic fundamentalism. Nor is there much difference in any other system that believes the entire body of an ancient mythical system, frozen in time, is rendered holy by antiquity, and is made more worthy of belief by faith and hope than by merit and proof. All religious fundamentalists, however called, are much the same under the skin. They may be highly dissimilar in methods and goals, and their words may be different, but their tune is the same. God is on their side, and therefore their beliefs are true and should be involuntary enforced on all members of society.[38]

Leaders of mainstream churches have been strangely silent on these issues. One church member has argued, for example, that mainstream Christians have let the religious right get away with peddling distortions and fantasies and with defining the election as a vote for Bush being a vote for Jesus. They should be asking questions such as "Was it God that put Bush in the White House, or was it the work of his powerful father?" Or "Where in the Bible does Jesus teach thou shall kill to spread my love?" This member then goes on to say that it is going to take some real noise to keep democracy and religion on course and in balance and that we must not become a nation of sheep.[39]

Yet religion was everywhere in the 2004 election. The candidates themselves had to interject religion into their campaigns, leading one pastor to remind voters that we are not electing a religious leader but that people should focus on how well candidates might serve the nation's common good as civil leaders.[40] Voter registration drives were held in some churches, leading to criticism from people concerned about church-state issues. And there was pressure on lawmakers to change a 50-year-old tax policy which says that churches can lose their tax-exempt status if they participate in political speech. Speaker of the House Dennis Hastert and Majority Leader Tom DeLay, among others, believed that clergyman should be allowed to speak from the pulpit freely on political issues even so far as to endorse candidates.[41]

For democracy to work requires inclusiveness, which in turn demands tolerance of other points of view, compromise, and the ability to work with others to arrive at joint solutions to problems. When one party with one worldview begins to dominate government, democracy disappears and we have some kind of dictatorship. People in a democracy must constantly be on guard lest somebody or some group that claims to know the solution to every problem begins to accumulate too much political power and stifles debate about critical issues of concern to that society. This is a sure path to disaster as the wisdom of a large part of the population is shut out of decision making and the policies of government reflect a narrow worldview that not everyone shares.

Democracy requires a secular point of view with respect to the world and how it works. There is no place for a worldview that advocates cutting down all the trees because Jesus is coming and he will turn water into wine and stones into bread. Thus we won't need trees or anything else the earth provides. People can believe this if they wish, but these beliefs should not become the basis for public or foreign policy. Policies of this nature should reflect the best science or intelligence that can be had; the wishes of the entire populace, not just a small segment; the views of governmental leaders; and other elements. Government policy is an amalgam of many elements and should not be based on any particular worldview, religious or otherwise. We as humans do not know the truth about these things and to claim otherwise is to claim to be like a God who knows all things.

Democracy requires experimentation. The states have often been described as laboratories where solutions to problems like poverty and welfare, environmental pollution, crime, and other social problems can be tried out to see what consequences result. If certain programs are successful, they may then be useful to try on a national level. No one really knows which programs are going to work or not, and there are always unintended consequences. But experimentation has no place in a fundamentalist worldview. If the truth has been revealed by God to certain people, there is no need to experiment as the truth is not up for question.

Furthermore, a democracy must be open ended with regard to the kind of society that evolves. There is so much diversity in our society that in a few years the white majority will be a minority like every other ethnic grouping. People with diverse backgrounds have many different ideas about the kind of society in which they would like to live and one particular group's vision of the good society should not be forced on them. Any group who has a clear vision of the kind of society it believes is right for all people should be feared. Society evolves over time and its goals change in response to new problems and causes. This is what keeps society interesting and viable, not some moral vision that would stifle creativity and the flexibility society needs to cope with new problems and situations.

These four elements—inclusiveness, secularism, experimentation, and open-endedness—form a unity of sorts, and if one of these begins to disappear, the others are under threat as is democracy itself. If government becomes the exclusive perview of one segment of society, particularly a religious segment, secularism disappears and with it any chance of experimentation and open-endedness with respect to society as a whole. The society then becomes inflexible, unable to cope with change. Creativity is stifled and dissent is not tolerated, and democracy, which is something of an experiment itself, no longer exists. This can happen very subtly and very quickly; thus democracy requires constant vigilance on the part of its adherents to keep it going for the next generation.

NOTES

1. Robert Kuttner, "What Would Jefferson Do?", *The American Prospect*, November, 2004, 31–32.

2. Walter Issacson, "God Of Our Fathers," *Time*, 5 July 2004, p. 62. See also Jon Meacham, "God And The Founders," *Newsweek*, 10 April 2006, 52–55; and "The faith of the Framers," *The Week*, 10 June 2205, 15.

3. Robert Boston, *Why The Religious Right Is Wrong* (Buffalo: Prometheus Books, 1993), 223.

4. John M. Suarez, "The Path to Theocracy: The Purgation of the First Amendment," in Kimberly Blaker, ed. *The Fundamentals of Extremism: The Christian Right in America* (New Boston Michigan: New Boston Books, Inc., 2003), 159.

5. Michael Shermer, *The Science of Good & Evil* (New York, Times Books, 2004), 261.

6. Richard Swift, "Fundamentalism Reaching for Certainty," New Internationalist, August 1990, as quoted in Herb Silverman, "Inerrancy Turned Political," in Kimberly, *The Fundamentals of Extremism*, 179.

7. Bruce Lincoln, *Holy Terrors: Thinking About Religion After September 11* (Chicago: The University of Chicago Press, 2003), 5, 50.

8. Shermer, *The Science of Good & Evil*, 261.

9. See an article by Evan Ratliff, who describes how the creationists are using the argument for intelligent design as a sort of Trojan Horse to sneak the teaching of creationism into the curriculum of public schools. Evan Ratliff, "The Crusade Against Evolution," Wired, October 2004, 157–205. In 2004 eight families from a school district in Pennsylvania filed a lawsuit against the district for voting to include the teaching of intelligent design in the ninth-grade science curriculum, claiming that this theory is a more secular form of creationism that may violate the constitutional separation of church and state. Martha Raffaele, "Lawsuit challenges teaching of alternative to evolution," *Denver Post*, 15 December 2004, 4(A). In 2006, another church-state issue appeared in the news. Colorado Christian University In Lakewood wanted its students to be eligible for state-funded scholarships to pursue a "Christ-centered" education. Colorado education officials turned them down citing a violation of the principle of separation of church and state which prompted a federal lawsuit and national attention. Subsequently, the U.S. Justice Department filed a friend-of-the-court brief siding with the university. Alicia Caldwell, "Money, state, church collide," *Denver Post*, 6 February 2006, 1(A).

10. Kuttner, "Jefferson," p. 37.

11. Arthur Schlesinger Jr., "Holy War," *Playboy*, November 2004, 42. In 2005, $2.15 billion in tax aid was directed to faith-based groups according to an administration report. In view of the cuts in social service spending by this administration, critics used these figures to argue that faith-based initiatives were being used as a cover for these cuts in social services for the needy. "Bush Resumes Push For 'Faith-Based' Initiative At Washington Gathering," *Church & State*, 59, no. 4 (April 2006): 15.

12. In June of 2004 a lawsuit was filed by a group in Wisconsin called the Freedom from Religion Foundation, alleging that the faith-based initiative program favors religious organizations in awarding federal contracts. Such favoritism, they say, violates the First Amendment. The defendants in the case are several Cabinet secretaries who oversee agencies with offices that have been set up to help religious groups apply for the grants. They are alleged to have cajoled religious organizations to come to them, telling them how to fill out forms and giving untried groups money. The suit asks that the use of taxpayer money for faith-based endeavors barred and that new rules be established to ensure that future appropriations do not go to social service

providers that include religion as an integral component of their services. JR Ross, "Group Sues Over Bush's Faith-based Initiative," *Denver Post*, 18 June 2004, 4(A).

13. Correspondence from the Interfaith Alliance, undated, 2.

14. Kuttner, "Jefferson," p. 37.

15. Kuttner, "Jefferson," 36.

16. Andy Pastzor, "James Watt Tackles Interior Agency Job With Reigious Zeal," *Wall Street Journal*, 15 April 1981, 1.

17. Stephen Mansfield, *The Faith of George W. Bush* (New York: Tarcher/Penguin, 2003), xiv–xv. Nicholas Kristof writing in the New York Times points out that there is a real "sex scandal" in the White House that involves millions of taxpayers dollars going to support "abstinence-only" sex education programs that cannot mention condoms or birth control. He argues that the real agenda of these programs is not to educate teens about sex, but to stamp our premartial sex altogether on the grounds that its sinful. According to Kristof this is religion rather than sane public policy. These policies are likely to lead to thousands more deaths from AIDS and tens of thousands of abortions, a real sex-scandal. Nicholas Kristof, "A sex scandal that really matters," *The Week*, 4 March 2005, 12.

18. Herb Silverman, "Inerrancy Turned Political," in Blaker, *The Fundamentals of Extremism*, 197.

19. Peter Singer, *The President of Good & Evil: The Ethics of George W. Bush* (New York: Dutton, 2004), 110-111.

20. Singer, *Good & Evil*, 111.

21. A. Scalia, "God's Justice and Ours," *First Things*, May 2002, 17–21, as quoted in Sam Harris, *The End of Faith* (New York: W.W. Norton, 2004), 156–57. Scalia also weighed in on the subject of the Ten Commandments. At one point he disagreed that the Ten Commandments were mostly a secular statement. They have, he argued, a religious meaning and to state otherwise is to water them down. With this interpretation many would have no argument, but then he went on to say that not only did he find the Ten Commandments to be religious, but they were also "a symbol of the fact that government derives its authority from God." The founders of the country might disagree with this statement as they believed that government derived its powers from the consent of the governed. Richard Cohen, "The miracle of Antonin Scalia, *Denver Post*, 13 March 2005, 5(E).

22. See Ivan Eland, *The Empire Has No Clothes: U.S. Foreign Policy Exposed* (Oakland, CA: The Independent Institute, 2004).

23. On September 1, 2001, Bush described the campaign against the terrorists as a "crusade . . . against a new kind of evil." This comment prompted so much adversity that four days later While House Press Secretary Ari Fleischer had to issue the following retraction: "To the degree that the word has any connotations that would upset any of our partners, or anybody else in the world, the president would regret if anything like that was conveyed. But the purpose of his conveying it is in the traditional English sense of the world. It's a broad cause." Talk about a confusing statement. But it does seem that this retraction was meant to deny that Bush was anti-Muslim in any of his statements and policies. Lincoln, *Holy Terrors*, 115. See also Alan Cooperman, "Bush's references to God carefully chosen, aide says," *Denver Post*, 16 December 2004, 29(A).

24. Lt. General William J. Boykin, in a slide show presentation at the First Baptist Church in Broken Arrow, Oklahoma on June 30, 2003, stated that the real enemy in the war on terror was none other than a spiritual enemy or Satan himself. The terrorists hate us because the United States is a Christian nation. In a January speech he recalled a Muslim soldier in Somalia who believed Allah would protect him in battle against the United States. In response Boykins is reported to have said, "Well, you know what I knew, that my God was bigger than his. I knew that my God was a real God and his was an idol." See Bill Berkowitz, "Boykin's Satanic comvergence," *Working for Change*, www.workingforchange.com/article.cfm?ItemID=15853 (25 November 2004). See also "What ever happened to tht General Boykin investigation" www.ariannaonline.com/forums/archive/index.php/t-8218.html (25 November 2004); and Freed Zakaria, "And He's Head Of Intelligence," Newsweek, 27 October 2003, 41. He was later reprimanded by a Defense Department investigation. See R. Jeffery Smith and Josh White, "Pentagon Probe: Speeches Improper," *Denver Post*, 19 August 2004, 15(A).

25. See Edward M. Buckner, "Winning The 'Battle Royal': Parallels And Solutions To The Growing Danger," in Blaker, *The Fundamentals of Extremism*, 211.

26. Lincoln, *Holy Terrors*, 13.

27. Nancy Gibbs, "The Faith Factor," *Time*, 21 June 2004, 33.

28. Schlesinger, "Holy War," 96. In Iraq itself Islamic fervor is ascendant, and Islamic fundamentalists are driving Christians out of the country. Iraq is on its way to becoming more Muslim, not more secular and certainly not more Christian. William Falk, *The Week*, 8 October 2003, 5. As attacks on churches and threats to families increased, some Christians called for the establishment of a "safe haven" in the northern part of the country while others wanted to form a militia to protect themselves. David George, "Iraq's Christians face fight or flight," *Denver Post*, 17 December 2004, 43(A).

29. Nicholas D. Kristof, "Jesus And Jihad," *New York Times*, 17 July 2004, 25. Evangelicals have strongly supported the War in Iraq. Before the invasion leaders such as Franklin Graham and Charles Stanley saw the war as an "exciting" opportunity to spread the Gospel and to vanquish "people who oppose" God. At that point 87 percent of white evangelicals supported the war, and at the beginning of 2006, 68 percent still professed such support. Charles Marsh, "Putting false faith in our president," *The Week*, 3 February 2006, 14.

30. Charles Krauthammer, "Today Tehran, Tomorrow the World," *Time*, 3 April 2006, 96; Jay Tolson, "Aiming For Apocalypse," *U.S News & World Report*, 22 May 2006, 34–35. See also Kevin Phillips, American Theocracy (New York: Viking, 2006). John Hagee, head pastor of an 18,000 member church in San Antonio, Texas, is the author of a best-selling book that purports to show that the Bible predicts a military confrontation with Iran. He argues that a strike against Iran will lead to the Arab nations uniting with Russia that will lead to an inferno exploding across the Middle East plunging the world toward Armageddon and the return of Jesus when the righteous are going to rule the nations of the earth. Sarah Posner, "Pastor Strangelove," *The American Prospect*, June 2006, 39–43.

31. Silverman, "Inerrancy Turned Political," 177.

32. Jerry Falwell, *Listen America* (New York: Doubleday-Galilee, 1980), 202, as quoted in Silverman, "Inerrancy Turned Political," 178.

33. Silverman, "Inerrancy Turned Political," 178–79.

34. Joseph L. Conn, "Power Trip," *Church & State*, October 1995, as quoted in Silverman, "Inerrancy Turned Political," 181.

35. Silverman, "Inerrancy Turned Political," 206.

36. Anna Quindlen, "Casting the First Stone," *Newsweek*, 31 May 2004, 82.

37. Cal Thomas argues that government can't be used to advance a moral and spiritual agenda, because it is the church and not the state that is commissioned to preach and observe God's message of love that alone can change human hearts. If the church seeks to attach God to political parties and earthly agendas it is doomed to futility. See Cal Thomas, "There are places that government can't go," *Denver Post*, 22 June 2005, 7(B).

38. Edwin Frederick Kagin, "The Gathering Storm," in Blaker, *The Fundamentals of Extremism*, 27.

39. Barrie Hartman, "Raising A Red Flag in Christendom," *Denver Post*, 3 October 2004, 5(E).

40. The Interfaith Alliance, *Roundup*, 10 September 2004, http://141.164.133/3/exchange/forms/IPM/NOTE.read.asp?command=open&obj= 000000. (11 September 2004).

41. The Interfaith Alliance, *Roundup*.

Part III

VALUES AND DEMOCRACY

Chapter Eight

Religion and a Democratic Society

THE RISE OF A THEOCRACY

The ultimate goal of fundamentalist Christianity is to reverse the restructuring of culture that has taken place in American society based on Enlightenment philosophy. According to some authors, religious fundamentalists want to restore religion to the controlling position it enjoyed in Puritan New England, which is indeed their heritage. They want to define communities and restore what they see as "traditional God-given values." After conducting a series of interviews with leaders of the religious right, Conway and Siegelman came to the conclusion that fundamentalist's goal are:

> To Christianize America, to fill all government positions with Bible believing Christians, to gain ascendancy over the national media, to have fundamentalist beliefs taught as science in public schools, to dictate the meaning of human life and ultimately to convert every person on earth.[1]

Some commentators argued that the Bush administration framed the 2004 election as a referendum on God and assembled an army of religious warriors to keep the president in office. In a speech to the White House Conference on Faith-Based and Community Initiatives, the president gave a sermon about the Good Book and the need to surrender one's life to a higher being. His faith-based czar, Jim Towey, told the crowd that a Kerry victory "could almost wind up creating a godless orthodoxy."[2] Another commentator stated that for three years the Bush administration has been waging a concerted campaign to tear down the wall between church and state.

This campaign goes far beyond Bush's frequent use of evangelical code words and his loyalists shocking suggestion that he was chosen for his position by God himself. Bush has used the power of the presidency to fill federal judgeships with right-wing Christian ideologues, to block stem-cell and other scientific research that doesn't mesh with fundamentalism, and to withhold billions in federal funds from family planning programs that offer such forbidden options as contraception and abortion. Those taxpayer dollars are now being funneled to faith-based groups whose primary mission is religious proselytization. Under this president, the secular state is under siege.[3]

Thus the culture war could also be characterized as fundamentalists vs secularists. The latter believe that secular control of government and society is necessary to promote freedom and liberty and for a society to flourish. Religious authority cannot be allowed to govern society. Having religion assume a dominant position within society does not put an end to conflict; indeed it ensures that conflicts will then assume a religious character and be more destructive than ever as history has proven over and over again. This could be exactly what is happening in this society as conflicts over abortion, stem cell research, and gay marriage are really conflicts over religious beliefs. Thus there is already something like a religious war going on in this country.

There is no such thing as a religious democracy. There is a great diversity of religious belief all over the world, and particularly in this country where religious diversity has been encouraged. Religions differ on all sorts of issues, and this diversity should be respected. But this administration is based on a particular fundamentalist faith that does not reflect the beliefs of many in the country. A faith-based presidency has to favor a particular brand of religion; all religions cannot all be amalgamated into some kind of general religious approach. When public policy reflects a particular religious worldview that is not shared by the entire country, we are going down the road towards a theocracy and democracy suffers.

Some commentators have said we ought to keep all this talk about religion in the public sphere where it belongs—in the churches. "It is one of the saddest ironies of our time that as America tries to calm the fires of theocracy abroad, it should be stoking milder versions of the same at home."[4] But is it possible to keep religion in churches? Are the fundamentalists going to be content again with confining themselves to saving souls and refrain from influencing public policy? And even more important should they be? To the extent we have a religious war going on in this country, does this war bring to the surface a underlying tension regarding religion and democracy that has been waiting to surface for many decades? The nature of religious faith is such that it requires a commitment on the part of its adherents; otherwise it would seem to be an empty faith that has no particular content. While religious adherents hold to transcendent beliefs in God and an afterlife, it is a fact that they still live in a world where all sorts of things are going on that do not square with the tenants of their faith. Do they not have an obligation to the faith they profess to try and change the world? Thus are Catholics who favor abortion really Catholics in the true sense of the word or are they Catholics in name only?

Surely the official position of the Catholic Church is against abortion in any form, and this has been true for many years. If some Catholic members, however, favor abortion or are against making it illegal, are they truly Catholics? Can they legitimately be refused communion by the church hierarchy or even be kicked out of the church? Must religion be solely a private matter and practiced behind closed doors or, as some argue, is the distinction between someone's private view on the morality of abortion and his or her public stance about its legality a distinction without a difference?[5]

These are interesting and legitimate questions for particular religions and for democracy. It seems that the fundamentalist churches were willing to content themselves with saving souls until the society decided to make abortion legal in Roe vs Wade. This may have been too much for them and a line was crossed that caused them to begin to take action in the political arena to change things. While Reagan did not pay much attention to their agenda, Bush has, and now that he has been reelected, they hope to push their agenda even further. Falwell is even reconstituting the Moral Majority to push their issues in the political arena.[6]

Their issues happen to coincide with the Catholic Church, and this combination is one the religious right hopes to foster. If the Catholic base of the Democratic Party is destroyed and Catholic supporters of these issues are integrated into the Republican Party, this will give them greater power to influence elections. But some are concerned about such a scheme. When religion and politics are fused, politics suffers and faith is corrupted. The space for personal conscience on these issues is erased. The most holy sacrament of the Catholic Church, communion, would have a partisan tinge and its religious meaning would be in question.[7]

Not all religions are the same, and if religion becomes involved more deeply in political life, this only deepens the conflicts in society. If the Mormons in this country whose numbers are growing, the Amish, and other religious movements including Muslims should become more involved politically, we would have conflict on a larger scale. The debate would then be over religious dogma and worldviews, a debate that has no resolution. Scientific findings would not help in resolving this debate as no amount of data is going to change one's religious beliefs. Nor are changing circumstances going to be persuasive for someone who believes in absolutes. Thus we would have such factionalism that democracy would be unworkable, and we would see the end of democracy as we know it at least.

RELIGION AND SOCIETY

While there are many differences between people in our society that divide it in multiple ways, there do seem to be some common differences between people who voted for Bush and those who supported Kerry in the last election. Many pundits and others concerned with these things see a geopolitical fault line running through American society that is marked by differences in cultural and religious values. Bush voters are most often seen as NASCAR-loving, gun-owning, God-fearing Republicans who are mostly found in the rural, suburban, and small-town heartland that runs from the Deep South through the Great Plains and into the western mountain states. Kerry supporters are characterized as highly secular, latte-sipping, diversity-embracing Democrats concentrated in the urban areas on the two coasts and around the Great Lakes.[8]

These characterizations are over simplified, to be sure, yet pollsters do note some differences in so-called core values between voters in states that voted for Bush and in states that went for Kerry, the red and blue states. Nearly twice as many voters in red states attend weekly religious services as do blue state voters, and 50 percent more voters in red states say they want their president to worship a higher being. And an overwhelming majority of red state voters think of that higher being in absolutists terms such as good versus evil. In the blue states the great majority think of that higher being as loving everyone in a "live and let live" attitude. For many red state voters, then, their stand on issues such as abortion, stem cell research, and gay marriage are not just about better policy choices; they are matters of personal morality and principle.[9]

The fundamentalists can take a good deal of credit for electing Bush to four more years as they turned out in record numbers to support their candidate. Evangelical Christians constituted nearly a quarter of the voters in 2004, and they backed Bush over Kerry by 78 percent to 21 percent. They were particularly significant in the battleground states of Florida and Ohio. Many of these evangelicals see two different Americas and see the vote as a protest against the assult on their values by secularism. Separation of church and state is like a code word understood by them to mean not allowing any religious values into the public arena. They are going to push hard for government to implement their agenda and support their values.[10]

This divide then, whether it is along the lines suggested by the pundits or involves absolutists versus pluralists and fundamentalists versus secularists, as I have suggested, does have some implications for democracy. There is something of a war over what kind of society we are to become, whether we will be a less secular, more scripture-guided society or whether we will become a more secular, science-guided society. At this point there does not seem to be much of a compromise between these worldviews as they are based on very different assumptions about the nature of the world and the nature of human beings, so we may be in for several more years of this divide before it plays itself out in some form or other. Whether religion and democracy can be mixed and the country still have a functioning democracy or whether they need to be kept separate to have a functioning democracy is the key question in this war for the future of the country.

MORALS AND VALUES

Morals and values are of particular importance, then, in this so-called war and deserve further discussion. To the extent that moral concerns were a major factor in the 2004 election and people did not vote their economic self-interest, then perhaps this reflects a search for meaning in a materialistic and commercialized society. Perhaps they feel betrayed by a society that seems to consider materialism and selfishness more important than moral values and concerns. While not denying that they have material needs such as a stable job, health care, and the like, they also have deeper needs and want their lives to have meaning. Thus they respond to candidates who seem to care about values and have some sense of a transcendent purpose.

In fundamentalist churches people are presented with a coherent worldview that speaks to these needs for meaning and purpose. People in many if not most, of these churches show a high level of caring for their members as long as they adhere to the "party" line, a level of mutual caring they rarely find in the rest of society. These churches provide a sense of community offered nowhere else in society other than the family, a community whose central theme is that life is valuable because it is connected to some higher meaning and purpose than just success in the marketplace.

Indeed, it is ironic that many of these same people share individualistic tendencies that support free market capitalism and are against government regulation of marketplace activities. They reject the notion that the government itself can supply a sense of community through policies that provide some of their material needs and a sense of economic security. Such a reliance on the marketplace makes the search for meaning and purpose through religion all the more important. The market itself does not create a community as the bonds which are created by the pursuit of self-interest are not those that make for a community that has a purpose beyond the materialistic values of the marketplace.

The society we are creating does not encourage diversity and a meaningful and interesting life in and of itself. People cannot be blamed for wanting a nice home to live in and places to shop where food and clothing are affordable. But what this means is that we create suburbs where everything is a boring sameness. Tract homes may be affordable for many people, but to make them relatively cheap means they must be built pretty much the same over a large area in order for efficiency to have an effect. People may have a few choices to individualize their homes, but not many, and thus much of suburbia is composed of street after street of houses similar to each other in every respect.

The commercial areas of suburbia also reflect this sameness. One sees the same restaurants (Red Lobster, Outback Steakhouse, McDonalds, etc.) and many of the same stores everywhere. Shopping malls have most of the same retail establishments no matter where you are, and thus one can be in any part of the country for all the difference it makes. Suburbia is thus very much the same in any part of the country, and other than climate and certain topographical features, there is not much difference from place to place. This has to contribute to a boring and uninteresting life that has little or no diversity and makes the search for meaning and purpose in other areas of life all the more important.

Add to all this the fact that most people have to sit in traffic for much of their day commuting to and from work and that the jobs that many people have are not very fulfilling and provide little or no meaning beyond the necessity to earn an income, and we have an American dream that may not be very attractive. Meanwhile we are industrializing more and more wilderness areas that provide an escape from all this boredom. Perhaps all this is why Americans seem to love violence in movies and other areas of life and such violence breaks out every now and then in a destructive manner. Perhaps many people are so bored and empty of feeling that it takes violence to wake themselves up and feel alive again.[11]

People who can afford to may move to a more desirable area, and this may work for a while. But sooner or later, other people also make the same move, and pretty soon crime, congestion, pollution, and other problems associated with urban communities catch up with them. Cities spend billion of dollars to expand freeway systems to handle traffic congestion, only to see the improvements change places where people live and their driving habits, and thus in a few years traffic congestion is just as bad as it was before the improvements. There seems to be no solution to these problems and after a while we become oblivious to them and go about our daily lives as best we can.

Thus it is no mystery why the search for meaning and purpose beyond all of this is so important. Perhaps this kind of existence also explains why people seem so interested in the end of times literature. They need to believe there is something better than this in an afterlife of some kind, where their lives will have meaning and purpose. But meanwhile we live in this life, and the kind of life most people lead makes them susceptible to authoritarian religious and political systems which simplify things into clear-cut choices between right and wrong, between good and evil, between the wheat and the chaff. Democracy requires citizens who think and take time to be involved and who are concerned about creating a better life in the here and now for themselves and their families.

Security

In addition to a concern about moral choices and values, there is also a concern about security in our country, a concern brought about by the 9/11 attacks. These attacks destroyed a certain innocence on the part of America and tapped into our sense of vulnerability. People have been scared of more such attacks ever since. The randomness of these attacks is beyond our control, and we know that no matter what measures we take to prevent them, we can never recapture the sense of security we had prior to these attacks. They have defined a generation and mark a change in the way we think about ourselves and our sense of security. The Bush administration was able to tap into these fears and continually projects the image of strong leadership that could better deal with these concerns and put Kerry at a disadvantage he could not overcome.[12]

And so we have all the bravado about winning the war on terror, to which people respond positively. But what does it mean to say we are going to win the war on terror? Are all the terrorists eventually going to be killed? Are they going to sign a document of unconditional surrender? Are they going to sign an armistice agreement? Are they going to lay down their arms and pursue a peaceful existence? Conventional wars have been won on these terms, but it is obvious that none of these means apply to the war on terror. So how will we know when the war is over? The Bush administration has provided no answer to this question and has given us no benchmarks for evaluating how the war on terror is proceeding.

The most realistic thing we can say is that the war on terror will never be over. Terror has been a fact of life ever since life has existed and will continue to be a problem as long as life exists. So we might as well get used to it and learn to get on with our lives in spite of the constant threat of terror. Perhaps Kerry had something of a realistic assessment when he talked about reducing terrorism to a nuisance, but to compare it to prostitution was not very sensitive to the way most of us think about terror. And if the terrorists ever get hold of atomic weapons and detonate even a dirty bomb in the middle of one of our major cities, this will be something more that just a nuisance. The 9/11 attacks were more than a nuisance, so such talk is not very helpful.

American citizens must not, however, give up their cherished freedoms and liberties that are the essence of democracy in a search for an elusive security. Politicians and others are going to promise security in order to get what they want, but we must be skeptical of these promises and not buy into them wholeheartedly. Should another terrorist attack occur on American soil, this will create even more of an environment of fear that can be tapped into by demagogues who promise to keep us safe from terrorists. But if we sacrifice our freedoms on the altar of security, the terrorists will have won and the war on terror will surely be over for us and other free societies around the world.

Pluralism

American society already can see the effects of the values debate in influencing what we can see on television. On Veterans Day in 2004 a large number of ABC affiliates chose not to broadcast *Saving Private Ryan* because of the language and violence depicted in the movie. It was shown in 2001 and 2002, but affiliates feared they would be fined by the Federal Communications Commission (FCC) that had begun to crack down on incidents like the Janet Jackson "wardrobe malfunction" during the Super Bowl halftime show. ABC offered to pay any fines they might incur, but that wasn't good enough as they were also concerned about negative reactions from viewers who were concerned about "moral values." This combination could have put their broadcasting licenses in jeopardy.[13]

Soon thereafter both NBC and CBS refused to air an ad by the United Church of Christ (UCC) that contained a message of inclusion. The ad was part of the denomination's new identity campaign that was soon to begin. It stated that like Jesus, the UCC seeks to welcome all people, regardless of ability, age, race, economic circumstance, or sexual orientation. The 30-second spot featured two bouncers standing guard outside a church and selecting which persons were permitted to attend Sunday services. A narrator then proclaimed the UCC's inclusiveness with an extravagant welcome to all people. According to the UCC, the ad was geared toward those persons who, for whatever reason, have not felt welcomed or comfortable in a church.[14]

In a written explanation CBS said the UCC was denied network access because the ad implied acceptance of gay and lesbian couples, among other minority constituencies and is therefore too "controversial." They stated that "because this commercial touches on the exclusion of gay couples and other minority groups by other individuals and organizations, and the fact the Executive Branch has recently proposed a Constitutional Amendment to define marriage as a union between a man and a woman, this spot is unacceptable for broadcast on the CBS and UPN networks." NBC simply stated that the ad is "too controversial."[15]

The Rev. John H. Thomas, the UCC's general minister and president stated "it's ironic that after a political season awash in commercials based on fear and deception by both parties seen on all the major networks, an ad with a message of welcome and inclusion would be deemed too controversial."[16] Leonard Pitts, a member of the UCC, writes that this rejection comes from the rise of gay bashing under the guise of religious conservatism. "Those folks," he writes, "would not be happy with an ad showing gays being welcomed anywhere, much less in church."[17]

In early 2005, IMAX theaters in several cities in the South including the Carolinas, Texas, and Georgia declined to show a film on volcanoes out of concern that some of its references to evolution might be offensive to those with fundamentalistic religious beliefs. The film called "Volcanoes of the Deep Sea" made a connection between human DNA and microbes that lived inside undersea volcanoes.[18] Such action seems ridiculous in a society that supposedly values science and education and hopes to maintain a scientific and technological edge over other countries. In any event we can expect more of the same as the values of the religious right become more and more dominant in society. As stated by one columnist:

> While religious minorities, especially devout ones, continue to enjoy protection of their rights in the United States, the spirit of rationalism is taking a real beating. Religious dogma dictates administration policy on stem-cell research, gay rights, and the use of condoms to combat AIDS, and the White House is determined to use religious groups as sponsors of tax funded social programs. The right detests "social engineering," except in service of the traditional family, heterosexuality, religious dogma, and worship itself. Centuries after the supposed triumph of reason and religious tolerance, the new millennium has begun with a return to religious fundamentalism and holy war.[19]

At a time the United States is resisting a Muslim holy war and trying to convince Arabs in the Middle East of the virtues of a pluralist democracy, the efforts of fundamentalists to inject God into government is bizarre. As one writer says, "What most differentiates America from the Islamist nations that we are trying to convert to Western style democracy is that they are theocracies while we respect civil rights and religious pluralism."[20] We must continue to respect these rights here at home and lead by example. The last thing we need is a holy war between fundamentalism and secularism in this country that divides us further, yet this is what we seem to have going on in this country.

THE FUTURE OF RELIGION

Arthur Schlesinger Jr. believes the 21st century promises to be the century of religious fanaticism. In the Islamic world such fanaticism is the breeding ground for terrorism. There are no more dangerous people in the world than those who believe they are doing the will of Almighty God. Such beliefs lead suicide bombers willingly to sacrifice their lives in order to kill as many infidels as possible. Religious fanaticism gives people courage to do things many of us find impossible even to contemplate. The men who led the 9/11 attacks were certainly not "cowards" as Bush described them; they were men of faith, faith that gave them the courage to stare death in the face to make a point. How many of us would have the strength of conviction these men must have had, a conviction that led to their own death in the service of a cause that in their minds was just and holy?

At least fundamentalism in this country has not yet produced that kind of religious fanaticism. But fundamentalism in this country has its own price in the triumph of faith over reason. We seem to have more and more public policies based on religious convictions than on reason in this country, whether it is stem cell research or gay marriage. And now the president has weighed in on the side of teaching intelligent design in public schools on a par with evolution as if intelligent design is a scientific theory that can be proved or disproved by scientific methods.[22] This administration's attitude towards science seems clear as scientific findings have been altered on everything from global warming to endangered species to correspond with the administration's preconceived notions.[23] Bush doesn't like to be confused by the facts; his mind is already made up and will not be changed. This kind of thinking got us into the Iraqi war, among other things.

The problem this world faces is that science and technology have given us the power to destroy life as we know it on this planet, if not through nuclear warfare then through environmental destruction. The things that saved the United States and the Soviet Union from destroying the world was the doctrine of Mutually Assured Destruction (MAD), the knowledge that if one side launched a preemptive strike, the other would have enough nuclear capacity left to destroy the aggressor. Reason triumphed because each side wanted to live rather than die, and the value of life was a value shared by both societies. Foreign policy could thus appeal to this thrust for life, if you will, as neither society wanted to see itself destroyed.

But what happens when nuclear weapons are under the control of a group who does not share such a value for life, where the promise of an afterworld is so strong that this life is of no consequence? Mutually assured destruction is exactly what they are after. What is going to stop a terrorist group from using nuclear weapons if they should ever get their hands on such weapons? The evil that reached our shores on 9/11 was not just the evil of terrorism; it was the evil of religious faith at its worst. It is time we recognized that we are in a conflict with radical Islamic fundamentalism, not just terrorism. And there is something about Islam that breeds terrorism. We should quit making excuses about Islam being a peaceful religion and claiming terrorists are misinterpreting Islam to suit their own interests.[24]

According to Sam Harris writing in The End of Faith, Islam has all the makings of a thoroughgoing cult of death, more than any other religion human beings have devised throughout history. On almost every page of the Koran, he states, there are instructions for observant Muslims to despise non believers, and thus it lays the ground for religious conflict. He has five pages of quotes from the Koran to support this conclusion and then states that anyone who reads these passages and still does not see a link between Muslim faith and Muslim violence probably should see a neurologist.[25] Why a neurologist rather than a psychiatrist is curious, nonetheless the point is the same.

Christianity and Judaism also have their problems as the God of the Old Testament is a God of wrath, and there are plenty of passages that are violent to the extreme.[26] As an interesting aside, those who are so concerned about posting the Ten Commandments in public places conveniently ignore the punishment for breaking those commandments.[27] The punishment for taking the Lord's name in vain is death (Leviticus 24:16). Working on the Sabbath is also punishable by death (Exodus 31:15) as is punishment for cursing one's father or mother (Exodus 21:17) and adultery (Leviticus 20:10). Should these punishments also be posted in our courts so judges can take them into account when it comes to sentencing?

The point is the Bible is full of violence and incites people to violence in defense of the faith. This leads Sam Harris to conclude, consistent with Schlesinger's point about religious fanaticism, that all reasonable men and women throughout the world have a common enemy that threatens to destroy the very possibility of human happiness, and I might add, the possibility of human life itself. That enemy is nothing other than religious faith.[28] Respect for other faiths or even worse the views of unbelievers is not an attitude that a God of any stripe endorses. Intolerance is intrinsic to every religious creed, and true believers cannot tolerate the possibility that other religions or no religion at all holds some truth about life and human happiness. Beliefs define one's vision of the world; they dictate behavior and one's emotional response to other human beings.[29]

Religion is a curious facet of human existence. We live our daily lives using our reason to figure things out and basing our activities on the things our experience with the world teaches us. Children eventually learn by gathering enough evidence that touching a hot stove is a painful thing to be avoided. But when it comes to religion, our beliefs about the world and its meaning and purpose can float entirely free of reason and evidence.[30] Even fundamentalists live by using reason to get through the day and need evidence to support most truth claims they encounter, yet when it comes to beliefs about the Bible as the literal word of God and the incredible claims it makes about the creation of the universe and the supernatural, they require no evidence whatsoever.[31]

Every religion, according to Sam Harris, preaches the truth of certain propositions for which no evidence is even conceivable.[32] Thus religion requires a leap of faith to believe in these propositions, a leap into a realm where rational discourse is impossible. Why this kind of leap seems to be necessary for so many people throughout the world is a mystery tied up in our past and in the human ego, among other things. It seems that people need a belief in something beyond this world and its experiences that gives them certainty, a sense of purpose, and provides meaning for their lives. But this is precisely the problem. When challenges to faith arise, as they inevitably do, one cannot engage in rational discussion and will end up using violent means, if necessary, to defend the faith. Thus religion has been one of the most pervasive sources of violence throughout history.

Thus far from religion being the solution to human hatred and violence, the practice of religion is the source for much of that hatred and violence. It gives justification for people to kill each other. Far from being the source of morality, it is the source for some of the most immoral acts humankind has ever committed. What we need is for a Reagan-type person to do to our perception of religion what Reagan did to government. Government is not the solution to our problems; he said, it is the problem itself, and this image stuck in the American psyche. What has to be done is to identify religion as the problem in the modern world; it is not the solution to life's problems.

We have come to the point with Islamic fundamentalism where religion breeds terrorism, but our response should not be to turn to Christian fundamentalism for answers and engage in some kind of holy war with Islam. Christians do not need to prove that their God is bigger than the God of Islam. This kind of fanaticism can only lead to more violence and more killing in the name of religion. Is a more moderate approach to religion the answer? Would this kind of approach put a damper on religious fanaticism that can lead to violence and help us tolerate each other's religious differences?

The difference between a fundamentalistic and a moderate approach to religion is that the former wants his or her particular brand of faith to inform every aspect of society. There should be no separation of church and state, but religion should permeate every part of governmental activity. The law should be based on religion, government policies in their entirety should be faith based, and there should be some kind of litmus test to make sure only true believers get into the highest levels of government and thus provide leadership for society. This is one of the most important decisions Iraq has to make in drawing up a new constitution. What role should Islam play in the country? Should it be a secular constitution or should it be based on Islamic beliefs?

It would seem that a moderate approach to religion would put a damper on the religious fanaticism that can lead to violence. In the moderate approach religion is just one part of life, like a section of a magazine, where religion has a place but is not pervasive through all of one's life. There are other sources of truth than the Bible or the Koran, and science has a legitimate place in the determination of public policy. The moderate has a tolerance of other religious approaches and does not need to believe he or she has the absolute truth that needs to be defended at any cost. This would seem to be a reasonable approach to religion that should be cultivated and might help to stem the tide of fanaticism.

However, according to Harris again, religious moderation will do nothing to lead people out of the wilderness. Moderation does not permit anything very critical to be said about religious literalism and does not call into question the core dogmas of religious faith. Religious moderates betray both faith and reason, and are the product of secular knowledge and scriptural ignorance. Religious moderates have no credibility to attack fundamentalism and thus offer no bulwark against religious extremism and religious violence.[33] Their beliefs provide the context in which scriptural literalism and religious violence can flourish without effective opposition and thus are in large part responsible for religious conflict in our world. The greatest problem according to Harris, is not only religious extremism, but the cultural and intellectual accommodation we have made to faith itself.[34]

The solution Harris advocates is for people to give up faith itself and find a way when faith without evidence disgraces anyone who would make outrageous religious claims and expect to be taken seriously. In an age where a single person or small group can cause millions of deaths or render a region uninhabitable for years, humankind has simply lost the right to live out our myths and hang on to our mythic identities. Beliefs people have, and we all have beliefs, must be open to evidence and argument and we must have a willingness to modify those beliefs in the light of new evidence. Such openness and a spirit of mutual inquiry will help secure a common future for humankind.[35] Religious dogma that has to be defended at all costs has to be given up in the interests of self-preservation.

While there is much to be said for this argument, it is not realistic to expect that people will give up their religious faith for any reason. Religion seems to have been a necessity for most people throughout history and will continue to be so for the foreseeable future. The best we can hope for, I think, is for some modifications to be more compatible with the age in which we live. Islam must change in such a way that it celebrates life more than death and must purge itself of those elements that make death appear so glorious. People who are brought up to glorify death have to hate themselves because they cannot embrace life, and thus if they are going to have to give up their life in the interests of their religion, they are naturally prone to take as many other people along with them as they can to get even with the cosmos. There are some psychological mechanisms at work here that are frightening.

Meanwhile, here in the United States, there is much to worry about. We are not going to progress as a nation if we teach intelligent design in our public schools. We need to teach our children how to question scientific findings to be sure, but this should not be replaced by religious dogma. Critical thinking is a skill needed to question both science and religion. Our children should be brought up to think for themselves and not accept the conventional wisdom in either science or religion. This is the path to progress—an openness to the future and a willingness to explore one's own mind and develop new ideas and new ways of thinking. No progress is possible if people have closed minds and are brought up to accept religious beliefs of whatever faith unthinkingly.

Religious fundamentalism needs to be seen for what it is—an authority system that needs no evidence to justify its claims but rests on the authority of a book called the Bible and of religious leaders and followers who buy into this system of beliefs in spite of all evidence to the contrary. The need for certainty and security plagues all of us, but to sacrifice our reason and humanness in the process seems outrageous. The best we can hope for is that people who need religion will at least get a religion consistent with 21st century and technology and is not rooted in ancient mythology. We cannot afford to carry around such primitive beliefs any more as they now threaten our very existence.[36]

NOTES

1. Edward M. Bruckner, "Winning The 'Battle Royal': Parallels And Solutions To The Growing Danger," in Kimberly Blaker, ed., *The Fundamentals of Extremism: The Christian Right in America* (Michigan: New Boston Books, Inc., 2003), 204.

2. "The election: A question of faith," *The Week*, 14 June 2004, 19.

3. "The election," p. 19. See also Richard Cohen, "President Bush mixing religion and politics," *Denver Post*, 26 May 2005, 7(B).

4. "Religion and politics: When God is your running mate," *The Week*, 5 November 2004, 8.

5. Andrew Sullivan, "Showdown at the Communion Rail," *Time*, 24 May 2004, 94.

6. Given the success of the 2004 vote, Falwell announced in November 2004 that he had formed a new coalition to guide an "evangelical revolution." Called the Faith and Values Coalition, Falwell characterized the new organization as a resurrection of the Moral Majority. The new group's mission would be to lobby for anti abortion conservatives to fill openings on the Supreme Court and lower courts, a constitutional amendment banning same-sex marriage, and the election of another "George Bush-type" conservative in the 2008 election. Hank Kurz Jr., "Falwell revives morality coalition," *Denver Post*, 10 November 2004, 3(A).

7. Sullivan, "Showdown," 94.

8. Jay Tolson, "How Deep The Divide," *U.S. News & World Report*, 25 October 2004, 42. One commentator has characterized the divide as a contest between the elite groups in society. See David Brooks, "A civil war within America's educated class," *Denver Post*, 20 June 2004, 4(E).

9. "Divided America," *U.S. News & World Report*, 25 October 2004, 37. See John Leo, "Don't discount moral views," *U.S. News & World Report*, 29 November 2004, 54 for a view that arguments about such issues which are based on religious beliefs should not be considered out of bounds because they come from people of faith. Also see Jennifer Wheary, "Who own America's moral values?" *Denver Post*, 2 January 2005, 3(E) for a different viewpoint.

10. Dan Gilgoff, "The Morals And Values Crowd," *U.S. News & World Report*, 15 November 2004, 42. See also Robert J. Barro, "The Political Power of the Pew," *Business Week*, 22/29 August 2005, 143; and Dan Gilgoff, "The Dobson Way," *U.S. News & World Report*, 17 January 2005, 62–71.

11. This statement is not meant to condone violence but only to suggest that violence does have the capability of stimulating people and awakening an emotional response.

12. According to one poll, 49 percent of those polled said they trusted only Bush to deal with terrorism which was 18 points more than those who said they trusted Kerry on this issue. Women were a key part of Bush's victory as Kerry carried the women's vote by only 3 percent in 2004, compared with Gore's 11 percent in 2000. Bush carried married women by 55 percent which was up from 49 percent in the 2000 election. These figures reflect women's concern with security. See Mortimer B. Zukerman, "A closer look at America," *U.S. News & World Report*, 13 December 2004, 68.

13. Dusty Sanders, "Retreat on 'Pvt. Ryan' silly," Rocky Mountain News, 15 November, 2004, 2(D). See also Marie Cocco, "Cultural jihadists of the right," *Denver Post*, 17 November 2004, 7(B); and Mike Littwin, "Ryan a casualty of battle on moral front," *Rocky Mountain News*, 13 November 2004, 6(A). See also James Poniewozik, "The Decency Police," *Time*, 28 March 2005, 24–31.

14. United Church of Christ Press Release, "Only recently did United Church of Christ learn of networks' ultimate refusal of ads," December 2, 2004, http://www.stillspeaking.com/news/release3.html. (3 December 2004).

15. United Church of Christ Press Release.

16. United Church of Christ Press Release.

17. Leonard Pitts, "Sleaze welcome on TV, but not love," *Times-Picayune*, 4 December 2004, B(7).

18. "Theaters pull film that refers to evolution," *Denver Post*, 24 March 2005, 10(A). In 2006, The Governor of Georgia signed a bill that would allow Bible classes in public high schools, and for the first time would set statewide guidelines and earmark public dollars for such courses. The Georgia school board has until February 2007 to decide how the course shall be taught, and no matter how it decides, the decision is expected to spark controversy and a flurry of lawsuits. Sarah Childress, "See You in Bible Class," *Newsweek*, 1 May 2006, 39.

19. Robert Kuttner, "What Would Jefferson Do?" *The American Prospect*, November 2004, 32.

20. Kuttner, "Jefferson," 38.

21. Arthur M. Schlesinger, Jr. *War And The American Presidency* (New York: W.W. Norton, 2004), 116.

22. Jean Torkelson, "President Bush boosts design theory's profile," *Rocky Mountain News*, 6 August 2005, 23(A). The religious people who object to evolution being a fact do not understand the nature of science. Of course evolution is not a fact, it is a scientific theory that is presently supported by the preponderance of evidence about how species change and adapt to changing environments. Perhaps someday another scientific theory will come along that will explain the facts better, but it is not intelligent design. Science looks for natural causes and explanations for things, and cannot deal with supernatural explanations. Intelligent design assumes a designer, a supernatural something that created the world. It is not a scientific theory that can be proven or disproven by data from the natural world. It is an article of faith and should not be taught in public schools. It is a sneaky and deceptive attempt by believers in creationism to "Chritianize" public education and extend their theocracy.

23. See Tom Yulsman, "Political interference with science real, troubling," *Denver Post*, 21 August 2005, 1(E).

24. See Irshad Manji, "When Denial Can Kill," *Time*, 25 July 2005, 78.

25. Sam Harris, *The End of Faith: Religion, Terror, And The Future Of Reason* (New York: W.W. Norton, 2004), 117–123.

26. Consider the following passage from Deuteronomy 20:10-18: "When you draw near to a city to fight against it, offer terms of peace to it. And if its answer to you is peace and it opens to you, then all the people who are found in it shall do forced labor for you and shall serve you. But if it makes no peace with you, but makes war against you, then you shall besiege it; and when the LORD you God gives it into you hand you shall put all its males to the sword, but the women and little ones, the cattle and everything else in the city, all its spoil, you shall take as booty for yourselves; and you shall enjoy the spoil of your enemies, which the LORD your God has given you. This you shall do to the cities which are very far from you, which are not cities of the nations here. But in the cities of these peoples that the LORD your God gives you for an inheritance you shall save alive nothing that breathes, but you shall utterly destroy them, the Hittites and the Amorites, the Cannaanites and the Hivites and Jebusites, as the LORD your God has commanded; that they may not teach you to do according to all their abominable practices which they have done in the service of

their Gods, and so to sin against the LORD your God." As quoted in Michael Shermer, *The Science of Good & Evil* (New York: Henry Holt and Company, 2004), 37–38.
27. Harris, *The End of Faith*, 155.
28. Harris, *The End of Faith*, 131.
29. Harris, *The End of Faith*, 12–13.
30. Harris, *The End of Faith*, 17.
31. Harris, *The End of Faith*, 19.
32. Harris, *The End of Faith*, 23.
33. Harris, *The End of Faith*, 20-21.
34. Harris, *The End of Faith*, 45.
35. Harris, *The End of Faith*, 48.
36. Alan Tacca in the *Kampala Monitor* advocates the abolishment of Christianity. "Most Western societies are now only nominally Christian. Even for churchgoers, 'God is clearly a cultural construct.' True believers are a dying breed, and Catholic and Protestant churches alike are struggling with a chronic shortage of priests and ministers. Rather than bemoaning this trend, the West should embrace it. Religion is doing little these days but provide fuel for conflicts: Muslims against Christians, Hindus against Buddhists, and everyone against the Jews. So let dispose of the Christian God, the way the Western colonial powers got rid of African deities long ago. Back then, colonizers 'actively undermined those gods until they were stripped of all dignity. It is now time to declare their God also primitive.' References to God should be removed from currencies and national anthems, sand-blasted off government buildings. Only after faith in the supernatural is gone can people take responsibility for generating 'virtue and beauty' in 'the human realm.'" Alan Tacca, "When a faith outlives its usefulness," *The Week*, 14 April 2006, 12.

Chapter Nine

Revitalizing Democracy

The revitalization of democracy requires the nation to address a number of issues that have surfaced in the past several years. These issues do not necessarily relate directly to the religious right, but some of them do provide opportunities for the religious right to try and dominate our political system. Regardless these are issues that should be dealt with in order to revitalize democracy in our society. These issues have to do with the future of the two-party system, the Electoral College, the redistricting of states to provide safe seats for incumbents, the money involved in campaigning which is related to the selling of candidates over television networks like products, voting procedures, and the courts.

THE TWO-PARTY SYSTEM

The counterpart of a rise of theocracy is the demise of the Democratic Party. What now becomes of the Democrats? They seem to be out of touch with a good many people in the country, although it must be remembered that Kerry did capture 48 percent of the popular vote and was only one state short of winning the election. But they lost seats in the House and Senate in the election of 2004 and they had only a thin line to stop anything the Republicans proposed in the way of legislation and judgeships. All they had was the filibuster in the Senate, and they even gave this away with respect to some judicial appointments.

The Democrats have some soul searching to do in order to keep the power they now have in Congress and capture the White House in the next election. It is vitally important to the country that they get their act together and provide more of a balance of power in the country as a one-party state would be disastrous. Absolute power corrupts absolutely whether we are talking about the status of our country in the world or whether we are talking about governance at the national level. If we become a one-party nation, this will destroy the diversity and plurality that is vital to a democracy. Two examples that took place at the end of 2004 after the elections show what can happen when one party has most of the power. In an unrecorded voice vote behind closed doors House Republicans changed a 1993 party rule that required leaders who are indicted to step aside. This rule was adopted when House Republicans were going after Democrats who had ethical problems. The rules were changed as the first order of business after the election of 2004 to allow Majority Leader Tom DeLay to keep his post even if a grand jury indicted him for alleged violation of federal laws in connection with fundraising activities for a political action committee.[1] In a related development, in late December 2004 House Speaker Dennis Hastert considered removing the House ethics committee chairman, Joel Hefley, a Republican from Colorado who had admonished DeLay in the fall and replacing him with Lamar Smith, one of DeLay's fellow Texans.[2]

The second example also involves Dennis Hastert, the Republican House speaker, who refused to bring a bill reforming the intelligence community to a vote because it did not have a majority of the majority party behind it even though it most likely would have passed with minority support. This was said to be the latest step in a decade-long process to marginalize the minority Democrats and run the House as virtually a one-party institution. The Democrats had earlier been barred from helping draft several major bills including the 2003 Medicare revision and the intelligence package itself. The Republican leadership held closed votes to shut out the Democrats, kept floor votes open past the time limit to win additional support, and barred Democrats from from genuine participation at the committee, floor, and conference levels. The amount of legislation submitted with special rules preventing amendments from the floor increased dramatically under Republican leadership.[3]

Some pundits have suggested that the Democratic Party has become too elite and has lost touch with the working class in our society. They need to find a way to connect with the heartland of America.[4] Others suggest that the Democrats are too identified with causes such as abortion and gay rights and that Kerry may have lost the election on November 18, 2003, when Massachusetts' highest court conjured up a right to gay marriage that spawned a backlash in which 11 states, including Ohio, passed a constitutional amendment banning such marriages. This issue mobilized people to turn out to vote, and most of them voted for Bush who favors a federal constitutional amendment that would prevent gay marriages.[5] Others suggest that the party missed the boat on value issues as some polls show that values played a major part in the 2004 election, particularly values with respect to issues such as abortion and same-sex marriage.

To the extent this is true, I suggest that the Democratic Party broaden the values debate to include other issues like the war in Iraq, the unequal distribution of income and wealth in this country, poverty, the environment, and other issues of concern. With regard to the war in Iraq, it is my contention that the Democrats missed the boat on this one, beginning with the congressional campaign in 2002. At that point they supported the president's request for authorization for the war in Iraq in the hopes of getting this issue behind them to focus on the economic issues they thought were more important and would win them control of Congress. But the war was the issue, and they should have opposed it on moral grounds. Apparently they were still rooted in the Clinton focus that "it is the economy, stupid."[7]

It was always a mystery why so many Democrats opposed the Gulf War when that seemed absolutely justifiable and then supported the Iraqi war, which had reasonable doubt written all over it with regard to weapons of mass destruction and links to terrorists. Perhaps they realized they were on the wrong side the first time and didn't want to make that mistake again. In any event Kerry was on the wrong side of the Iraqi war and got taken to task for his changes during the campaign. He never could get it straight. Even though he had voted for the war in Congress, he could have admitted at the beginning of his campaign that he had made a mistake and did not see the moral implications of invading a country that had not attacked us and that Bush's doctrine of preemption was of questionable morality given the uncertainty of our intelligence.

Then when given an out when asked if knowing what we know now about no weapons of mass destruction, would he still have supported the war, he answered in the affirmative adding that he would have used the power more effectively than the current administration.[8] Was he afraid of alienating voters if he answered in the negative? He should have answered as did Hillary Clinton, that the vote would never have come before Congress if the lack of WMD was an established fact. But he got himself mired in contradictions, with his later statements about the wrong war at the wrong time in the wrong place. Consistency of message was not one of his strong points.

Whatever criticism of the war he did mount was not about morality but more about effectiveness, that Bush did not have a plan for peace and was conducting an ineffective effort to establish stability in Iraq. Kerry claimed he would be more effective by bringing other nations into the effort and sharing the burden. But he did not question the morality of the war as he had during the Vietnam War after he returned from duty. He seemed to have lost his moral compass. Neither party has debated or discussed the idea of a preemptive or preventive war, but this debate must occur at some point, and the merits and demerits of such an approach to war must be put on the table and discussed. The Bush doctrine should not be accepted and become conventional wisdom. It is too radical a departure from what has been established practice for centuries.

This brings up another point. The Democrats need to go on the attack and change the image of the Republican Party. They should not let them continue to get away with calling themselves conservative. Conservatism in the best sense of the word means just what the word implies, a cautious approach to change and a bent to preserving the institutional structures that have been in existence for some time and have proven themselves. As stated by Jerry Z. Mueller, a history professor at the Catholic University of America, "The conservative defends existing institutions because their very existence creates a presumption that they have served some useful function, because eliminating them may lead to harmful, unintended consequences, or because the veneration which attaches to institutions that have existed over time makes them potentially usable for new purposes."[9]

By any measure one wants to use, the federal government is bigger and more powerful and in many ways more intrusive than when Bush took office. Domestic spending has increased at a greater rate than under any president in several decades. Bush has not vetoed a single spending bill that has come across his desk. He pushed hard for the prescription drug bill that was the most expensive and extensive revision to Medicare since its inception. The national debt is at record levels and climbing. And he is engaged in nation building, something he lambasted during the 2000 campaign.[10] This is hardly a conservative administration in any sense of the word.

This administration is more accurately something along the line of radical revolutionaries. They have overthrown the idea of the sovereignty of nations, a doctrine that has been in place for centuries to govern the relations between countries. They are in the process of overthrowing any semblance of progressivity in our tax system and want to make the tax cuts which favor the wealthy permanent. Taxes on unearned income from dividends and capital gains have been drastically reduced, and we have moved towards more of the tax burden being placed on wages and the middle class. Now there is even talk of a flat tax or consumption tax which would be even more regressive. They have taken away rights of American citizens with the Patriot Act and have waged a war on the environment in overturning many regulations related to clean air and water as well as disposal of toxic substances. And then they tried to change Social Security into something that is not social and certainly not secure.

This is anything but a conservative administration, and the Democrats need to keep harping on this every way they can and change the image of the party. If the country has turned conservative, the Democrats need to advertise themselves as the true conservatives and take away this ground from the Republicans. They need to become the party of fiscal conservatism in particular as the Republicans abandoned any semblance of fiscal responsibility years ago in the Reagan administration. The Democrats need to tag the Republicans with a "borrow and spend" image and shed their own image of "tax and spend" by becoming the party of fiscal responsibility. Many disgruntled Republicans in the country are concerned about the fiscal health of the country and really do not have a party at this point. They may still vote Republican based on the image they carry in their minds, but they can be peeled away if the Democrats change this image.

This is a moral issue as well as an economic issue, and the Democrats need to get this message across. It is immoral for this country to keep on living beyond its means and expect the rest of the world to foot the bill and keep financing our debt. It is also immoral for more of the tax burden to be placed on the middle class and continue to pass tax policies that so overwhelmingly favor the already rich. If the rich get richer and the poor poorer, this is hardly a formula for harmony in our society. Prosperity should be shared by all, and any policies that skew the game in one class's favor are immoral to the core. Taking away basic rights of Americans is immoral as is destruction of our environment in the interest of the profits of oil and gas companies. The Democrats need to frame all these issues in moral terms and remind citizens that there are more moral issues than abortion, stem cell research, and same-sex marriage.

Regarding campaign strategies, the Democrats might as well write off the South and much of the West. Perhaps Florida is still a possibility for Democrats, but the rest of the South is so hopelessly dominated by the religious right that it is not worth the effort, at least in the presidential campaign. Campaigns for Congress might be a different matter. But for president, the Democrats do not need the South anyhow. As for the West, Nevada, Colorado, and New Mexico seem to be the best possibilities, but the rest of the West may also be open for Democratic gains. So all the Democrats need to do is keep the blue states they won in the last election, and work on Ohio, Indiana, Iowa, and Missouri in the Midwest and three states in the West. Winning all or even one of these states like Ohio would give them the balance of the votes in the Electoral College.

As stated before, the Democrats have a moral obligation to get their act together and find their soul again. Or to put it more crudely, they need to rediscover their intestinal fortitude. Perhaps the best thing that happened to the

Democrats in the 2004 election is the defeat of Tom Daschle, who proved to be a gutless wonder over and over again. Perhaps the new leadership will show more intestinal fortitude in opposing the president's policies. Working with Republicans to pass legislation they oppose on principle is not going to help them. They need to be obstructionist when appropriate and stand up against ideas they oppose.[11] The Democrats need to quit looking at polls and act on the basis of Democratic principles. And if they don't know what they are anymore, they need to have a discussion to recover them. The way to make a president unpopular is to oppose his policies on principle and get this message across to the American people.

Arthur Schlesinger Jr. states that the long-term problem of the Democrats is to deal with the image of government that started with Ronald Reagan, who eviscerated the notion of affirmative government by stating that government is not the solution to our problem, that government is the problem.[12] Ever since, we have had representatives in government who do not believe in government and see it only as a means to grant favors to lobbyists who keep them in office with donations. The idea that government can and has solved problems that cannot be solved in any other way needs to be revived. Government can do good things for people that need doing, and the Democrats need to project a positive image of government to counter the Republican negativism.

THE ELECTORAL COLLEGE

The Electoral College is a disaster waiting to happen. While the issue was on the table in the 2000 election because Gore won the popular vote and yet lost the electoral votes and the election, it is not likely to get much attention now that Bush seemingly won in a definitive fashion. But it must be noted that a switch of only 60,000 votes in Ohio would have given its 20 electoral votes to Kerry and thus the majority of the electoral votes and the election. This 60,000 votes represents only .05 percent of the total votes cast in the nation as a whole. Bush would still have won the popular vote by 3.5 million but would not be president. This would have been a far more serious matter than Gore's 550,000 vote margin in 2000 and would have given the Republicans every right to protest the results. It might have split the country even more than did the 2000 vote.

Something needs to be done about this problem. The Electoral College as presently constructed is an anachronism. Either it needs to be abolished entirely or the electoral votes distributed on some other basis than a "winner take all" arrangement. The reform that is talked about the most is to go with the popular vote and do away with the Electoral College. Going with the popular vote would best respect the "one man-one vote" principle and provide a direct link between the voters and the elected candidates. This appealed to me as well, as a direct vote seemed best to reflect the wishes of the electorate. However, after reading a book by Arthur M. Schlesinger Jr. entitled War and the American Presidency, I came to be disabused of this notion.

Schlesinger points out that the abolition of the state-by-state, winner-take-all electoral system would hasten the disintegration of the party system and encourage splinter candidates and parties that would take votes away from the major parties. Since it would be likely that no candidate would get anywhere near a majority of the popular vote under these conditions, a runoff election of the top two candidates would be the result. Splinter parties with their accumulated votes would be in a position to extract concessions from the runoff candidates in exchange for their support in the runoff election. One national election is bad enough, Schlesinger says. A double national election with horsetrading going on might mean that the winner of the first round might lose in the second round depending on the deal made with splinter parties. In addition there is the problem of organizing a nation wide recount in the case of close elections.[13]

To avoid the problem of a popular-vote loser being the electoral-vote winner, Schlesinger proposes that the popular vote winner be given a bonus of two electoral votes for each state and the District of Columbia; thus there would be a pool of 102 electoral votes awarded to the winner of the popular vote. This bonus plan was already proposed in 1978 by the Twentieth-Century Fund Task Force on Reform of the Presidential Election Process. Schlesinger claims that this plan would virtually guarantee the popular-vote winner would also be the electoral-vote winner and at the same time preserve both the constitutional and practical role of the states in presidential elections.[14]

Other ways of reforming the system have to do with preserving the electoral system as it is but allocating the electoral votes based on the popular vote in some manner. The "winner take all" system disenfranchises too many people, especially those states where the vote is close. Imagine being a Republican voter in New York or California where so many electoral votes are at stake, and yet Republicans effectively do not have a say in the presidential election. This does not seem fair on the surface, suggesting that the electoral votes ought to be allocated on some other basis.

The state of Colorado had an amendment on the ballot in the 2004 election that would have awarded the state's nine electoral votes proportionally to each presidential candidate based on the popular vote. This amendment did not pass, but if it had been in effect in 2000, the election would have gone to Al Gore. The states of Nebraska and Maine already allocate their electoral votes differently, in giving two electoral votes to the candidate who wins the popular vote in the state and one electoral vote for each congressional district in which a candidate receives a majority.

Other ideas have been suggested to deal with this problem. Congress should appoint a blue ribbon bi-partisan commission to look into this situation and suggest solutions for Congress and the nation to consider. This situation should not be allowed to continue until a real disaster happens. And while we are at it, the right for each individual citizen to vote in national elections should be affirmed in a constitutional amendment. As it now stands, individual citizens have "no federal constitutional right to vote for electors for president unless and until the state legislature chooses statewide election." Individuals in 135 nations have the constitutional right to vote, but the United States does not recognize this fundamental right in its constitution.[15]

REDISTRICTING

In 2004 Tom DeLay pushed a controversial redistricting plan through the Texas legislature that resulted in four new Texas GOP members being elected to the House of Representatives. This was just the latest, and perhaps the most blatant, attempt to redraw district lines to favor one party over another. However, both parties are guilty of redrawing Congressional district lines to provide safe havens for the incumbents. The result is that political competition is eliminated in these districts as the incumbents have an advantage that cannot be overcome. Of the 435 seats in the House that were theoretically in play in 2004, only 33 were actually competitive.[16]

Voters in these districts are effectively disenfranchised and are not given a real choice. Meanwhile the candidates do not have any reason to explain themselves in response to a credible candidate. There is no real democracy in the House, and instead of the voters choosing their representatives, in most of the districts the representatives choose their voters. Redistricting has become a science as computer technology is used to sift through demographic data to draw district lines that maximize partisan advantage. District maps take on a surreal character as they snake all over the state in order to pack as many Republicans and Democrats as possible into different districts.

Gerrymandering dates back to the early days of the country, but it has not been the problem it is today. The Republicans have pushed the envelope even further with a new strategy that has been called re-redistricting. Supposedly, redistricting takes place every 10 years when a new census is taken and such redistricting is supposed to reflect changing population trends. But in 2002 when the Republicans took control of the state legislature in Colorado, they tried to transform two competitive districts into party strongholds. The state supreme court struck down this move by holding that the state constitution limited redistricting to once a decade.[17]

No constitutional ban existed in Texas, however, to prevent DeLay from redrawing congressional lines once Republicans gained control of the Texas legislature. In such states redistricting can take place the moment one party comes to dominant the governorship and state legislature. Such shifts of power in statehouses can take place quickly, as when the Democrats took control of the state legislature in Colorado during the 2004 election. This situation raises the specter of continuous redistricting wars that can further polarize the political landscape.[18]

Such a situation means, according to some analysts, that moderates from both parties are not likely to get elected. Because the majority of districts are controlled by one party or the other, the winner of the primary contest usually is at one end of the political spectrum to appeal to the dominant majority in the district, either Democratic liberals or Republican conservatives. Thus people get elected to the House that are more ideological than moderates, making compromise more difficult. They are beholden to a district that is not diverse and is more ideologically oriented than would otherwise be the case.[19]

What is the solution to such a problem, in which it is difficult for new people to run for the House with any hope of winning? How can new voices hope to run against incumbents given the advantage the latter has in House races? In some states like Arizona there has been a backlash against such unchecked partisanship. This state adopted a constitutional amendment in 2000 that moved primary responsibility for redistricting from the legislature to a blue ribbon commission. An even better way exists in Iowa, where a nonpartisan panel draws districts that do not give incumbents a competitive edge. In any event there are ways to deal with this problem that some think threatens democracy to its core.[20]

MONEY

In an interview with two correspondents from Time magazine, retiring Senator Fritz Hollings of South Carolina mentions money as the biggest problem in Congress. He stated that the body politic has got a cancer of money and that, even as a senator with a six-year term, he had to spend most of his time trying to raise money. In 1998, for example, he raised $8.5 million to get re elected, which amounted to about $30,000 a week, each week, every week, for six years. Consequently, he could only listen to the people who gave him money and had no time for other people or for his Senate colleagues. He had time only for money, to hurry up and raise money so he could get on television and get re elected.[21]

In 2002 a House incumbent raised an average of $900,000 to campaign for re election, up from $650,000 in the 1998 election. The typical challenger, however, was able to raise only $197,000 for his or her campaign. Thus money is another reason incumbents have the edge, money from special interests to which they have become beholden. Some 98.2 percent of House incumbents won reelection in 2002, and senators are only slightly more vulnerable. Running for office is growing more and more costly, and the gap between challengers and incumbents is widening, with Congress becoming more a club of the rich or near rich who are dependent on special interest money to keep their seats.[22]

Overall, almost $4 billion was spent on the 2004 election with more than $1.6 billion spent on TV ads alone. Some $2.2 billion was spent just in the presidential election. The Democrats nearly matched the Republicans in money spent on the election, but the Republicans seem to have spent their money more effectively. While Kerry and the Democrats increased their vote total by 6.8 million votes, Bush and the Republicans increased their total by nearly 10.5 million.[23] The amount of money spent on this election is staggering, and one has to question the wisdom of our system when in a time of increasing budget deficits we spend this much money to promote and defeat candidates running for political office.

Our legislative system could be seen as the best Congress money can buy. Without a personal fortune to tap into, most incumbents rely on money from trade unions, lobbyists, and corporations for their money, and these groups expect a return on their investment. The average voter does not have such influence. To deal with this problem, some analysts suggest fixing and broadening public funding, helping challengers by requiring local television stations to provide free air time to candidates, overhauling the Federal Election Commission to do its job more effectively, and encouraging small donors to give more money to campaigns.[24]

An organization called the Institute for Democracy and Electoral Assistance located in Stockholm reports that 63 percent of democracies in the world provide free access to the media, thus doing away with one of the major reasons for raising money. Most of these democracies also limit campaign contributions, as does this country, but one-fourth of them also limit campaign expenditures. While the Supreme Court feared the latter would undermine our democracy, some argue that political equality requires creating barriers between money and the ballot box.[25]

Molly Ivans would ban all corporate donations from any part of the election process. She argues that this would eliminate much of the bribery that goes on in the system as she calls the way campaigns are financed in this country rank and open bribery. Politicians tend to dance with the ones who got them elected, and corporate money gets many candidates elected to office. While corporate political action committees traditionally split their contributions between candidates of both parties, a new study completed in 2004 found that large corporate PACS gave at least $3 to Republicans for every $1 given to Democratic candidates, helping to keep the Republicans in office.[26] This growing allegiance of business to the GOP was said to be the result of ideological compatibility, respect for majority power, and the efforts of Republican leaders and conservative activists.[27]

Part of the problem is, of course, the voters themselves. The way candidates are elected in this country is getting to be a disgrace. Candidates are sold on television like a product, and creating an image is all important rather than dealing with the issues with any degree of substance. For many voters this may be the only way they learn anything about the candidates, which is why television advertising is so effective. Everyone complains about negative advertising, but the reality is that it works to influence votes. The Swift Boat ads hurt Kerry in 2004 and he eventually had to respond to them. People like the negative. Just consider the kinds of things that make the nightly news. Politicians, like newscasters, know what appeals to people.

One would hope for a more informed electorate, but that may be wishful thinking. People who work two jobs and have kids to raise do not have the time or energy to devote much effort to learning about the candidates and their position on issues, so they rely on television advertising just like they do for buying products. Perhaps one way to counter this trend is to have more debates where the candidates have to deal more substantively with issues and problems. But the fact of the matter is if television advertising were not so effective, it would not take so much money to run for office since such advertising makes up the bulk of campaign expenditures.

VOTING PROCEDURES

When most of us vote, we think we are participating in a nation wide single election for president, yet actually, some 13,000 counties and municipalities across the country conduct elections all with different ballots, standards, and machines. Some analysts have called this a dysfunctional decentralization that accounts for most of the problems with elections in this country. The Supreme Court in Bush vs Gore called for equal protection of voting rights and said that equal protection applies not only to who is allowed to vote but also the manner in which people vote. Depending on where they live, voters use different methods to vote, and if machines are involved, they are of widely varying accuracy and efficacy. The nation as a whole does not have uniform standards for voting as authority has been delegated to the lowest and often poorest level of government.

The Help America Vote Act (HAVA) was passed in 2002 to correct some of these problems, but the only provisions of the law that were implemented in the 2004 election were provisional ballots and ID requirements. These provisions may have caused more problems than they solved. The law states that first-time voters who register by mail must present identification when registering or voting. Some states went further than the law by requiring that all voters, not just new ones, show identification at the polls. Four of those states required photo identification. These identification requirements were arbitrarily and incorrectly enforced, and some voters were wrongfully turned away from the polling place or forced to cast provisional ballots that may or may not have been counted.[29]

Provisional ballots were cast when a voter's name was not on the registration list, a particular problem in the 2000 election when many eligible voters were turned away because their names did not appear on the rolls. These ballots were supposed to be counted once election officials could confirm their validity. Under the new law the right to cast a provisional ballot and have it counted depends on being a registered voter in the jurisdiction, which was supposed to mean the geographic area responsible for voter registration and not the precinct or polling site. This usually means the county, but this is not how many state election officials interpreted the law.[30]

In several states election officials ordered counties to reject provisional ballots that were cast in the wrong polling place. Some 28 states threw out provisional ballots that were cast in the wrong precinct, even with regard to selection of candidates for statewide offices. Some allegations have been made that the vast majority of provisional ballots cast in Florida were disqualified, some because of being cast at the wrong polling place. In Cleveland one-third of the provisional ballots were supposedly invalidated. If these problems with provisional ballots appeared in all 50 states, the number rejected could have been significant.[31]

Other problems surfaced with respect to registration and voting. In Ohio, the secretary of state issued a directive that all voter registration forms be on 80-pound paper stock because anything lighter could be shredded by postal equipment. Thus if someone downloaded an application from the Board of Elections Web site and submitted it, that registration may have been rejected. This directive was later rescinded.[32] Election officials in many jurisdictions failed to supply an adequate number of voting machines, leading to long lines and wait times than may have constituted an unconstitutional denial of voting rights. Such voting machine disparities have the effect of imposing differential barriers to voting in different polling places.[33]

Many of these problems appeared because voting itself has become a partisan issue as voting procedures can be manipulated for partisan purposes. Many countries have nonpartisan national election commissions while others have political parties share responsibility for the conduct of elections. The United States is one of the few democracies that lets the incumbent government put itself in charge, granting responsibility to what can be a highly partisan secretary of state. Thus election directives can and have been issued that tend to favor the party in power and work against the registration and actual voting of people who are likely to vote for the other party. Thus many techniques have been used to disqualify voters who do not support the party in power.[34]

Suggestions have been made to deal with these problems. Some say it is time for Congress to insist on national standards that would alleviate some of these disparities in voting. The country should also have a nationwide registration list instead of the thousands of separate lists that currently exist, many of which are inaccurate. HAVA requires that by 2006 all states must have computer-based interactive statewide lists, but this will work only if everyone agrees not to move out of state.[35] Voter registration should be made easier and provisional voting rules must be clarified. Electronic voting machines must have a technology that allows for auditing and voter verification. And finally, there must be some kind of nonpartisan governance of elections to reduce manipulation of the process for political purposes.[36]

THE COURTS

The three branches of government—legislative, executive, and judicial—are supposed to provide checks and balances on each other to prevent abuse of power, but the judiciary has a special role to play in our system of government. While the legislative and executive branches are expected to be political because they are elected officials, the judiciary has an image of being above politics. The core ideals of the judiciary involve fairness, objectivity, and decisions based on principle. The long black robes judges wear are supposed to convey these ideals—that judges will decide each case that comes before them on the merits of the case and will decide cases on the basis of legal principles and precedent after hearing all the evidence. They are not to prejudge cases on the basis of ideology or partisan politics. Faith that our courts will be impartial is crucial to the proper functioning of a democratic system.

Yet reality is quite different. In the 38 states where judges are elected rather than appointed, judicial candidates are acting just like politicians. They run attack ads on television, state their beliefs about issues up front to win supporters, and look for big donors, doing all those things that were once considered beneath the dignity of the office. The process of installing federal judges has become bitterly partisan as both liberals and conservatives make accusations of racism, sexism, and religious intolerance against candidates they don't want as judges in the federal court system. The judicial process has thus come to reflect the same division that exists in American society and is as bitterly polarized and political as any other branch of government.[37]

Granted that the courts have never been entirely divorced from politics and that the ideal of judges being legal scholars cloistered above politics has never really existed, some still believe that political considerations have never been as influential as they are today. In a poll conducted in 2001 and 2002 by the Justice at Stake Campaign, a nonpartisan watchdog group, 48 percent of the 894 elected judges polled said they felt under a "great deal" of pressure to raise money for their election. Asked about the influence political contributions had on their decisions, some 4 percent said "a great deal of influence," another 22 percent said "some influence," and just 20 percent said "just a little influence." The answer should have been "no influence at all," an answer that received only 36 percent of the responses.[38]

Many of the unwritten traditions of civility and nonpartisanship that used to govern federal judicial appointments have eroded. Republican staffers for the Senate Judiciary Committee infiltrated the computers of their Democratic counterparts and reviewed thousands of confidential files that contained strategy documents. President Bush broke ranks with his predecessors and has not consulted with the Democratic leadership on potential nominees. There was a custom that judicial nominees had to win at least one vote from the minority party to be appointed, but that has been discarded. And the Democrats made unprecedented use of the fillibuster to block controversial candidates, so much so that the Republican leadership of the Senate threatened to change the rules regarding the ability of a minority party to fillibuster.[39]

Special interest money involved in judicial races has increased dramatically as these groups have increasingly come to view the judiciary as just another branch of government to be bought and captured. A little known Supreme Court decision handed down in 2002 overturned a state law that forbade candidates for judgeships from taking positions on controversial issues that might come before them on the bench. This decision makes it easier for candidates to comment on policy issues and sent signals to special interests on how they would rule on particular issues. This prompts interest groups to solicit candidates' views on certain issues of interest and use this information to decide which candidates to support.[40]

The problem is that judges are not supposed to be politicians whose job it is to advance the interests of those who vote for them. Judges are not supposed to represent anyone; their job is to represent the law itself. But the ideal that we are a nation of laws and not men is rapidly eroding, and the notion that one can get a fair hearing from any judge is disappearing. The trick is making sure your case is heard by the right court that has a judge who is likely to rule in your favor. Thus battles over jurisdiction are of critical importance in many cases.

Few countries in the world allow judicial elections because of these problems, yet the appointments process also has its problems as most people who are appointed judges have political connections. The reasons states allow judges to be elected by the voters is to ensure that they are held publicly accountable for their decisions. Perhaps the way to go, then, is to have publicly financed judicial elections to destroy the influence of special interest money over the election process. The American Bar Association is in favor of this, and in 2004 North Carolina became the first state to fund judicial campaigns fully.[41]

In any event, the politicization of our court system is a threat to democracy that needs to be corrected. It diminishes the ability of the courts to fulfill their role of upholding the principles embedded in the Constitution, in federal and state statues, and in common law in a fair and impartial manner. The Supreme Court may have done the country great harm by becoming involved in the 2000 election and setting the tone, so to speak, for partisan warfare. It should have stayed out of this controversy and let the state settle its own interstate power struggle.[42] By interjecting itself into this controversy, the high court broke the bonds between the people and their elected representatives in what most people believe was a partisan decision. The result is that the voting process itself has become politicized.[43]

This same Supreme Court became the key battleground between liberals and conservatives over the appointment of a new Supreme Court justice and perhaps as many as four new judges, depending on who retires and who maintains their health. These judges will influence the way the country goes for years to come. It has been years since I felt that candidates for these positions were nominated on the basis of their qualifications rather than their ideology or their stance on certain issues such as abortion, affirmative action, and now gay marriage. There are undoubtedly many people like me in the country at large. This is not good for democracy if many of its citizens have given up on an impartial judiciary. It is a problem that needs to be addressed by both parties for the good of the country and its system of government.

NOTES

1. See Charles Babington and Helen Dewar, "House GOP changes rule to help DeLay keep post," *Denver Post*, 18 November 2004, 2(A). See also Gloria Borger, "A whiff of arrogance," *U.S. News & World Report*, 6 December 2004, 42. Delay was eventually indicted in Texas on a felony money-laundering charge and was forced to relinquish the post of minority leader. In April 2006, he announced that he would not run for re-election and would resign from Congress in the next few months. While he had won the Republican primary, he thus avoided losing in the general election. By winning the primary he denied his Republican challengers the chance to succeed him as he regarded them as gadflies and traitors according to one source. The Abramoff scandal was getting close to him as two former aides pleaded guilty to criminal charges and a third was under investigation. Under the federal campaign rules, any re-election money that is raised by a lawmaker can be used to pay legal fees stemming from official duties. R. Jeffrey Smith and Jonathan Weisman, "Sources say DeLay put off leaving to lock up primary," *Denver Post*, 5 April 2006, 2(A); Robin Toner, "Texan drove GOP agenda for a decade," *Denver Post*, 5 April 2006, 2(A); and Edward T. Pound, "Who's Next," *U.S. News & World Report*, 17 April 2006, 33–34.

2. Mike Allen, "Ethics official faces ouster," *Times-Picayune*, 30 December 2004, A(2). Just a day or two later, House Republicans introduced rule changes that would make it harder to bring ethics complaints against lawmakers. Richard Simon, "GOP poised to ease ethics inquiry rules," *Denver Post*, 3 January 2005, 6(A). Fred Wertheimer, president of Democracy 21, said these changes would mean "one-party veto power" over complaints. See Mike Allen and Charles Babington, "House GOP leaders seek ethics rules change," *Times-Picayune*, 1 January 2005, A(3).

3. Charles Babington, "Majority role a party line in House," *Times-Picayune*, 27 November 2004, A(2); Sam Rosenfeld, "Then Came the Hammer," *The American Prospect*, December 2004, 51–54. See also John Aloysius Farrell, GOP acts like Dems of old," *Denver Post*, 27 March 2005, 25(A).

4. See "The Democrats: Now what?" *The Week*, 12 November 2004, 9; Dan Thomasson, "Democrats must find a way to connect with heartland," *Denver Post*, 7 November 2004, 7(E); and Gloria Borger, "Democrats need a twang," *U.S. News & World Report*, 22 November 2004, 30. There has been no end of suggestions as to what the Democrats need to do to become a viable political party. For a sampling see Joe Klein, "A New Idea of Democrats: Democracy," *Time*, 11 April 2005, 17; Gloria Borger, "Standing for Something," *U.S. News & World Report*, 10 October 2005, 38; Gloria Borger, "A Confederacy of Dunces," *U.S. News & World Report*, 19 December 2005, 42; Garance Franke-Ruta, "Remapping The Culture Debate," *The American Prospect*, February 2006, 38–44; Robert Kuttner, "Is Corruption Enough?" *The American Prospect*, February 2006, 3; Robert B. Reich, "Beyond 'No'," *The American Prospect*, July 2005, 64; and Michael Tomasky, "Party in search of a Notion," The American Prospect, May 2006, 20–27.

5. John Leo, "What now, Democrats," *U.S. News & World Report*, 15 November 2004, 82. Sarah Wildman argues that the Democrats failed to frame the gay marriage

debate in terms of discrimination that is immoral and unconstitutional. This might have countered religious concerns about gay marriage by bringing out a significant anti discrimination vote from moderates. See Sarah Wildman, "Wedding-Bell Blues," *The American Prospect*, December, 2004, 39–40.

6. Alan Brinkley, "What's Next?" *The American Prospect*, December, 2004, 18–23.

7. Senator Robert C. Byrd says, "Some high-priced pollster had apparently convinced the Senate Democratic leadership that we could 'get the war behind us' and change the subject to that of the flagging economy, where the election prospects would appear to be more favorable to the Democrats. What nonsense." Senator Robert C. Byrd, *Losing America: Confronting A Reckless and Arrogant Presidency* (New York: W.W. Norton, 2004), 174.

8. David Epso, "Kerry reaffirms vote for Iraq war," *Denver Post*, 9 August 2004, 4(A).

9. Jerry Z. Muller, *Conservatism: An Anthology of Social and Political Thought From David Hume to the Present* (Princeton, NJ: Princeton University Press, 1997), 5. Edmund Burke, who has arguably written the single most influential work of conservative thought, put it this way: " . . . the existence of an institution creates a prima facie case that it has served some human need, and that historical continuity is intrinsically valuable because it increases the emotional hold of an institution upon its members." Muller, *Conservatism*, 24.

10. Andrew Sullivan, "Why the Old Labels Don't Stick," *Time* 1 November 2004. 51. For most of the last century conservatives argued that power ought to reside with the states and local governments, while liberals worked for the expansion of federal power. Some argue that these roles are now reversed. See Steve Chapman, "Switching sides on the virtues of government," *The Week*, 11 March 2005, 14.

11. E.J. Dionne, "Power of negative thinking," *Denver Post*, 12 November 2004, 5(E). See also Bill Press, "Senate Democrats caving in before Republican counterparts," *Rocky Mountain News*, 2 April 2005, 13(C).

12. Arthur Schlesinger Jr., "Opportunity Knocks," *The American Prospect*, December, 2004, 24–25. See also "Tax & Spend: The unapologetic case for big government," *The American Prospect*, May 2005, A1–A23.

13. Arthur M. Schlesinger, Jr., *War And The American Presidency* (New York: W.W. Norton, 2004), 100–102.

14. Schlesinger, *The American Presidency*, 102–103.

15. Schlesinger, *The American Presidency*, 103.

16. "Republicans strengthen their control of Congress," *The Week*, 12 November 2004, 7.

17. Special Report, "Does Your Vote Matter?" *Business Week*, 14 June 2004, p. 66.

18. Special Report, "Does Your Vote Matter?" 66.

19. Special Report, "Does Your Vote Matter?" 66.

20. Special Report, "Does Your Vote Matter?" 66.

21. Michael Duffy and Douglas Waller, "What We'll Miss And What We Won't," *Time*, 29 November 2004, 32–34.

22. Special Report, "Does Your Vote Matter?" 74.

23. Thomas B. Edsall and James V. Grimaldi, "On Nov. 2, GOP Got More Bang For Its Billion, Analysis Shows," *Washington Post*, 30 December 2004, A(01).

24. Special Report, "Does Your Vote Matter?", 74–75.

25. Robert A. Pastor, "America Observed," *The American Prospect*, January 2005, A3.

26. Molly Ivins and Lou Dubose, *Bushwhacked: Life in George W. Bush's America* (New York: Random House, 2003), 297.

27. Thomas B. Edsall, "Study says corporate PACs gave GOP more," *Times-Picayune*, 26 November 2004, A(12)

28. Pastor, "America Observed," p. A2.

29. Tova Andrea Wang, "2004: A Report Card," *The American Prospect*, January 2005, A4–5.

30. Wang, "A Report Card," A5.

31. Wang, "A Report Card," A5–6.

32. Wang, "A Report Card," A4.

33. Wang, "A Report Card," A6.

34. See Wang, "A Report Card," A6–7. See also Steven Carbo, "Color It Wrong," *The American Prospect*, January 2005, A14–16.

35. Pastor, "America Observed," A2–3.

36. Wang, "A Report Card," A7. See also Miles S. Rapoport, "The Democracy We Deserve," *The American Prospect*, January 2005, A8–10. See also "The New Ballot Box," *The American Prospect*, May 2006, A1–A11.

37. Mike France and Lorraine Woellert, "The Battle Over The Courts," *Business Week*, 27 September 2004, 38.

38. France and Woellert, "Courts," 26–27.

39. France and Woellert, "Courts," 40.

40. In 2004 the Illinois Civil Justice League which is backed by corporations, asked all judicial candidates in the state about their views on everything from class-action rules to the constitutionality of punitive damages. The League of Christian Voters in Alabama asked state supreme court candidates to provide answers to questions involving whether they are born-again Christians, go to church, and define marriage as a union between a man and a woman. France and Woellert, "Courts," 41.

41. France and Woellert, "Courts," 44.

42. See George F. Will, "Bush v. Gore, Ticking Bomb," *Newsweek*, 25 October 2004, 114.

43. See Mike France, "One Man, One Vote, Two Lawyers," *Business Week*, 25 October 2004, 43.

Chapter Ten

The Future of America

There was a great deal of speculation after the 2004 election as to what kind of president Bush would be in his second term. During the campaign in 2000 Bush promised to unite the country and overcome the partisan bickering that had overtaken Washington during the Clinton administration. Yet he divided the country more than ever during his first term and governed from the right in pushing a conservative agenda relative to tax cuts, the war in Iraq, and other policies. The big question was whether this stance would change in the second term or whether Bush would pursue an even more partisan agenda since this time he seemed to have at least something of a mandate. Would he live up to the promises he made in the 2000 campaign to be a more compassionate conservative, to run a humble foreign policy, and to be a uniter not a divider?[1]

One school of thought held that in their second term, presidents think more of their legacy than in pushing a new and risky agenda and become more conciliatory and willing to cooperate with the opposition. This school expected a mid-course correction on things like Iraq that had not gone well and an admission of errors that would help to soothe feelings about this endeavor. In a second term it was also believed that Bush would not push for major changes in the tax code and Social Security but would settle for smaller changes along the lines of tax simplification and perhaps some demonstration projects on privatization of Social Security. Since Bush did not have to worry about another term, there would be less pressure to prove his conservative credentials.

The other school of thought scoffed at this notion and believed Bush would continue to be who he is; tough, faith based, and unyielding on things in which he believes. Thus Bush was expected to hang tough on Iraq and continue to pursue an aggressive foreign policy that would involve confronting

Iran and North Korea about their nuclear arms programs. He was expected to push for dramatic changes in the tax code and aggressively pursue privatization of Social Security as well as tort reform. And rather than adopt a conciliatory approach to the appointment of judges to appease Democrats, he would continue to ask for the appointment of hard right-wing conservatives to the bench in order to reward the religious fundamentalists who seemed to have provided him with his margin of victory. They were expecting action on abortion and gay marriage.[2]

Then there is what might be called the pragmatic school which believed that no matter what Bush might want to do, he was hemmed in by certain realities that even he could not ignore. With respect to foreign policy the U.S. does not have the military resources to continue an aggressive, unilateral foreign policy based on the threat of military force rather than diplomacy. We are stretched thin in this regard and may not even be able to maintain our troop level in Iraq at its current level, to say nothing of further commitments elsewhere. Thus our foreign policy will have to be less aggressive, less militant, less unilateral, and less arrogant.[3] With regard to domestic policies the country does not have the money to afford any bold new policies that will add to the nation's debt, which is at record levels.[4] Finally, this school believes Bush would have to heal the wounds in this country if he wanted to get anything done as contentiousness is no longer in his interest. He was elected by only 51 percent of the people, which is hardly a landslide and does not constitute a clear mandate to do anything.

Which of these schools of thought is most realistic? Perhaps Bush gave the country a clue in his first press conference after the election, when he was anything but humble. In response to questions about what he was going to do in a second term, he replied, "I earned capital in the campaign, and now I intend to spend it."[5] In the article announcing Bush as Time Magazine's Person of the Year, the authors portray Bush as a man prepared to leave the "death of compromise" as his second-term legacy. He is reported to have said at his moment of victory, "I've got the will of the people at my back." With regard to bipartisanship he stated, "I'll reach out to everyone who shares our goals," meaning those who fall in line with his policies. He made it clear that he was not about to change his mind with regard to Social Security and the tax code in pursuit of his "ownership society."[6]

Actions followed these words. At the end of December it was announced that Bush planned to nominate for a second time 20 people whom the Democrats prevented from coming to a vote on their nomination for federal judgeships. Among these 20 were 12 people renominated for the U.S. Court of Appeals, including Priscilla Owen to the 5th Circuit Court of Appeals in New Orleans. Missing from this list was Charles Pickering Sr., who was elevated to the appeals court by a recess appointment which did not need congressional approval. Pickering decided to retire and not seek nomination for a permanent seat. Nonetheless it seemed as if this action signaled that the president intended to renew partisan warfare.[7]

His appointments of Condoleeza Rice as secretary of state and Alberto Gonzales as attorney general can be read as an emphasis on wanting people in these positions who are loyalists and were not going to give Bush much, if any, opposition to the things he wants done. He wants unity in his administration if not in the society at large. Then came the push for Social Security reform and a "full speed ahead and dam the torpedos" attitude towards the federal deficit. The transition costs of giving younger workers the option to invest some of their Social Security payments in the stock market would be anywhere from $1 to 2 trillion, a sum that the administration said would be borrowed rather than paid for in some fashion. With these actions it seems clear in which direction Bush was headed in his second term.

FISCAL POLICY

The Bush agenda included at least four major policy areas where he wanted to make changes: (1) changing Social Security to allow young workers to invest some of their funds in the stock market, (2) making the tax cuts approved in his first term permanent, (3) reforming the tax code which could mean simply tax simplification or more radical measures such as enacting a flat tax or perhaps a national sales tax, and (4) tort reform to reduce the exposure of doctors and businesses in liability lawsuits. All of these were somehow related to Bush's concept of an ownership society in which people are allowed more control over their lives and which others saw as an "every man for himself and the devil take the hindmost" attitude.

All these changes, however, must be seen against the backdrop of the financial situation facing the nation. During its first term the Bush administration had seen the projected $5 trillion surplus disappear to be replaced with some $5 trillion in new debts over the coming decade. The Congressional Budget Office estimates that making the 2001 and 2003 tax cuts permanent will cost about $4 trillion over the next decade, making them the most critical part of this long-term fiscal threat. Add to this the $2 trillion cost to finance the transition of Social Security privatization, which will add $200 billion a year to the federal deficit, and it seems clear that federal spending is out of control.[8]

The $236 billion surplus of 2000 has become a $400 billion annual deficit. Making the tax cut permanent means that deficits will continue for another 10 years according to the Congressional Budget Office.[9] The Bush administration and its Republican allies in Congress have lowered taxes, increased defense expenditures, increased benefits, and increased discretionary spending. They have presided over an explosion of government spending. Overall federal spending has risen 33 percent since Bush took office, twice as fast as under Clinton and faster than any other president since Lyndon B. Johnson.[10] The federal debt limit as been raised four time under the Bush administration to nearly $10 trillion, almost double the $5.7 trillion when Bush took office. According to some commentators, it is hypocrisy for Republicans to define themselves as fiscal conservatives.[11]

All the Republicans can to is continue to cut taxes. In May 2006, they sent Bush a $69 billion package for tax reduction that would extend until 2010 the 15 percent tax rate on capital gains and dividend income. These cuts initially passed in 2003 were set to expire in 2008. Previously these rate had been as high as 20 percent and 38.6 percent respectively. the bill also contained a one-year reprieve for the roughly 15 million taxpayers who would be faced with paying the alternative minimum tax originally designed to prevent wealthy citizens from escaping taxes entirely. Taken as a whole, this tax package would give an average cut of $47 to families earning between $40,000 and $50,000 and $42,766 to families with incomes of more that $1 million. To say that the benefits are extremely skewed towards the rich is an understatement.[12]

Does anyone care about this deficit.[13] This budget deficit, along with our expanding trade deficit, means that this county soaks up about 80 percent of the world's savings. We have to sell some $2 billion treasury securities every day to the world's financial markets to finance these deficits. The question is how long the world will continue to finance our life style or will it find other priorities. As the world loses confidence in our ability to get our fiscal house in order, the dollar may continue to decline more than it already has, and eventually other countries are going to demand a higher interest rate to finance our debt. This would most likely lead to a decline of our economy as low interest rates are necessary to spur private investment that increases growth of the economy.

Are the Bush administration's economic policies leading us to a fiscal armegeddon? Alan Greenspan, former chairman of the Federal Reserve, warned that accumulating deficits are dangerous to our economic health. While at the moment we may be all right, "net claims against residents of the United States cannot continue to increase forever in international portfolios at their recent pace." In other words we cannot go on forever relying on foreign investors to support our free-spending ways. Rather than increasing spending, we should be reducing budget deficits and reigning in spending.[14]

Even the Heritage Foundation, a conservative group if there ever was one, has to admit that while economic freedom is expanding around the world, it is stagnant in this country. Based upon findings in the 11th edition of The Index of Economic Freedom, jointly produced by the Heritage Foundation and the Wall Street Journal, Dr. Ed Feulner, president of the Heritage Foundation, says that our government is losing its leadership on the very thing that has been the foundation of our strength; economic freedom. The United States has allowed higher government spending and protectionist measures to drag our economy down.[15]

No one in the administration seems to be alarmed about these trends as they push ahead with their agenda. They continue to engage in "creative accounting" practices to make it appear that the president can fulfill his promise to cut the deficit in half by 2009. For example, they decided to measure their progress against the $521 billion deficit that was previously predicted rather than the actual shortfall of $413 billion, a move that allows them to say they have already reduced the deficit by $100 billion and claim success if the deficit falls to $260 billion. In addition they assume that there will be a surge of $200 billion in tax revenues in 2005, the largest one-year jump in history, and an increase of $700 billion by 2009.[16] And the budget excluded the costs for the wars in Iraq and Afghanistan, which reached $100 billion in 2005 as well as the $200 billion cost of privatizing Social Security. Congress passed a law to require corporations to be more honest in their accounting practices in light of the corporate scandals of a few years ago. Apparently we need a similar law passed for the government itself.

And there are other problems. The middle class faces a squeeze as even two-income families have less discretionary income and less savings potential than did a single-income family of a generation ago. People who work for $65,000 or less, which is roughly 80 percent of our working population, see themselves falling further and further behind.[18] One problem is the exposure to well-educated workers in low wage environments like China and India that are now connected to us by real-time technology.[19] Two million jobs were lost during Bush's first term, and a record 45 million people lack health insurance. Some 35.9 million Americans are living in poverty, an increase of 4 million since Bush became president.[20] Meanwhile the gap widens between the income of middle-class families and those of the wealthy and higher reaches of management. How long will Americans continue to tolerate this situation?

SOCIAL SECURITY

The Bush administration chose to focus its initial efforts of reform of the Social Security system by creating a crisis situation where many think none exists. The basic plan is to allow workers to shift a portion of their payroll taxes from the Social Security system to their own investment accounts. Workers under 55 would be able to divert 4 percentage points of their 12.4 percent annual payroll tax that goes to Social Security into private accounts up to a maximum of $1,000 a year.[21] The idea is to allow workers to benefit from the higher returns the stock market can provide and build up a nice nest egg for themselves to use for retirement purposes.

The problem is that such a plan would reduce the amount of money available to pay benefits to current retirees and shrink promised benefits for future pensioners. With respect to the first problem, the transition costs are estimated at anywhere from $1 to $2 trillion, a staggering sum by anyone's standards. These costs arise because Social Security is a pay-as-you-go-system, or an intergenerational transfer, meaning that the money paid in by workers today is used to pay benefits to current retirees. There is no investment fund of any kind used to pay benefits. Thus if younger workers in the future divert part of the taxes into private investment accounts, there will be less money available to pay current retirees.

Since Bush has promised not to raise taxes to cover this shortfall, this means the money would have to be borrowed and would add to already record deficits as stated earlier. The Bush administration has floated an idea that is typical of its approach to fiscal matters. It claims that any transition costs would be offset by a corresponding decrease in long-term debt because benefits to future retirees would be reduced. Thus there is no net change in government borrowing because the money borrowed would eventually be put back into the system and the money that would have to be borrowed to pay current retirees should not be counted in the budget.[22] Never mind that his offset wouldn't happen for several decades while the money that is borrowed enters the system immediately and adds to the deficit burden the government is carrying. The money has to be borrowed from somewhere and interest paid on the money borrowed.

The second problem arises because if younger workers put part of the payroll taxes into private accounts, they cannot expect to get full benefits from Social Security. Some estimates show that today's 20-year-olds would see their benefits cut by nearly half, leaving them a check when they retire that would equal only 15 percent of their annual income.[23] The reason for such a drastic reduction is that the administration would also change the way benefits are calculated. Under today's system first-year benefits are tied to increases in average wages during the retiree's working experience. Under the proposed system, they would be tied to price inflation. Since prices grow more slowly than wages, this seemingly innocuous shift would mean that by 2075 benefits would decrease by close to 40 percent.[24]

The Bush administration claims that the system is in crisis and needs fixing before a disaster results. More and more baby boomers are getting ready to retire over the next few decades, and the ratio of workers paying taxes to retirees collecting benefits will drop dramatically. In 1955 the ratio was 8.6 workers for every retiree. In 2040 the ratio is expected to drop to 2 workers for every retiree.[25] This situation is not sustainable and has to be corrected before it becomes a real problem, so claims the administration. If nothing is done, the system may not have enough money to pay today's young workers their full benefits.

But what is the actual situation? The system has been running a surplus for some years now because birth rates were down during the depression years, and thus current workers have been putting more into the system than retirees have been taking out in the form of benefits. This surplus is expected to continue until 2018 when baby boomers retire and demand more cash from the system. Thus the surplus will start to be drawn down, but the system can still pay all promised benefits until 2042, according to a Social Security Administration estimate. The Congressional Budget Office puts the date at 2052 because of different economic and demographic assessments. Even after that date, Social Security taxes would cover about 70 percent of planned benefits.[26]

So is there a crisis? Some claim that this so-called crisis is no different than the runup to the war in Iraq. This administration, it is said, falsely hypes every issue as a crisis. We have been through this kind of propagandizing before and should not fall for these kinds of scare tactics again.[27] The push for private accounts is likely to be a replay of the presidential campaign. On the one side are the Democrats and their allies who want to defend their most sacred legacy from the New Deal-coalition and claim that the Bush administration plan will benefit Wall Street and wipe out a plan that has worked so successfully. On the other side are the Republicans and their allies who will push for the ownership society and privatization of social programs.

About 48 million Americans receive Social Security benefits. While Roosevelt never intended the system to be the sole source of retirement funds, for about 20 percent of retirees it has become just that. About two-thirds of retirees count on it for about half their income[28] so any drastic changes to the program will affect the lives of millions of Americans for better or worse. These changes should be done carefully and honestly, and it is the latter where most people who are engaging in the debate seem to be lacking. There are two aspects to this dishonesty, the real nature of the Social Security trust fund and the real nature of stock market returns.

While indeed Social Security may be solvent until 2042 or 2052, it must be noted that the so-called surplus that has been built up in the system has been used to fund the federal budget. The government has actually borrowed that money from the Social Security trust fund by issuing bonds that pay about 2 percent interest on average. This kind of borrowing does not raise interest rates because the government gets the money from itself and does not have to compete for savings in the capital markets.[29] Thus the surplus is nothing more than IOUs from one part of the government to another. There is no money invested in anything that can be drawn down to pay benefits.

This situation will change already in 2011, when the surplus will drop rapidly. At that time the government will have to start borrowing to make up the difference between the $100 billion a year it has been borrowing and the dwindling surplus. By 2018 when the Social Security system starts taking in less money in payroll taxes than it pays in benefits, the system will have to start cashing in its government bonds to keep on paying benefits. According to one estimate, the government will have to raise an additional $225 billion a year in current dollars by 2030 to pay off the bonds coming due in that year alone.[30]

This seems to be the real crisis; that the government has an unfunded liability that will add significantly to the deficit if something isn't done to change the system. While private accounts are being touted as the solution to the problem, one has to wonder if the most important feature is the proposal to index benefits to prices rather than wages. According to one estimate, this feature would reduce benefits for younger people so drastically that by 2050 the system would begin generating huge surpluses.[31] This feature has not been trumpeted by the administration, and for good reason. It is another attempt to place the burden of the government's increasing deficit on future generations.

All this would be well and good if future retirees could indeed build up a nice nest egg for retirement by investing in the market, but the way this program is being touted by the administration gives the impression that the stock market never takes a downturn. While it may return 7 percent annually on average, that is an average, not a guaranteed yearly return. The stock market has had some significant downturns in its history, and there were many periods when the return was negative for several years. It seems as if we have already forgotten recent history when the bubble burst at the turn of the century.

Some people who are retiring are going to be caught in this downturn and lose a significant amount of their nest egg just when they need it for retirement. And then what is going to happen? If there are significant numbers of people involved who represent enough votes to affect an election, they are going to go hat in hand to government and ask for a bail out by the government. And if the government has directed the way money can be invested by restricting it to so called "safe" investments, they will have a good argument in saying the government should have let them invest their money any way they wanted and they might have been able to get positive returns in a downturn. There is an even bet that politicians will respond to this situation, and what we will end up with is privatization of the gains and socialization of the losses, further increasing the government's debt burden.[32]

All in all, private accounts do not make sense. They take both the social and security aspects out of the system. The idea behind Social Security was to make some kind of contract between generations and build in a promise that the young would take care of those who worked all their lives and deserve to retire in dignity. The security part is that there would be some money there to retire on that did not depend on the fluctuations of the market. It would be guaranteed by the government of the United States and would keep pace with inflation. And since benefits are tied to the amount of wages the retiree earns in his or her lifetime, there is also a degree of fairness to the system.

Fairness was at issue in another Bush proposal that would have cut benefits for upper-and middle-income people and preserve them for the poorest 30 percent. Workers earning more than $36,500 would have their benefits cut in the interests of providing benefits for the poorest people in society. This was a ploy to put the Democrats in a bind, who have traditionally been champions of the poor and downtrodden. How could they oppose a plan that targeted poor people? The problem was, as critics pointed out, that this plan changed Social Security into a welfare program which higher-income workers would come to resent. Support for the system would decline and eventually Congress would find reason to scrap the system, which is probably what Bush had in mind.[33]

If the Bush administration were serious about fixing just the Social Security system, there are many less radical alternatives could be proposed. Because people are living longer and are in better health, the retirement age could be raised to say age 70, which might be more realistic. Another alternative is to raise the ceiling on taxable income. Currently only the first $90,000 of income is subject to the payroll tax, and raising this to say $140,000 would raise more money for the system and affect only a small percentage of the workforce. The payroll tax itself could also be increased from the current 12.4 percent (the worker's share is 6.2 percent of wage and salary income), but this would disproportionately affect working-class and middle-class families and is not very popular.[34]

Another proposal would change existing individual retirement accounts (401K plans) to make them more attractive to lower-income workers. This would be accomplished by turning the current tax exclusion for annual contributions into a credit, which would benefit people in lower tax brackets. People are not saving enough for retirement, but rather than change the Social Security system, this kind of add-on account would encourage more private saving and take place outside the Social Security system. Variations of this idea include a government match for the contributions of low-income workers and making them automatically part of the scheme unless they choose to opt out.[35]

Then there is the argument that the problem may take care of itself. The projections about the shortfall in Social Security funds are far out into the future. After all 2042 and 2052 are decades away, and much can change during that time. The shortfall occurs in part from pessimistic projections of a steep slowdown in economic and population growth. But if the country matched its growth rates of the past 75 years for the next 75 years, according to projections by the Social Security Administration (SSA), there would be no shortfall. The SSA has adjusted its numbers every year since the mid 1990s, lowering the shortfall and pushing doomsday back every time. So why not wait and see how all this plays out rather than making a major change to the system at this point?[36] There is also something of a paradox here in that if the economy does not grow enough to wipe out the shortfall, the stock market is not going to be doing well either, so private accounts are no solution.

The best solution, however, is to take the Social Security surplus that is currently accumulating and invest it in a relatively safe place to earn a higher rate of return than Treasury securities are earning. Alan Sloan, for example, wants to amend the law so the Social Security fund can buy mortgage-backed securities, high-grade corporate bonds, and other such investments and in addition make the government pay cash interest on the $1.7 trillion of Treasury securities that the fund now owns. Under this plan by 2017 Social Security would have $3 trillion of mortgages and corporate bonds, and the interest on these securities would cover the program's cash deficit until 2026, buying time for a more permanent fix to the system. Of course this would mean that the government could not use Social Security surpluses to reduce the federal deficit, meaning the deficit for 2004 would have been a staggering $558 billion. Sloan realizes his proposal does not have a chance as Bush wants to continue to disparage the trust fund while using the surpluses to offset revenue losses from massive tax cuts.[37] So much for fiscal sanity.

The Republicans came up with a variation of this theme by proposing to divert the surplus to create individual investment accounts for workers under 55 unless they opted out of the program. Workers who chose such accounts would have their benefits reduced by the amount placed in their accounts plus interest. Initially investments would be limited to Treasury bonds, which pay the same as current benefits, but in 2008 workers could diversify their investments. The program would gradually decline and end in 2017 when the surplus is projected to vanish. This proposal contained no cuts in benefits, no increases in taxes, and no changes in the retirement age, thus avoiding the hard choices that may be necessary to fix the system. This plan has been criticized as having all the faults of the Bush plan. It does nothing to deal with the long-term solvency of the system, and only hastens the trust fund's demise.[38]

It seems clear that what Bush really wants to do is destroy the Social Security system as we know it and increase the risk of retirement for most Americans. The opportunity society is only an opportunity for the rich to get richer while the rest of the people struggle to keep their heads above water. The American public seemed to realize this as they failed to buy into the Bush plan despite the administration's efforts. Their propaganda machine failed on this count, and Social Security reform seems to be a dead issue.[39] If the Bush administration were really serious about tackling long-term problems with entitlements, it would focus its efforts on Medicare, which many think is much more of an immediate problem because the projected shortfall is triple that of the Social Security System.[40] Instead it made the Medicare situation worse with its prescription drug plan for seniors.

THE VISION THING

After the 2004 election Bush triumphantly announced that he had earned political capital he intended to spend. Why he would choose to spend so much of that capital on Social Security reform, however, was a mystery to many people. Granted that Social Security needs attention given the retirement of baby boomers, but why such a drastic reform that would change the system into something different when mere tinkering with the existing system would seem to solve the problem? It is in this effort that the Bush administration and its Republican allies in Congress may have shown their hand and revealed what kind of future they envision for the country. Couple this effort with other actions this administration has taken and we have a plausible scenario of where the Republicans would like to take the country.

The Social Security program is the backbone of the New Deal of Franklin Roosevelt. It is perhaps the key program of all those put into place in response to the Depression. It assured some retirement income for everyone who had ever worked in our society whether or not they had saved anything for retirement. It was not initially meant as the only source of retirement income, but as a supplement. However over time it became the only source for many people. Destroy Social Security and the door is wide open to do away with all the programs of the New Deal and subsequent efforts of the Democrats to build on this legacy with other entitlement programs. It is the cornerstone of the

Democratic Party's efforts to win the hearts and minds of the disadvantaged classes in our society and build a coalition that kept them in power for years.

What the Bush administration and its Republican allies seem to want is to turn back the clock to a time before the Roosevelt era, and by that I mean even before the time of Teddy Roosevelt, who after all had concern for the environment and worried about the power of big business. They want to return us to a period before the Interstate Commerce Act of 1897 and the Sherman Act of 1890 when capitalism was more or less unfettered and capitalists could do most anything they pleased without government interference. They want to recreate an aristocracy like that which existed in those years, where the Carnegies, Rockefellers, Morgans, and other like-minded aristocrats ran society and the government had to bend to their wishes.

The rationale behind all this is that giving free enterprise a free hand without government interference will result in economic growth that will benefit everyone. The phrase used most often to describe this rationale is that "a rising tide lifts all boats." Some boats may indeed be lifted much more than others as inequalities become greater, but everyone benefits to some extent and all are going to be better off than they were before. The problem with this metaphor is that the poorest people in our country don't even have a boat. It is unaffordable, so they drown or have to be evacuated as happened in New Orleans where the poor did not have a way to get out of town. And the boat for the middle class is so leaky they are barely able to keep afloat. Meanwhile the rich sail by in their bigger and fancier yachts, swamping anybody who gets close to them.

The case that this is the vision driving the Bush administration is compelling. Medicare is another staple of the Great Society program of the Democrats, and it would seem the prescription drug plan the Republicans were so anxious to pass gives evidence of their commitment to continue and strengthen this program. The devil is in the details, however, and as it got closer to the time to implement this provision, the motivation behind this plan became clearer. The Republicans are no bleeding heart liberals to be sure, and they did not pass this plan to benefit seniors who are struggling to pay for their drugs. As a senior who is on Medicare, I fully expect to pay more for health care in the future as Medicare premiums increase. The drug benefit will not offset these increases.

Seniors were confronted with a bewildering array of choices from many different companies all touting their drug benefits. They covered different drugs, have different deductibles, and other differences such that a senior was expected to be a whiz at statistics to figure out which plan will best serve his or her needs.[41] Many just threw up their hands and stuck with their current plan, especially if they had supplemental insurance that did have some drug coverage. The confusion was even greater than that which surrounded the issuance of drug cards which saved most of us a miniscule amount of money. The government did not seem overly concerned to simplify these choices and enforce some uniform rules that can be easily understood by seniors. Let free enterprise have its day by giving us more choices than we could possibly handle.

It is becoming more and more clear that in addition to the pharmaceutical companies the real beneficiaries of this program are the Health Maintenance Organizations (HMOs), who are being subsidized to the tune of billions of taxpayer dollars to offer seniors a choice, so to speak, of joining their program to receive the array of health benefits they have to offer. Never mind that they could not make money off seniors on their own such that many, if not most companies, pulled out of this market several years ago and left seniors in their plans high and dry. The real intent of this program is to wean, or perhaps even force, seniors out of traditional Medicare into HMO programs. The Bush administration and its Republican allies are willing to set aside their free market principles and go to any expense in the interests of destroying another entitlement program that has been successful in providing medical care to millions of seniors. But as people join HMOs, traditional Medicare will become more and more expensive and less of an option for more and more seniors. They will be forced to give up their choice of doctors to join a plan heavily subsidized by the government. Medicare as we know it will disappear.

The Bush administration will seize on every opportunity to cut programs that help the disadvantaged in society. Hurricane Katrina supposedly put the issue of poverty back on the national agenda, and the president promised bold action to deal with this problem. But again the devil is in the details. Conservatives used the storm as an excuse to suspend requirements that federal contractors who received no-bid contracts to rebuild New Orleans and the Gulf Coast have affirmative action plans and pay locally prevailing wages. The rationale was to help the rebuilding proceed quicker by removing bureaucratic road blocks. The reality is that it will help Bush's corporate cronies make more money at the expense of the poor and disadvantaged.[42]

The cost of rebuilding New Orleans and the Gulf Coast may be as much as $200 billion, and Bush called for spending cuts to offset this cost with no plans to rescind the tax cuts still on the agenda or do away with the pork in the energy and highway bills that were recently passed. Instead compassionate conservatism was at work again, as Republican leaders in Congress targeted Medicaid and food stamps for spending cuts. While the spending cuts in Medicaid and food stamps that were part of the congressional budget resolution reached in the spring of 2005 were put on hold, the chairman of the House Budget Committee wanted to raise these cuts by several billion dollars. Conservatives argued that the storm exposed the failure of programs to help the disadvantaged and have proposed tax-free zones for business and school vouchers as alternatives. Mike Pence, a Republican from Indiana who leads the conservative caucus, even had the audacity to suggest that tax reductions for the rich are a key to fighting poverty, despite the fact that the poverty rate has risen every year since Bush took office.[43]

Entitlement programs are thus a target of this administration, but not only entitlement programs are threatened. The whole structure of government's ability to regulate business and other institutions in society is under threat. This threat comes from changes in both personnel and the judicial philosophy dominating our courts, particularly the Supreme Court. In a book entitled "Radicals In Robes," by Cass R. Sunstein, this threat is spelled out in great detail. The author claims that since the election of Ronald Reagan, high-level Republicans in the White House and Senate have been able radically to transform the federal judiciary. A judiciary with a tendency towards left-wing activism has been replaced by one tending towards right-wing activism.[44] And the issues at stake include a lot more than just abortion.

Their agenda includes the following: (1) to reduce the power of the federal government including Congress itself, (2) to scale back the rights of those accused of crime, (3) to strike down affirmative action programs, (4) to eliminate campaign finance laws, (5) to diminish privacy rights, above all the right to abortion, (6) to invigorate the Constitution's Takings clause in order to insulate property rights from democratic control, (7) to forbid Congress from allowing citizens to bring suit to enforce environmental regulation, and (8) to protect commercial interests, including commercial advertisers, from government regulation.[45]

These groups believe that the American Constitution has been in exile at least since the 1930s when the New Deal of Franklin Roosevelt took effect. Before 1932 the national government had sharply limited power and the system of constitutional rights was radically different from what we see in effect today. With the Great Depression and the New Deal, the Supreme Court abandoned its commitment to the Constitution as it was originally written. Thus the real Constitution, sometimes called the Constitution in Exile, must be restored and affirmative action programs, campaign finance regulation, and environmental regulations, among other things, must be struck down. The Constitution means what it meant when it was ratified, and we must return to that interpretation even if it results in a radical change in our institutions and in certain rights American have come to take for granted.[46]

Thus constitutional questions become historical ones, and it must be read to fit with the original understanding of the founding fathers. If it was not originally understood to ban sex discrimination or racial segregation, protect privacy, or protect the environment at the expense of property rights, then judges have no authority to depart from this original understanding.[47] From this view comes the idea of strict construction, that judges should not legislate from the bench but should follow the strict guidelines laid down in the Constitution. They should not impose their own values and preferences when making judicial decisions.

But there are many problems with this view which the strict constructionists ignore. For one thing many provisions of the Constitution are stated in general terms suggesting that broad principles are involved. Terms like "equal protection" and "freedom of speech" are not spelled out specifically as to their meaning, and thus new issues that come along which the framers could not possibly have foreseen have to be judged as to whether they fall under these broad principles. Does wiretapping, for example, fall under the Fourth Amendment's ban on unreasonable searches and seizures? Since it isn't specifically mentioned in the amendment, a strict constructionist would have to say no, a position most reasonable people would reject. The point is we live in a different world from the ratifiers, a world they could not possibly have envisioned. We have to decide whether specific issues in our time fall under the broad provisions of the Constitution, and we cannot appeal to a so-called original understanding of the framers or ratifiers of the Constitution.

Political neutrality is a pretense as those who adhere to a so-called original understanding of the Constitution have adopted a certain kind of judicial or political philosophy and argue that this is the only approach that deserves to be taken with respect to interpretation of the Constitution. Even assuming we could accurately discern the original understanding of the ratifiers, why should people living today be bound by the decisions of those who lived many generations ago? The group who ratified the Constitution was a small subset of the population; it did not include any women, the vast majority of blacks, many of those without property, and others who were not permitted to vote. As Sunstein states, "Does the ideal of democracy strongly argue in favor of binding current generations to the understandings of a small portion of the population from centuries ago?"[48]

Sunstein argues that those who adhere to some kind of original understanding of the Constitution, what he calls fundamentalists, offer an unmistakable partisan vision of the Constitution that fits with the extreme right wing of the Republican Party. Their view of the Constitution casts serious doubts on affirmative action programs, gun control laws, restrictions on commercial advertising, environmental regulations, campaign finance reform, and laws that permit citizens to sue to enforce the federal law. It questions the existence of many federal agencies such as the Environmental Protection Agency. It questions a right to privacy and allows the federal government to discriminate on the basis of race. It permits states to benefit religious believers and perhaps even to establish churches. And it imposes sharp limits on Congress's power to regulate interstate commerce and to enforce the guarantees of the Fourteenth Amendment.[49]

Over the past two decades, Sunstein claims, such fundamentalism has had a large influence on the Supreme Court as the Rehnquist Court invalidated about three dozen congressional enactments from 1985 to 2005, a record of activism unparalleled in the nation's history.[50] But the fundamentalists want a lot more, and they may get it with the Supreme Court appointments of the Bush administration. We may wake up one day to find that we live in a much different country than we had thought, where basic liberties and freedoms we have taken for granted are in jeopardy. The questions for the country to ask are: Is this the kind of society in which we want to live? Would it be a just society that promotes the ideal of equal opportunity for all its citizens? Would it be a society that cared about environmental problems that could affect future generations and their ability to live a good life? There are many other similar questions that need to be asked.

The sixties were a time of social revolution, and I consider myself a product of these years, having been involved in the Civil Rights Movement and working for consumer and environmental causes. Our goal in those years was nothing less than to build the great society, to use Lyndon Johnson's phrase, and government was the instrument to accomplish these goals. We were going to eliminate poverty with government programs, promote equal opportunity through civil and equal rights legislation, protect consumer rights and clean up pollution through government regulation, create safe workplaces with government inspections, and many other such measures. The problem was that government became overbearing, government was everywhere, and this became a problem for business and some individuals.

Reagan got into office by arguing that government is the problem and not the solution, and this philosophy took root in providing the foundation for the modern conservative movement. It is the philosophy that prevails in the federal government today and finds its culmination in the Bush administration and its Republican allies who want to turn back the clock a century or more to an era of unfettered capitalism. What Reagan began Bush wants to complete. The evidence is rather compelling that this is the vision that is slowly but surely being implemented in our society.[51]

Thus one final way of looking at the divide in our society is to think of it as a divide between those of us who want to hang onto the ideals embedded in the New Deal of Franklin Roosevelt and the the Great Society of Lyndon Johnson and those who don't. Granted the government may have become too pervasive in society, but we do not want to give up equal opportunity, elimination of poverty, retirement with dignity, a clean environment, worker and consumer protection, and other such ideals. On the other side of the divide are those who would do away with entitlement programs to help the disadvantaged, abolish any form of affirmative action, severely limit the government's ability to regulate business in the interests of a clean environment, and so forth. It is a divide that continues to get deeper as the goals of the conservative movement are realized more and more throughout our society. This battle is being fought on many fronts.

The Democrats, however, do not seem to understand they are engaged in a war for the future of the country and are not just competing for particular offices in government. For the Republicans politics is war by other means and the Democrats do not seem to understand the nature of the war in which they are engaged. The issue is not just abortion, but the role of government and religion in society. Democrats do not have a competing vision for the country that can energize them and engage voters. They keep giving away what few weapons they have as they did with the fillibuster allowing more federal judges to be appointed who can further undermine what they stand for. If they can't get their act together now that they have control of Congress and begin to counter the Republican offensive, then I think it may be time for a third party.

This third party could draw the moderates from both the Republicans and Democrats, the centrists who are concerned with fiscal responsibility and are not locked into hardened positions on social issues but who can actually intelligently discuss abortion and gay marriage as well as stem cell research and other social issues. They are people concerned about the growing inequality in our society and realize that the environment has to receive more attention than it has in the Bush administration. This third party would not have to win control of the House and Senate to gain influence but only capture enough seats in both chambers to wield the balance of power by denying either major party a majority. Nothing could get done without their support, and thus they could insist that their agenda be addressed in bills passed by either chamber. While I do not have a name for this third party, I do have an agenda to suggest.

INTELLIGENT DESIGN

The conservative agenda is bankrupt to deal with the new issues emerging in our society and the world. The liberal agenda focusing on entitlement programs and social issues is equally bankrupt. It seems to me we are in the midst of a radical discontinuity in history; new issues are emerging that involve radical changes in the way we live and work and go about our daily routines. We cannot cope with these issues by simply making minor changes to the way we do things and the way we think about our lives. Existing programs and institutions that have served us so well in the past may not be relevant to the changes needed in the current world in which we live. While all this may seem a bit grandiose, let me make the case for such a discontinuity.

While intelligent design is in the news a good bit these days, it is a theology as currently understood that some want to teach in public schools. What intelligent design needs to become is a policy that finds its way into what governments at every level do in their policy decisions, what business organizations do in their planning for the future, and what individuals do as they live out their daily lives. We need to redesign almost everything in this society to respond to the twin issues of energy and climate change. These are the two issues more than anything else that make our time one of a radical discontinuity with the past.

Higher energy prices are here to stay given increasing world demand and dwindling supplies, and we are not going to drill our way to energy independence by opening up the Arctic National Wildlife Refuge or any other area for that matter. Nor is ripping the mountains apart in western Colorado to get at the oil shale deposits the answer. These efforts may make a lot of money for oil and gas companies, but they are not going to bring energy prices down to previous levels. And climate change is real and cannot be wished away or ignored. Whether or not carbon dioxide is the culprit, the earth is warming and this has implications for where people live and how we build and protect vulnerable cities along coastal areas.

We need to redesign the way our houses are built to take more advantage of solar energy. The technology to do this has been available for years, but we have not built energy-efficient houses on anything like a large enough scale. The same goes for apartment buildings and condo complexes. The condo building in which I live in Denver should have solar panels on its roof that could supply a good deal of energy for the building. The sun shines in Denver on more days than it does in Miami, and yet this energy is wasted because we do not build the capacity to collect and use it to supply our energy needs on a large enough scale.

We need to redesign our cities to be more energy efficient and reduce urban sprawl that necessitates longer and longer commutes. As people search for an affordable home and their piece of the American dream, they are driven further and further away from their jobs in the city, turning the daily rat race into a marathon. Extreme commuters defined as those who drive more than 90 minutes to work one way, are the fastest growing group of commuters. More than 3.4 million people have that long a commute, double the 1990 rate. Nearly 10 million people drive more than an hour to work, up 50 percent from the 1990 rate. The average commute is 25 minutes, up 18 percent from two decades ago. There are more than 226 million cars and trucks on the nation's roads, up from 59 million a half century ago. Moving jobs to the suburbs isn't the answer as commuters continue to drive away from them as well.[52]

There was a major project that was recently finished in Denver to widen Interstate 25 from downtown Denver to the southern edge of the city. It was called T-Rex for a reason and cost billions of dollars and took many years to complete. Supposedly it is to relieve traffic congestion on the interstate, but what people who make the decisions about these projects fail to realize is that they are dealing with a dynamic situation. My guess is that in just a few years after completion of the project, the interstate will be as congested as ever. All it will do is to encourage more people to move to the southern suburbs in the hopes that the commute will be easier, but as more and more people make this move, it will become just as congested as before.

During the period I lived in New Orleans, the north shore of Lake Ponchatrain experienced rapid growth as people left the city to live in a more pleasing and safe environment. The existing causeway across the lake became more and more congested, of course, as people commuted to and from work in the city. The solution was to build another causeway to relieve the congestion. If this were to be built, it would only encourage more people to move to the north shore and in a few short years the congestion would be as bad as ever, requiring another solution, which would most likely be another causeway.

Rather than building highways to relieve existing traffic congestion, we need to build highways with a projection of what decisions people will make with respect to that highway. Planners need to ask whether they want more people to move to the suburbs. That's what the highway rebuilding is really all about. Do people in southeastern Louisiana want more people to move out of New Orleans to the north shore? Of course the latter may be a moot point now in light of hurricane Katrina, but the example still holds. We do not seem to ask the right questions when it comes to highway projects and then are surprised when the expected results do not happen.

We just keep doing the same things over and over again. We keep drilling for oil and gas on every available square inch of federal land, we keep building the majority of our houses and office buildings the same way, we keep building the majority of our cars the same way, we keep living and thinking the same way. All of this may have to change if we are to survive and continue to have something of a satisfactory life. While changes are taking place relative to alternative energy sources and more fuel efficient cars, they are not taking place fast enough and on a large enough scale. We don't want major change nor do we want to upset our version of the American dream. But the environment in which we live is changing whether we like it or not, and we have no choice but to change in response. The question is will it be an intelligent response.

THE VALUES DIVIDE REVISITED

The values divide in this country is many things as shown in the table below; it is not just one set of values over which we differ. The divide is over traditional American values that I grew up with and that served this country well during the last century. It is between those who believe in a more aggressive military posture and support preemptive and preventive wars despite all their problems versus those who adhere to a more defensive military posture that uses military force only in response to an actual attack. It is between those who want to do away with all taxes on capital, a policy that favors the rich, and those who still believe in a progressive tax system. The divide is between those who are willing to sacrifice freedom for security and those who will not sacrifice certain freedoms under any circumstances. It is between those who see the natural environment as something that provides resources to be exploited as fast as possible and as a place to dump our waste into without worrying about the consequences versus those who believe nature needs to be protected from abuse and preserved for future generations.

Regarding religion, the divide is between those who think truth is absolute and from only one source, that being God's revealed truth in a holy book like the Bible, and those who believe there are many sources of truth including science and experience among other things. It is between those who think society should be religious through and through and religious belief ought to guide everything society does versus those who believe in a secularist approach to society where religion is just one part of a complex mix of factors that go into decision making. It is between those who would tear down the walls between church and state and fund more faith-based programs and support the teaching

The Values Divide

Traditional Values

Preemptive or Preventive Wars	Defensive Wars in Most Cases
Security at Expense of Freedom	Certain Freedoms are Sacred
Tax System That Favor the Rich	Progressive Tax System
Exploit and Use Nature	Protect and Conserve Nature

Religious Values

Absolute Approach to Truth	Pluralistic Approach to Truth
Religious Approach to Society	Secularist Approach to Society
Religion Dominates the State	Separation of Church and State

Political Values

One-Party Dominance	Division of Power
Unfettered Capitalism	Regulated Capitalism

of intelligent design and creationism in public schools and those who want to see religion kept out of the state's affairs.

Finally, with respect to the government and the future of the country, the divide is between those who want to create a one-party state that has complete control of the government into perpetuity and those who want to revitalize democracy with a viable two-party system if not even a third party to reflect the diversity in the country. And it is between those who want to create an unfettered capitalistic society by destroying government programs and severely restrict its ability to regulate business versus those who want to preserve those programs that work and recognize that regulations are needed to protect the environment and balance the rights of citizens against corporate power.

People may find themselves on different sides of this divide with respect to different issues, but I suspect research would show that many if not most, people in our society adhere to the full set of values on one side or the other. The left side in the above table roughly represents the conservative position and the right side the liberal position as these positions are now understood in our society. The meaning of these terms, of course, changes over time. What used to be called liberal no longer exists. What was moderate is now liberal, what was conservative is now moderate, and the conservative position these days used to be called the far right. In any event the divide over these values is real and is most apparent when it comes to the election of government officials.

This brings me to a final comment. What kind of government do we want in the future? The conservative revolution that began in the Reagan years has a very negative view of government. Government is the problem, not the solution. Government only interferes with the efficient working of the free market system and should get off the backs of business. It is not something that can play a positive role in society but should be reduced in size until it can be drowned in a bathtub, to use the words of Grover Nordquist, the head of a group devoted to cutting taxes and reducing the size of government. Reagan even advocated that people considering government service should see it as a second career to be gone into only after they have made a success in the private sector. Public service is not something young people out of college should consider as it is not worth their time and effort.

We get the kind of government we want and after some years of this attitude we get a government that appoints incompetent people to head organizations like the Federal Emergency Management Administration (FEMA) and so, sure enough, it fails miserably in response to hurricanes—so miserably, in fact, that I find myself thinking the government ought to get out of the business of responding to disasters that hit the nation. Do away with FEMA, and while we are at it, the Homeland Security Department. The private response to Hurricane Katrina was overwhelming, so maybe it would be better to let private organizations direct the response effort, which they did to a large extent, and make it easier for private individuals to donate to these organizations. Do away with these government bureaucracies. The point is this negative view of government becomes a self-fulfilling prophecy.

What we have now, it seems, is a government composed of too many people who don't believe in government. They campaign and win elections by being against government and promising to cut spending and government programs. Would business or any other organization hire people who didn't believe in what the organization is doing and have a positive approach towards the organization? Yet they like being where they are, the pay, the perks, and the power, so they will do anything necessary to get reelected. They are professional politicians, many of whom might not be able to make such a success of anything else. They care more about getting reelected than in serving the public, and so whoever can contribute the most to their campaigns calls the shots. What we have is crony democracy at its worst as those corporations and individuals who donate most to the party in power are favored when it comes to government policy. This is the kind of government we get after years of considering government in such a negative manner. Will we ever recapture a sense of government doing good things in being able to respond to public needs as it did during the Depression? Will we be able to attract competent people to run for office and serve in the government and make public service a viable option for the best and the brightest in our society?

After all is said and done, it should be clear that God is not directing the affairs of this nation; the Bush administration and the Republican Congress are providing this guidance. It is unfair to blame God for their foolishness. It seems that the Bush administration is one whose mind is made up and will not let itself be confused by the facts, whether they be the findings of the UN inspectors or science with regard to environmental problems. The Bush administration has been able to make this fault into a virtue by projecting the image of a strong leader who has a vision and is able to stay the course. Hopefully the American people have begun to see this philosophy for what it is, simple stubbornness and inflexibility in the face of new evidence and an inability to adapt to changing circumstances. They must begin to focus less on these so-called leadership qualities and focus more on where this leadership is taking the country.

The recent elections have given America the opportunity to catch its breath and take stock of itself. The Democrats can now block the radical Republican agenda regarding privatization of social security and making tax cuts for the rich permanent along with the appointment of more radical judges to our courts. Perhaps they even begin to get the budget under control and curb runaway federal spending. There may be some ability for the new Congress and the president to work out compromises on social security and immigration reform. But even it nothing gets done a divided government can be a blessing as each party can block the more radical proposals of the other.

We have had enough "adventures" over the last six years and need some time to settle down and consider the issues this book has raised. The values divide is real and whose values will prevail for the future is the most important question facing the country. People need to realize just what is at stake, and hopefully this book has clarified some of these value issues so people have a better understanding what the values divide is all about. When we choose our next leaders of Congress and the White House we need to take a close look at the values they hold and their vision for the country and decide if this is what we want for the future of America.

NOTES

1. Several pundits hoped that Bush would unite the country after the election and had suggestions to accomplish this objective. See Jonathan Alter, "Bush Could Bring Us Together," *Newsweek*, 15 November 2004, 29; Jeffrey E. Garten, "Uniting, Not Dividing: A Blueprint for Bush," *Business Week*, 15 November 2004, 33; and Andrew Sullivan, "Let's Have a Truce," *Time*, 15 November 2004, 120.

2. Richard S. Dunham and Howard Gleckman, "Can the GOP Get Down to Business?" *Business Week*, 22 November 2004, 43; John Aloysius Farrell, "Bush's debt to right may vex 2nd term," *Denver Post*, 17 November 2004, 29(A).

3. Fareed Zakaria, "Writing Prose For a New Term," *Newsweek*, 15 November 2004, 33.

4. Peronet Despeignes, "All Hail The Free-Lunch President," *Fortune*, 24 January 2005, 24.

5. Kathleen Parker, "Get off your high horse first, Dubya," *Denver Post*, 11 November 2004, 7(B).

6. Nancy Gibbs and John F. Dickerson, "Person Of The Year," *Time*, 27 December 2004, 34.

7. Deb Riechmann, "Bush stands by judicial nominees," *Times-Picayune*, 24 December 2004, A(2).

8. The storyline the administration pushed is that borrowing $2 trillion in the short run will save the system $11 trillion in unfunded liabilities in the long run, which may be as long as 75 years. These savings, however, are hypothetical while $2 trillion of additional borrowing will have to be financed immediately. See Robert Kuttner, "What Killed Off the GOP Deficit Hawks?" *Business Week*, 27 December 2004, 32.

9. Mike Allen and Matthew Cooper, "Hey, Big Spender. . . " *Time*, 30 January 2006, 34–36.

10. Edmund L. Andrews, "Camps bickering over federal spending," *Denver Post*, 6 April 2006, 19(A).

11. See Mortimer B. Zukerman, "Hypocrisy on Stilts," *U.S. News & World Report*, 22 May 2006, 60.

12. Kevin G. Hall and James Kuhnhenn, "GOP to send Bush $69 billion package for tax reduction," *Denver Post*, 11 May 2006, 19A; Silla Brush, "The GOP'S Tax Windfall," U.S. News & World Report, 22 May 2006, 25. Meanwhile, Republicans leaders proposed cuts in food stamps that would remove 225,000 people in working households with children from the program, cuts of $379 million in foster care payments to relatives who take in children removed from their parent's homes, and $9.4 billion in Medicaid cuts which would grow to $45 million over a ten year period. All of these cuts would affect people at the bottom of the income scale and are an example of "compassionate conservatism" in action. See E.J. Dionne, "Budget leader's secrets," *Denver Post*, 6 November 2005, 5(E).

13. See Robert J. Samuelson, "A Deficit of Seriousness," *Newsweek*, 16 May 2005, 39 and Peter G. Peterson, "Hear no deficit, see no deficit, speak no deficit," Fortune, 23 August 2004, 48–50.

14. David Gergen, "Speaking truth to power," *U.S. News & World Report*, 6 December 2004, 88. In one of his final appearances before Congress Greenspan also warned lawmakers that their profligate spending is threatening an otherwise healthy economy. See Marilyn Greewax, "Lawmakers told to cut spending," *Denver Post*, 4 November 2005, 8(C). Congress seems unable to reign in spending, and Bush has yet to veto a bill because of excessive spending. The energy bill, which will do nothing to reduce our dependence on foreign oil, contains billions of dollars in incentives to promote "clean coal" and domestic oil and gas production, incentives for an industry that is already earning record profits because of the increase in gasoline prices. And the highway bill, also passed in 2005, contains money for all kinds of pet projects that squander taxpayer's money.

15. Rebecca Hagelin, "Economic Policies are Moral Issues," 7 January 2005, www.heritage.org/Press/Commentary/ed010705a.cfm. (9 January 2005).

16. There was only an $84 billion increase in estimated tax receipts in 2005 which did reduce the deficit from a projected $427 billion to $343 billion. This includes a 42–percent increase in revenues from corporate profits. The administration claimed, of course, that these figures proved their policies were working and that we would grow ourselves out of the deficit. The Congressional Budget Office warned, however, that these revenue improvements probably would not be sustained and the fiscal outlook for the coming decade remained unchanged. See Andrew Taylor, "Budget projections finally bring good news for Bush," *Denver Post*, 16 August 2005, 5(A).

17. Edmund L. Andrews, "Bush gears budget to hit deficit goal," *Denver Post*, 2 January 2005, 24(A). In this same budget request Bush will give priority to military expenditures and domestic security while advocating cuts in social welfare programs like housing assistance for low-income families. See Robert Pear, "Bush budget to limit benefits," *Denver Post*, 9 January 2005, 2(A). See also John Parvensky, "Bush's budget may leave more homeless," *Denver Post*, 27 March 2005, 3(E); Dr. Stephen Berman, "Attempts to trim federal budget hitting America's kids hardest," *Rocky Mountain News*, 16 April 2005, 13(C).

18. See Paul Krugman, "The joyless U.S. economy," *Denver Post*, 6 December 2005, 7(B); "Issue of the week: Why the economy gets no respect," The Week, 16 December 2005, 38.
19. Mortimer B. Zukerman, "An opportunity lost," *U.S. News & World Report*, 20 September 2004, 76.
20. Robert Sam Anson in The New York Observer as quoted in "Kerry: A Campaign in search of a message," *The Week*, 17 September 2004, 18.
21. Arron Bernstein, "Social Security: Are Private Accounts A Good Idea?" *Business Week*, 24 January 2005, 66–67. Apparently there was some debate in the administration over what to call these accounts, but since there was some negative reaction to calling them private accounts, the new politically correct wording is to call them personal accounts, which people seem to like better. See Molly Ivins, "GOP rules for debate getting 'personal,'" *Denver Post*, 30 January 2005, 7(E).
22. Bernstein, "Social Security," 70.
23. Bernstein, "Social Security," 67.
24. Howard Gleckman, "The Beltway Battle Ahead," *Business Week*, 24 January 2005, 73.
25. Karen Tumulty and Eric Roston, "Social Security: Is There Really A Crisis?" *Time*, 24 January 2005, 26.
26. Bernstein, "Social Security," 68.
27. Tumulty and Roston, "Social Security," 25. See also Richard Cohen, "The Social Security crisis," *Denver Post*, 21 December 2004, 7(B).
28. Tumulty and Toston, "Social Security," 24. See also Michelle Singletary, "After 70 years, Social Security still a savior for millions," *Denver Post*, 14 August 2005, 13(K).
29. Shawn Tully, "Tending To Social Security," *Fortune*, 7 February 2005, 16.
30. Tully, "Social Security," 16.
31. Tully, "Social Security," 16.
32. Mortimer B. Zuckerman, "A 'cure' worse than the cold," *U.S. News & World Report*, 31 January/7 February 2005, 75–76. There is something of a double-edged sword here, in that the government wants to make sure people do not speculate with these private accounts or get taken by an unethical broker. Most people do not have the time or knowledge to make good investment decisions on their own and thus should not have complete freedom to invest in anything they choose. But if the government directs these investments in any way, it is subject to the argument that it is responsible for any losses people experience.
33. Froma Harrop, "Social Security isn't welfare," *Denver Post*, 5 May 2005, 7(B).
34. Tumulty and Roston, "Social Security," 27. Some claim that a 2 percent increase in the payroll tax would eliminate totally the shortfall of $3.7 trillion, as would paring the tax cuts of 2001 and 2003 back by less than 50 percent and transferring the added revenues to the Social Security system. See Laura D'Andrea Tyson, "Social Security Crisis? What Crisis?" *Business Week*, 17 January 2005, 24. Others argue that we should recapture the revenue lost as rising inequality pushed a greater share of aggregate U.S. wages out of reach of the 12.4 percent cutoff. Foregoing this extra revenue means that Social Security taxes only 85% of collective payroll earnings, not 90

percent. Thus Congress should put the aggregate taxable income level back to 90 percent. This move would eliminate 40 percent of the projected Social Security deficit. See Aaron Bernstein, "Why the Greenspan Fix Didn't Work." *Business Week*, 30 May 2005, 60–61.

35. Howard Gleckman and Richard S. Dunham, "Social Security: It'll Take A Helluva Sales Job," *Business Week*, 7 February 2005, 33.

36. Bernstein, "Social Security," 67. At the beginning of 2005 the Congressional Budget Office already altered its forecast and stated that the system would take in more money annually than it pays out in benefits until 2020, two years later than its earlier estimate. David Espo, "Social Security should be solvent until 2052, CBO says," *Denver Post*, 1 February 2005, 2(A).

37. Allan Sloan, "A Piggy Bank for Social Security," *Newsweek*, 4 April 2005, 49.

38. "New Social Security plan has old faults," *Denver Post*, 27 June 2005, 7(B); Marie Cocco, "Trust fund does exist," *Denver Post*, 29 June 2005, 7(B).

39. Not quite dead. Bush's privitization plan for Social Security was snuck into the 2007 budget. The proposal included an estimate of $712 billion over seven years for transition costs. The plan also included plans to save $3.4 billion over 10 years by eliminating the token $225 lump-sum death benefit and cutting off monthly survivor benefits to teenagers who drop out of high school. In short, the plan would cut benefits to surviving spouses and orphans. See "Bush's 'pittance' for widows, widowers," *Denver Post*, 10 February 2006, 6(B). Other think Social Security needs to be put back on the table for discussion. See "Social Security: O.K. Gang, Back to the Table," *Business Week*, 9 January 2006, 102. For an extensive discussion of the issue see Lee Walczak and Richard S. Dunham, "I want my safety net," *Business Week*, 16 May 2005, 24–34, and Bush's house of Cards: The privatization fraud," The American Prospect, February 2005, A1–A23.

40. See Howard Gleckman, "The Real Retirement Time Bomb," *Business Week*, 31 January 2005, 72; Robert J. Samuelson, "Medicare, not Social Security, is the real problem for America," *Rocky Mountain News*, 15 January 2005, 13(C); David Broder, "Fixing health care should come first," *Denver Post*, 7 April 2005, 7(B); and Ricardo Alonso-Zaldivar and Joel Havemann, "Medicare's fiscal future worsening, report says," *Times-Picayune*, 2 May 2006, A(5). The Bush administration wants to slow the growth of Medicare spending by pushing health savings accounts which would make people pay more for health care. See Kevin Freking, "Bush aims to shift health bill to patients," *Denver Post*, 7 February 2006, 15(A). Some studies show that the rising costs of Social Security and Medicare will by 2030 easily consume a third of workers' future wage and salary increases because of higher taxes to support these programs. See Robert J. Samuelson, "Rising costs of Medicare, pensions eat up wages," *Rocky Mountain News*, 9 April 2005, 33(A).

41. See Jane Bryant Quinn, "Time to Cram For Medicare," *Newsweek*, 24 October 2005, 44; Robert J. Samuelson, "The Coming Drug Bust?" *Newsweek*, 28 November 2005, 45.

42. Jason Deparle, "Katrina plan may cut into aid for poor," *Denver Post*, 11 October 2005, 1(A). See also Hope Yen, "Review: Government ties brought Katrina contracts," *Denver Post*, 20 October 2005, 9(A).

43. Deparle, "Katrina," 1(A). See also Robert Pear, "Health programs face cuts," *Denver Post*, 30 October 2005, 2(A).

44. Cass R. Sunstein, Radicals In Robes: *Why Extreme Right-Wing Courts Are Wrong for America* (New York: Basic Books, 2005), 15.

45. Sunstein, *Radicals In Robes*, 10–11.

46. Sunstein, *Radicals In Robes*, 3–11.

47. Sunstein, *Radicals In Robes*, 26.

48. Sunstein, *Radicals In Robes*, 74.

49. Sunstein, *Radicals In Robes*, 243.

50. Sunstein, *Radicals In Robes*, 245. See pp. 15–16 for an enumeration of specific actions the Rehnquist Court has taken in this regard.

51. The demise of pensions also fits into this vision. See Laura Karmatz, Lisa McLaughlin, and Dody Tsiantar, "The Broken Promise," *Time*, 31 October 2005, 33–47 for the story of how more and more companies are walking away from their promise of retirement and health care benefits with congressional assistance. The trend is towards individual workers assuming more and more of the risks for their retirement just as they had to 100 years ago and going without needed health care because they have no insurance.

52. Keith Naughton, "The Long And Grinding Road," *Newsweek*, 1 May 2006, 53–59. See also Mark Morrison, "Living Too Large in Exurbia," *Business Week*, 17 October 2005, 36–40.

Sources

In preparing this book I read all the books in the Bibliography and am indebted to these authors for the insights and information they provided. While most of these books are against the war in Iraq or at least raise questions about it and are critical of the Bush administration, several are pro-Bush and provide useful information about his religious background. There have been more books written about this administration and its policies than of any other administration I can remember, and I tried to keep up with most of them or at least those that seemed to be most important. It has been interesting reading all these books and getting different perspectives on what is going on in this administration.

In addition to these books I read four newsmagazines every week including *Time*, *Newsweek*, *U.S. News & World Report*, and *The Week*. These sources provided an incredible amount of information that is referenced in the book. Of course I also read the daily newspaper which in this case happened to be *The Denver Post* which carries many news stories from the Associated Press and editorials from various other newspapers. On occasion, I also read other newspapers such as *The New York Times*, *Washington Post*, *The Times-Picayune*, and a second Denver newspaper, the *Rocky Mountain News*.

A third group of source material consisted of general interest magazines and journals that I read on a regular basis. As far as magazines are concerned, these included *The American Prospect*, *E Magazine* (The Environmental Magazine), and *Scientific American* which from time to time had some useful information for this book. Journals included *Foreign Affairs*, *The Wilson Quarterly*, and *Dissent*. *Foreign Affairs* in particular had some very useful information on Iraq and other issues of concern to society that provided useful insights and information that I incorporated into this book.

For whatever reason I was highly motivated to read all this material as I find this period in the nation's history fascinating and frightening at the same time, and I am indebted to all the authors of these books and articles for keeping me interested and providing me with the material for this book. It has been a most interesting journey and one that I hope will prove fruitful as people read this book and digest its contents.

Bibliography

Ackerman, Bruce. *Before The Next Attack: Preserving Civil Liberties In An Age Of Terrorism* (New Haven: Yale University Press, 2006).
Albright, Madeleine. *The Mighty & The Almighty: Reflections on America, God, and World Affairs* (New York: HarperCollins, 2006).
Altman, Daniel. *Neoconomy: George Bush's Revolutionary Gamble With America's Future* (New York: Public Affairs, 2004).
Anonymous. *Imperial Hubris: Why The West Is Losing The War On Terror* (Washington, D.C.: Brassey's, 2004).
Blaker, Kimberly. *The Fundamentals of Extremism: The Christian Right in America* (New Boston, MI: New Boston Books, 2003).
Bremer, L. Paul III. *My Year in Iraq: The Struggle to Build a Future of Hope* (New York: Simon & Schuster, 2006).
Brzezinski, Zbigniew. *The Choice: Global Domination Or Global Leadership* (New York: Basic Books, 2004).
Bush, George W. *A Charge To Keep* (New York: William Morrow, 1999).
Byrd, Senator Robert C. *Losing America: Confronting A Reckless And Arrogant Presidency* (New York: W.W. Norton, 2004).
Carter, Graydon. *What We've Lost* (New York: Farrar, Straus and Giroux, 2004).
Carter, Jimmy. *Our Endangered Values: America's Moral Crisis* (New York: Simon & Schuster, 2005).
Center for Constitutional Rights. *Articles of Impeachment Against George W. Bush* (Hoboken, NJ: Melville House Publishing, 2006).
Clark, General Wesley K. *Winning Modern Wars: Iraq, Terrorism, and the American Empire* (New York: Public Affairs, 2003).
Clarke, Richard A. *Against All Enemies: Inside America's War on Terror* (New York: Free Press, 2004}.
Corn, David. *The Lies of George W. Bush: Mastering the Politics of Deception* (New York: Crown, 2003).
Dean, John W. *Conservatives Without Conscience* (New York: Viking, 2006).

Dennett, Daniel C. *Breaking the Spell: Religion As A Natural Phenomenon* (New York: Viking, 2006).
Dershowitz, Alan M. *Why Terrorism Works: Understanding the Threat, Responding to the Challenge* (New Haven: Yale University Press, 2002).
Edgar, Bob. *Middle Church: Reclaiming the Moral Values of the Faithful Majority from the Religious Right* (New York: Simon & Schuster, 2006).
Eland, Ivan. *The Empire Has No Clothes: U.S. Foreign Policy Exposed* (Oakland, CA: The Independent Institute, 2004).
Franken, Al. *Lies And the Lying Liars Who Tell Them: A Fair and Balanced Look at the Right* (New York: Dutton, 2003).
———. *The Truth: With Jokes* (New York: Dutton, 2005).
Freiling, Thomas M., ed. *George W. Bush on God and Country: A President Speaks Out on Faith, Principle, and Patriotism* (Washington, D.C.: Allegiance Press, 2004).
Frum, David & Richard Perle. *An End To Evil: How To Win The War On Terror* (New York: Random House, 2003).
Gerges, Fawaz A. *Journey of the Jihadist: Inside Muslim Militancy* (New York: Harcourt, 2006).
Harris, Sam. *The End Of Faith: Religion, Terror, and the Future of Reason* (New York: Norton, 2004).
———. *Letter to a Christian Nation* (New York: Knopf, 2006.
Hightower, Jim. *Thieves In High Places* (New York: Viking, 2003).
Ivins, Molly and Lou Dubose. *Bushwacked: Life in George W. Bush's America* (New York: Random House, 2003).
Johnson, Haynes. *The Age of Anxiety: McCarthyism to Terrorism* (New York: Harcourt, 2005).
Kengor, Paul. *God and George W. Bush: A Spiritual Life* (New York: HarperCollins, 2004).
Kennedy, Senator Edward M. *America: Back on Track* (New York: Viking, 2006).
Kennedy, Robert F. Jr. *Crimes Against Nature: How George W. Bush and His Corporate Pals Are Plundering the Country and Hijacking Our Democracy* (New York: HarperCollins, 2004).
Khalidi, Rashid. *Resurrecting Empire: Western Footprints and America's Perilous Path in the Middle East* (Boston: Beacon, 2004).
Krugman, Paul. *The Great Unraveling: Losing Our Way in the New Century* (New York: W.W. Norton, 2003).
Leone, Richard C. and Greg Anrig, Jr. (eds.) *The War on Our Freedoms: Civil Liberties in an Age of Terrorism* (New York: Public Affairs, 2003).
Lerner, Michael. *The Left Hand of God: Taking Back Our Country From The Religious Right* (New York: HarperCollins, 2006.
Lewis, Bernard. *From Babel To Dragomans: Interpreting The Middle East* (New York: Oxford University Press, 2004).
———. *The Crisis of Islam: Holy War and Unholy Terror* (New York: Modern Library, 2003).

Lincoln, Bruce. *Holy Terrors: Thinking about Religion after September 11* (Chicago: University of Chicago Press, 2003).

Linker, Damon. *The Theocons: Secular American Under Siege* (New York: Doubleday, 2006).

Lynn, Barry W. *Piety & Politics: The Right-Wing Assult On Religious Freedom* (New York: Harmony Books, 2006).

Mansfield, Stephen. *The Faith of George W. Bush* (New York: Tarcher/Penguin, 2003).

Micklethwait, John and Adrian Wooldridge. *The Right Nation: Conservative Power in America* (New York: Penguin Books, 2005).

Miller, Mark Crispin. *Cruel And Unusual: Bush/Cheney's New World Order* (New York: W.W. Norton, 2004).

Mooney, Chris. *The Republican War on Science* (New York: Basic Books, 2005).

Muller, Jerry Z., ed. *Conservatism: An Anthology of Social and Political Thought From David Hume to the Present* (Princeton, NJ: Princeton University Press, 1997).

Newhouse, John. *Imperial America: The Bush Assault On The World Order* (New York: Knopf, 2003).

O'Reilly, Bill. *Culture Warrior*. (New York: Boardway Books, 2006.

Packer, George. *The Assassins' Gate: America in Iraq* (New York: Farrar, Straus and Giroux, 2005).

Phillips, Kevin. *American Dynasty: Aristocracy, Fortune, And The Politics of Deceit In The House Of Bush* (New York: Viking, 2004).

———. *Wealth and Democracy: A Political History of the American Rich* (New York: Broadway, 2002).

———. *American Theocracy: The Peril and Politics of Radical Religion, Oil, and Borrowed Money in the 21st Century* (New York: Viking, 2006).

Pope, Carl and Paul Rauber. *Strategic Ignorance: Why the Bush Administration is Recklessly Destroying a Century of Environmental Progress* (San Francisco: Sierra Club Books, 2004).

Prados, John. *Hood Winked: The Documents That Reveal How Bush Sold Us a War* (New York: The New Press, 2004).

Rampton, Sheldon and John Stauber. *Banana Republicans: How the Right Wing Is Turning America into a One-Party State* (New York: Tarcher/Penguin, 2004).

Rich, Frank. *The Greatest Story Ever Sold: The Decline And Fall Of Truth From 9/11 To Katrina* (New York: Penguin, 2006).

Risen, James. *State Of War: The Secret History of the CIA and the Bush Administration* (New York: Free Press, 2006).

Shermer, Michael. *The Science of Good & Evil* (New York: Times Books, 2004).

Singer, Peter. *The President of Good & Evil: The Ethics of George W. Bush* (New York: Dutton, 2004).

Soros, George. *The Bubble of American Supremacy: Correcting the Misuse of American Power* (New York: Public Affairs, 2004).

Schlesinger, Arthur M., Jr. *War And The American Presidency* (New York: W.W. Norton, 2004).

Stern, Jessica. *Terror in the Name of God: Why Religious Militants Kill* (New York: HarperCollins, 2003).
Sunstein, Cass R. *Radicals In Robes: Why Extreme Right-Wing Courts Are Wrong for America* (New York: Basic Books, 2005).
Suskind, Ron. *The Price of Loyalty: George W. Bush, the White House, and the Education of Paul O'Neill* (New York: Simon & Schuster, 2004).
———. *The One Percent Doctrine: Deep Inside America's Pursuit Of Its Enemies Since 9/11* (New York: Simon & Schuster, 2006).
Tolchin, Martin & Susan J. *A World Ignited: How Apostles of Ethnic, Religious, and Racial Hatred Torch the Globe* (Lanham, MD: Roman & Littlefield, 2006).
The 9/11 Commission Report. *Final Report of the National Commission on Terrorist Attacks Upon the United States* (New York: W.W. Norton, 2004).
Tushnet, Mark. *A Court Divided: The Rehnquist Court and the Future of Constitutional Law* (New York: W.W. Norton, 2005).
Unger, Craig. *House of Bush/House of Saud: The Secret Relationship Between the World's Two Most Powerful Dynasties* (New York: Scribner, 2004).
Whitman, Christine Todd. *It's My Party Too: The Battle for the Heart of the GOP and the Future of America* (New York: Penguin Press, 2005).
White, Mel. *Religion Gone Bad: The Hidden Dangers of The Christian Right* (New York: Tarcher/Penguin, 2006).
Woodward, Bob. *Bush and War* (New York: Simon & Schuster, 2002).
———. *Plan of Attack* (New York: Simon & Schuster, 2004).
———. *State of Denial: Bush at War, Part III* (New York: Simon & Schuster, 2006).
Zakaria, Fareed. *The Future of Freedom: Illiberal Democracy at Home and Abroad* (New York: W.W. Norton, 2003).

Index

Abdullah, Crown Prince of Saudi Arabia, 22, 40n73
abortion, 107, 111, 114, 119, 164–65, 181, 194
Abramoff, Jack, 195n1
absolutism, 110–12, 166
Abu Ghraib, prisoner abuse at, 51–52, 134
Adams, John Quincy, 35n21
affirmative action, 194
Afghanistan, 5, 9, 12, 17, 22, 24, 26, 29, 47, 48
Ahmadinejad, Mahmoud, 151
AIDS, 171
Air National Guard, 21
Allawi, Ayad, 14
al Qaeda, 23, 27, 48, 52, 55, 65, 150; suspected link between Saddam and, 11–13, 134; 9/11 attacks and, 5, 34n7
Alternative Minimum Tax (AMT), 74
Altman, Daniel, 78
aluminum tubes, 6–7
Alzheimer's disease, 112
American Bar Association (ABA), 194
American Broadcasting Company (ABC), 170
American Civil Liberties Union (ACLU), 53, 114, 148

American dream, 80, 168, 215
American Political Science Association, 77
American Prospect, 225
American public: support for Iraqi War, 19
Amnesty International, 52
Anderson, Terry, 99
Annan, Kofi, 13, 36n27
Anonymous, 16
Ansar al-Islam, 22
anthropomorphism, 112–16
apocalyptism, 126n1, 126n2
Appeals Court. *See* Court of Appeals, U.S.
Arctic, 90
Arctic National Wildlife Refuge (ANWR), 95–96, 98, 215
Argriculture Department. *See* Department of Argiculture
aristocracy, 75–76, 180, 209
Arizona, 188
Arlington National Cemetery, 134
arsenic, 88–89
Ashcroft, John, 148
Askariya Mosque, 15
Associated Press, 5
Atta, Mohammed, 13

Baath Party, 16, 139
Bacevich, Andrew J., 24–25
Baghdad, 18
Balzar, John, 100
Bible, the, 147, 178n18; as explanation, 113–14; infallibility of, 109; literal interpretation and, 110–11, 116–18, 174; mythology and, 118; violence and, 173, 178n26; as Word of God, 110
Bill of Rights, 47
bin Laden, Osama, xii, 5, 22, 49; goals of, 23, 63–65, 126n8, 150; Saddam and, 12, 26
binary logic, 119
biological diversity, 85
biological weapons, 7, 11
Blade Runner, 97
Boykins, Lt. General William J., 150, 158n24
Brahimi, Lakhdar, 18
bribery, 189
Bremer, L. Paul "Jerry," III, 37n42, 139
Britain, 15
Brooks, David, 110
Brzezinski, Zbigniew, 30–31
Bureau of Land Management (BLM), 93
Breaux, John, 132
Burke, Edmund, 196n9
Bush administration: belief in God and, 132–33; certainty and, 135; digital thinking and, 135; environment and, 84, 87–96; freedom and, 44–45; intelligence and, 6–7; international law and, 8–9; Iraqi War and, 3–5; morals and, 135, 138–39; rationales for war, and, 5–10, 13, 21–22; politics of fear and, 57; religion and, 129–40; self-righteousness and, 136–38; surveillance and, 54–57; values and, x
Bush, George H.W., 28, 129, 138
Bush, George W.: absolutism and, 130–32; claims of Saddam-al Qaeda links by, 12–13; as commander in chief, 48, 53; Crown Prince Abdullah and, 22; debates and, x; environment and, 84, 87–96; freedom and, 44, 47, 132–33, 141n13; Geneva Conventions and, 50, 52–53; Guantanamo Bay detainees and, 47–51; Iraq stategy and, 27–28, 42n108; macho attitude and, xii; "Mission Accomplished" speech, 18; rationale for war and, 13, 21–22, 35n20; "preemption doctrine and, 8, 10, 29–30, 183; religious faith of, 129–30; second-term agenda of, 198–214; second-term appointments of, 199–200; science and, 95–96, 139, 142n32; signing statements and, 53–54; taxes and, 82n23; Texas National Guard and, 21; 2000 election of, 185–86; 2002 State of the Union address of, 7, 137; 2004 campaign of, 78; 2004 election of, x; 2004 inaugural speech of, 44; WMD and, 6–7
The Bushes: Portrait of a Dynasty, 150
Bush Doctrine, ix, 8, 10, 29–30
Byrd, Robert, 140, 196n7

California, state of, 90
campaign contributions, 77–78
capital gains, 76
capitalism, 209, 218–19
carbon dioxide, 89, 215
categorical exclusions, 43
Catholic Church, xii, 153, 165
Catholic University of America, 183
Carter, Graydon, 140
Carter, Jimmy, 24, 30, 129
Center on Budget and Policy Priorities, 71
Central Intelligence Agency (CIA), 6–8, 15, 27, 56, 65; intelligence failures in, 6; prisons and, 50–51; WMD investigations of, 12
Center for Strategic and International Studies, 27

Clean Air Act, 88, 90–91
Clean Air Interstate Rule, 92
Clear Skies, 90–92, 95
Cheney, Dick, 21, 53, 82n23, 131; Gulf War and, 28; PNAC and,4; claims of Saddam-al Qaeda link by, 13; claims about WMD by, 6–7
Chicago Divinity School, 148
China, People's Republic of, xiii, 48, 89, 202
Christian Coalition, 152
Christianity, 108–9, 179n36
Churchill, Winston, 61
CIA. *See* Central Intelligence Agency
citizen participation, 94
Citizens for Tax Justice, 71, 73
civil liberties, ix
Civil Rights Movement, 213
civil war, 15, 26, 29, 33
civility, 131–32
climate change, 45, 87–90, 102n15, 102n19, 139, 172, 215
Clinton, Bill, 20, 91, 93, 127n17, 129, 182, 198
Clinton, Hillary, 136, 182
Cold War, 23, 62
Colorado, state of, 186–88
Columbia Broadcasting System (CBS), 170–71
Commander in Chief, 48, 53
commons, 99–101
community, 167
commuting, 215–16
compassionate conservatism, 137, 210, 221n12, 221n17
competitive system, 98
concentration of income and wealth, 75, 76
Congress, U.S., 72, 131, 136, 189; Iraq War authorized by, 6; makeup of, 77; terrorism and, 27, 44, 46–47, 57
Congressional Budget Office (CBO), 72–73, 76, 200–201, 204, 223n36
conservatism, 183–84, 196n9, 196n10, 218

constitution, Iraq, 14
Constitution, U.S., 24, 48–49, 53–55, 57, 211–12; religion and, 144
Constitutional Amendment, 171
Constitutional Convention, 144
containment and deterrence doctrine, 8–10
conversation, ix
consumption tax, 79, 183
corporations: taxes and, 74, 81n16
Council on Foreign Relations, 33
Court of Appeals, U.S., 47–48, 199
courts, 192–94
Crawford, Texas, 100, 130
creationism, 109, 156n9
crusade, 150, 157n23
culture wars, ix, 164

Daschle, Tom, 185
data-mining, 54
death tax, 71
Declaration of Independence, 144
deficits, 72–73, 200–202, 221n16
DeLay, Tom, 148, 154, 181, 187–88, 195n1
democracy, 44, 169; experimentation and, 155; inclusiveness and, 154; Iraq and, 5, 16, 38n54; open-endedness and, 155; religion and, 140, 163–80; revitalization of, 180–97; secular point of view and, 154
deism, 144
Democratic party, 180–85, 195n4
Democrats, x, xii, xiii, 6, 84, 214
Denver, 215–16
Denver Post, 225
Department of Agriculture, 93, 146
Department of Health and Human Services, 146
Department of the Interior, 93, 95–96
Department of Justice. *See* Justice Department
Department of Labor, 146
detainees, 47–54

234 *Index*

Detainee Treatment Act of 2005, 53
Dewey, John, 117, 121, 127n13
dirty bomb, 48, 51
discontinuity, 215
Dissent, 225
District of Columbia, 186
diversity, 64, 168, 218
dividend taxes, 72–73
Dover Air Force Base, 134
Draft, 19, 61
Duelfer, Charles, 11–12, 131, 134, 137

E Magazine, 225
ecology, 99
economic growth, 99
economic theory, 98
egocentrism, 115
Egypt, 17
Eland, Ivan, 22–24
elections, Iraqi, 14, 18
elections, U.S.: of 2000, 185–86; of 2002, 189; of 2004, x, 21, 139, 189, 198; of 2006, 219–20; money and, 188–90
Electoral College, xii, 185–87
electronic voting machines, 192
The Empire Has No Clothes, 22
The End of Faith, 173
The End of Nature, 84
endangered species, 172
enemy combatants, 47–48, 50
energy independence, 41n100, 215
energy policy, 45
Energy Task Force, 41
England, Lyndie, 51
Enlightenment, 16, 143–44
entitlement programs, 208–9, 211
environmental issues, ix
Environmental Protection Agency (EPA), 87, 89–92, 95, 212
equal protection, 212
estate tax, 71, 75, 81n5
ethics, 195n2; the environment and, 86–87; fundamentalism and, 122, 124; instrumentalism and, 86

Evangelicals. *See* Fundamentalism
evolution, 178
exit stategy, 27

Fahrenheit 9/11, 149
Falwell, Jerry, 110, 113–14, 121, 151, 165, 177n6
faith: the presidency and, 130, 164; public policy and, 130
Faith and Values Coalition, 177n6
faith-based initiatives, 146–47, 156n11, 156n12
family planning programs, 164
Federal Bureau of Investigation (FBI), 46, 53
Federal Communications Commission (FCC), 170
Federal Election Commission (FEC), 189
Federal Emergency Management Administration (FEMA), 218
federal judges, 107, 164, 193, 199–200, 214
Federal Reserve Board, 80
Feulner, Dr. Ed., 202
Fifth Amendment, 95
fillibuster, 193, 214
First Amendment, 144
Fiscal policy, 200–202
flat tax, 79, 183, 200
Florida, state of, 191
Food stamps, 210
Foreign Affairs, 8, 225
Foreign Intelligence Surveillance Act (FISA), 54–55
Foreign Intelligence Surveillance Court, 55
foreign policy, 4
Forest Management Act, 93
Forest Service, 93
Founding Fathers, 47, 143–45
Fourth Amendment, 54, 212
Fourteenth Amendment, 213
Franklin, Ben, 144
Franks, General Tommy, 139

freedom, 17, 44–45, 132–33, 135, 141n13; democracy and, 145–47; security and, 57–62; of speech, 212
Freedom of Information Act, 45, 50, 53
Freedom Medal, 139
Friedman, Thomas, 62–63
Fundamentalism, ix,xi; absolutism and, 110–12; certainty and, 120–21; characteristics of, 109–26; dehumanization and, 118–19; democracy and, 145–47, 153–54; digital thinking and, 119; environment and, 128n25; ethics and, 122–24, 128n24; gay marriage and, 111, 164, 171–72, 181, 194, 195n5; intolerance and, 123; moral values and, 111; politics and, 144, 152–54, 159n37; public policy and, 107, 147–49, 164, 172; self-righteousness and, 121; war and, 149–51, 158n29, 158n30

Gates, Bill, 72
Geneva Conventions, 45, 49–50, 52
gerrymandering, 187
GI Bill, 77
glaciers, 90
Glacier National Park, 90
global warming. *See* climate change
globalism, 64
God: anthropomorphism and, 112–16; Bush administration and, 132–33; as personal, 113; power of, 120
Gonzales, Alberto, 52, 55, 200
Gore, Al, x, 185–86
Goss, Peter, 56
government, 218–19
Graham, Billy, 129
Great Britain. *See* Britain
Great Depression, 62, 211
Great Society, 213
Greenspan, Alan, 79, 201
Griles, J. Steven, 94–95
Guantanamo Bay, detainees at, 45, 47–50, 52–53

Gulf Coast, 210
Gulf War, 28, 130, 182

Halliburton, 25
Hamdan v. Rumsfeld, 49
Hamadan, Salim, 49
Hamdi, Yaser Esam, 48, 66n15
Harris, Sam, 173–75
Hastert, Dennis, 154, 181
Hayden, General Michael V., 56
health insurance, 202
Health Maintenance Organizations (HMOs), 210
Healthy Forests Restoration Act, 93
Hefley, Joel, 181
hegemony, 4
Help Americans Vote Act (HAVA), 191–92
Hendrickson, David C., 8
Heritage Foundation, 202
Hollings, Fritz, 188
Homeland Security Department, 61, 218
House Budget Committee, 210
House of Representatives, 187
household income, 80
Hughes, Karen, 137
Hurricane Georges, 114
Hurricane Katrina, 61, 210, 216, 219
Hussein, Saddam, xii, 3–5, 8, 15, 22, 26, 44, 135; brutality of regime and, 10; defensive strategy of, 18; disposal of, 137; fall of, 26; 9/11 attacks and, 6, 113–14; suspected link between al Qaeda and, 6, 12–13, 41n102, 134; WMD and, 6–7, 10–12, 130–31, 136

idealism, 32, 136
ideology, 131
Illinois Civil Justice League, 197n40
IMAX, 171
imperialism, 22–24
inaugural address, 44
Independent Institute, 22
Index of Economic Freedom, 202

India, 89, 202
individualism, 167
incumbents, 187–89
inequality, ix, 75–76, 202, 209
Inspector General of EPA, 91–92
Institute for Democracy and Electoral
    Assistance, 189
insurgency, 14, 17–19
intelligence, 6–7, 35n20, 130
intelligent design, 107, 156n9, 172, 176,
    178n22, 214–16
International Court of Justice, 21
international law, 8, 13
Interior Secretary. *See* Secretary of
    Interior
interrogation techniques, 52
interstate commerce, 213
Interstate Commerce Act of 1897, 209
Iowa, state of, 188
Iran, 30, 43n117, 199
Iraq, 115, 198–99; alleged Niger uranium
    deal of, 7; casualties, 134; civil war
    and, 15, 26, 29, 33; congressional
    authorization for war with, 6;
    constitution for, 14; democracy in, 5,
    13–21, 38n54, 132–33; elections in
    (*see* elections Iraq); ethnic conflict in,
    15–16; insurgency in, 14, 17–19;
    Kissinger on, 16, 30; lack of U.S.
    strategy in, 26; life in, 38n51; postwar
    planning for, 26, 32; power vacuum
    in, 14; sectarian conflict in, 15–16;
    U.S. embassy in, 42n108; WMD in
    (*see* weapons of mass destruction
    [WMD])
Iraqi insurgents, 14, 17–19
Iraqi Interim Governing Council, 14, 18
Iraq Survey Group, 11
Iraq War, ix, 3, 172; commitment to,
    3–5; consequences of, 25–33; costs
    of, 19–20, 39n62, 39n64, 61;
    justification of, 5–10; legitimacy of,
    8–9; oil and, 24–25; rationale for, 13,
    21–22, 35n20
Islam, 14, 27, 171, 173, 175–76

Islamic fundamentalism, xi, 23, 174
Islamic state, 15
Islamic terrorism, 65
Ivans, Molly, 189–90

Jackson, Janet, 170
Jefferson, Thomas, 143–44
jihads, 14, 64
Johnson, Lyndon, 20, 138, 213
Johnson, Steve, 92
judicial elections, 194
Justice at Stake Campaign, 193
Justice Department, U.S., 48, 52, 146

Kay, David, 11
Kennedy, David M., 32
Kennedy, Edward, 138
Kennedy, John F., 32, 58, 129
Kennedy, Robert F., Sr., 100
Kent State, 20, 138
Kerry, John, 166, 190; 2004 election
    and, x, xii, 78, 135, 153, 163, 180,
    185; environment and, 84; Iraq war
    and, 136, 182; military service and,
    21, 190; terrorism and, 169
Kissinger, Henry, 16, 30
Klein, Joe, 19
Koran, 173
Koyto Protocol, 89–90
Kurds, 22
Kuwait, 6

Labor Department. *See* Department of
    Labor
League of Christian Voters, 197n40
Lebanon, 17
Left Behind literature, 150
legitimacy, 8–9, 31, 137–38
Lewis, Bernard, 145
The Lexus and the Olive Tree, 62–63
Libby, I. Lewis "Scooter," 7
liberals, 218
libertarian, 99–100
London, 60
Los Angeles Times, 57, 100

macho attitude, xii
materialism, 64
McCain, John, 53
McClellan, Scott, 52
McKibben, Bill, 101
medicade, 210
medicare, 74, 138, 183, 208–9, 223n40
mercury emissions, 87, 92, 102n28
middle class, 70, 72, 184, 202
Middle East, 15, 27–28, 137; democracy and, 4–5, 17, 31, 44, 61, 132, 171; oil and, 25; power and, 29; terrorism and, 23, 62
military tribunals, 45, 49–50
military, U.S.: recruitment, 29, 42n112
miracles, 116, 117, 133
Mitchell v. Helms, 146
Moral Majority, 151, 165, 177n6
moral issues, 135, 167–69
moral outrage, 20
moral values, 111, 122, 139
Moore, Michael, 149
Mormons, 143
Mountain States Legal Foundation, 95
Mueller, Jerry Z., 183
Muhammad (Prophet), 150
Mutually Assured Destruction (MAD), 172
mythology, 118, 125

National Academy of Sciences, 89
National Broadcasting Comany (NBC), 170–71
national debt, 183
National Environmental Policy Act (NEPA), 93
national forests, 92–94
National Forest Management Act, 93
National Guard, 28
National Intelligence Council, 15, 26
national parks, 101
national sales tax, 200
National Security Agency (NSA), 54–56
National Security Council, 7
National Security Strategy, 10

natural environment, 84–86, 97
negative advertising, 190
neoconservative, 4–5
Neoconomy, 78
New Orleans, 114, 210, 216
Newsweek, 73–74, 139, 225
New Deal, 204, 208, 211
New Source Review (NSR), 91
New York Times, 7, 54, 110, 225
Niger, 7
9/11 attacks, 5, 10, 29, 44, 54, 57–62, 113, 120–21, 126n7, 134, 140, 169, 170, 172–73
9/11 Commission, 37n39, 60, 69n56
nitrogen oxides, 91–92
Nixon, Richard, 129
Nixon administration, 54, 138
Nobel laureates, 96
no-fly zones, 22
Nordquist, Grover, 218
North Carolina, state of, 194
North Korea, 9, 30, 199
Norton, Gale, 94–96
NSA. *See* National Security Agency
nuclear weapons, 173

O'Connor, Sandra Day, 49
Office of Faith Based Services, 147
Ohio, in election of 2004, 191
oil, 24–25
oil drilling, 216
oil shale, 215
Oklahoma City bombing, 58
Old Testament, 108
O'Neill, Paul, 3, 5, 7, 131
Ottoman Empire, 29
Owen, Priscilla, 199
ownership society, 199
ozone, 91–92

Padilla, Jose, 48, 51
Paige, Rod, 148
Patriot Act, 45–47, 57, 183
Pearl Harbor, 57, 59–60
Pell Grants, 77

Pence, Mike, 211
Pentagon, 25, 51–52, 58–59
pensions, 224n51
People for the American Way, 114
Persian Gulf, 24
pledge of allegiance, 146
Phillips, Kevin, 75–76, 130
Pickering, Charles Sr., 199–200
Pitts, Leonard, 171
pluralism, 16–17, 112, 145, 166, 170–72
Political Action Committees (PACs), 190
Political Economy Research Center, 99
Pope, Carl, 87, 95, 100
popular vote, 185–87
Powell, Colin, 21, 35n20, 50, 53
power, xiii
power vacuum, 14, 16, 26, 136
"preemption" doctrine, ix, 8, 10, 29
Prague, 13
prayer, 115, 127n11
preemptive strike, 6, 8–10, 12, 34n12, 36n27
prescription drug plan, 183, 209–10
"preventive war," 8, 10, 12, 34n12
prisoner abuse, 61, 134
private property, 100, 104n50
progressive income tax, 75, 80, 183
Project for a New American Century (PNAC), 4, 32
propaganda campaign, 6, 37n39
property rights, 98–99
protests, 138
provisional ballots, 191
public lands, 92–94, 103n45
public policy, 107, 147–49, 164, 172
public service, 218
Puritans, 143, 163

Radicals In Robes, 211–13
Rather, Dan, 21
rationing, 61
Rauber, Paul, 87, 95, 100
Reagan, Ronald, 23, 95, 138;
    government and, 174, 185, 213, 218;

judiciary and, 211; religious right and, 144; taxes, and, 73
Reagan administration, 73, 147, 151, 184
realism, 32, 136
redistricting, xii, 187–88
recruitment, 29, 42n112
Reformation, 16
Rehnquist Court, 213
religion, xii, xiii; democracy and, 140, 163–80; end of, 179n36; future of, 172–76; in public life, ix, 107; moderaton and, 175; society and, 166–67; violence and, 174–75
religious dogma, 176
religious fanaticism, 172–75
religious fundamentalism. *See* Fundamentalism
religious right, xi, 131, 151–52, 180
renewable energy, 87
Republican party, xi, 78, 132, 152, 181, 183–84, 212
Resolution 1441, 8
Restoring Scientific Integrity Campaign, 96
resurrection, 116
Revelation, book of, 108
Rice Condoleezza, 21, 100
Roadless Area Conservation Rule, 88, 103n30
Robertson, Pat, 110, 113–14, 145, 152
Rocky Mountain National Park, 83
Rocky Mountain News, 225
Roe v. Wade, 151, 165
Roosevelt, Franklin D., 61–62, 208, 211
Roosevelt, Teddy, 209
Royal Institute of International Affairs, 15
Rumsfeld, Donald, 6, 21, 53; PNAC and, 4
Russia, 90, 141n13

Samarra, mosque bombing in, 15
San Diego, 18
Saudi Arabia, 22, 25

Saving Private Ryan, 170
Scalia, Antonin, 49, 66n17, 148, 157n21
scandals, 122
Schaeffer, Eric, 95
Schlesinger, Arthur, Jr., 150, 172–73, 185–86
Schrer, Michael, 34n7
school vouchers, 146
science, 95–96, 139, 142n32, 175, 219
Scientific American, 225
second coming, 117, 150–51, 153
Second World War. See World War II
secret prisons, 50
Secretary of Education, 148
Secretary of the Interior, 94, 147
Secretary of State, 26
sectarian violence, 15–16
secularism, 112, 166, 171
security, 169–70
Senate Intelligence Committee, 36n35
Seante Judiciary Committee, 193
separation of church and state, 166, 175
sex education programs, 157n17
Sherman Act of 1890, 209
Shermer, Michael, 123, 145
Shiites, 14–15, 29, 38n52
Sierra Club, 87, 89
signing statements, 53–54
Singer, Peter, 148
Sistani, Grand Ayatollah Ali al-, 14
Sixties, 213
Skull and Bones Society, 77
Sloan, Alan, 207
Smith, Lamar, 181
smog, 91
Social Security, 74, 138, 183, 198–99, 202; benefits, 202, 204; private accounts and, 203, 206, 222n21, 222n32, 223n39; reform of, 200, 202–8, 220n8, 222n34; surplus, 72, 204–5
Social Security Administration (SSA), 204, 207
solar heating, 215

Soros, George, 44
sound science, 95–96
sovereignty, 10, 29
Soviet Union, xiii, 8, 23, 45, 172
species extinction, 97
State of the Union address: of 2002, 7
stem cell research, 107, 111–12, 164, 171–72
Stevens, John Paul, 50
Stott, John, 110
Strategic Ignorance, 87–88, 95
Straw, Jack (British Foreign Secretary), 35n20
strict constructionists, 212
suburbia, 168
suicide bombers, 22, 172, 176
sulfur dioxide emissions, 87, 91–92
Sunnis, 14–16, 38n52
Sunstein, Cass R., 211–13
superabses, 42n108
Superfund, 101n3
supernatural, 87, 116–17
Supreme Court, U.S., 149, 177n6, 189, 193, 211–13; detainees and, 48–49, 51, 57; 2004 election and, 194; religion and, 146
surveillance, 54–57, 68n40, 68n46, 68n50, 69n52
Suskind, Ron, 34n11
Swift Boat Veterans for Truth, 21, 190
Syria, 12

takings clause, 95
Taliban, 5–6, 9, 48
tax code, 199–200
tax cuts, 70, 82n25, 138, 183, 200; consequences of, 71–76, 79–80; dividends and, 72–73; proposals, 70, 72
tax policies, ix, 184
Tax Policy Center, 72
technology, 64, 84–85
television advertising, 190
Ten Commandments, 146, 173

Tenet, George, 139; on Iraq WMD, 6–7; "slam dunk" reference to WMD, 34n11
Terrorists, terrorism, ix, 27, 31, 44, 48, 177n12; definition of, 45–46; Iraq and, 17, 22, 26, 41n103; roots of, 62–66; war on, 61, 169; United States and, 23–24
Texas, 5, 21, 187–88
Texas Air National Guard, 21
Texas Rangers, 8, 21
Tillich, Paul, 126
Time, 19, 28, 132, 188, 199, 225
Tito, Josip Broz, 15
theocracy, 145, 163–66, 178n22
third party, 214, 218
Thirty Years War, 29
Thomas, Cal, 159n37
Thomas, John H., 171
Times Picayune, 225
toleration, 17
tort reform, 200
Towey, Jim, 163
torture, 51–54
toxic substances, 183
trade deficit, 201
"tragedy of the commons," 99
Treaty of Westphalia, 29, 45
tribalism, 64
Tucker, Robert W., 8
Turley, Jonathan, 57
Twentieth Century Fund Task Force on Reform of the Presidential Election Process, 186
Tyson, Laura D'Andrea, 76

unilateralism, xiii, 5, 10, 31
Union of Concerned Scientists, 96
United Church of Christ (UCC), 170–71
United Kingdon. *See* Great Britain
United Nations, xii, 6, 13, 30, 36n27, 52, 90, 137; Security Council of, 8, 13; UN Charter, 8; weapons inspectors of, 6, 11, 130, 219

United Nations Convention Against Torture, 52
UPN, 171
unlawful combatants, 47–48, 50
uranium, 7, 137
urban sprawl, 215
USA Today, 55
U.S. Fish & Wildlife Service, 96
U.S. News & World Report, 225
Utah, state of, 93
utilities, 91–92

values, 63–64, 66, 98, 167–69, 182
value added tax, 79
values divide, ix, x, 170, 213–14, 217–20
value judgments, 85
Veterans Day, 170
Vietcong, 14
Vietnam, xiii, 17, 20, 23, 138
Vietnam War, 14, 17, 23
volatile organic compounds, 91
Volcanos of the Deep Sea, 171
voter registration, 191–92
voting procedures, 190–92

Wall Street, 204
Wall Street Journal, 202
War and the American Presidency, 186
war on terror, 39n61, 48
warlords, 9
Washington, George, 17
Washington Post, 225
Watt, James, 95, 147–48
Wealth and Democracy, 75
weapons of mass destruction (WMD), 7, 130–31, 137, 142n18, 182; Cheney and, 6–7; CIA investigations of, 12; George W. Bush and, 6–7; Kay's Congrssional testimony on, 11; as not found, 11–12; Saddam's alleged possession of, 134, 138; Tenet's "slam dunk" reference to, 6
weapons inspectors, 6, 11, 34n14

The Week, 225
wetlands, 87
What We Have Lost, 140
White House Conference on Faith-based and Community Initiatives, 163
White House Office of Faith-based and Community Initiatives, 146
Whitman, Christine Todd, 87, 89–90
wilderness, 92–94, 97, 101
Wilkerson, Lawrence, 53
Wilson, Joseph C., 7
Wilson, Woodrow, 22, 40n74
Wilson Quarterly, 24, 225

Wisconsin, state of, 83
Wise Use Movement, 95
Woodward, Bob, 60, 133
World Trade Center, 58–59, 63
Wolfowitz, Paul, 4, 16, 21
World War II, 59–60
World War IV, 24

Yale University, 77
yellow ribbon patriotism, 19
Yugoslavia, 15

Zakaria, Fareed, 29, 31

About the Author

Rogene A. Buchholz is the Legendre-Soule Chair in Business Ethics Emeritus in the College of Business Administration at Loyola University of New Orleans. He has published over seventy-five articles and is the author of ten books in the areas of business and public policy, business ethics, and the environment. Before moving to Loyola, he taught in business schools at the University of Minnesota, Washington University in St. Louis, and the University of Texas at Dallas, where he was also Associate Dean and Undergraduate Program Director.

Regarding education, he received his B.S. Degree for North Central College, an M.S. in economics from the University of Illinois, a M.D. degree from Perkins School of Theology at Southern Methodist University, and a Ph.D. in business from the University of Pittsburgh. He also worked for State Farm Insurance Co., Southland Corporation, and Alcoa in the field of management information systems, and was in the campus ministry and pastor of a church in Pittsburgh for three years. He also served for four years in the U.S. Air Force after graduation from high school. Dr. Buchholz is currently retired and lives with his wife in Denver, Colorado.

THE UNIVERSITY OF MICHIGAN

DATE DUE

DEC 0 2 2007